PRAISE FOR *42 FAITH*

"I can't wait to read this book because I have always had great respect for Jackie and his faith. His personality was to fight everything tooth and nail, but that was totally at odds with what he had to do to integrate baseball. So I think his faith in God was central to him finding a way to focus on the greater good."

—JIM BROWN

NFL HALL OF FAMER AND

CIVIL RIGHTS PIONEER

"*42 Faith* is a book about courage, struggle and, ultimately, victory over bias. The stories Ed Henry tells about Jackie Robinson's ordeal put you right on the field of play. Unforgettable book."

—BILL O'REILLY

ANCHOR, FOX NEWS CHANNEL

"Ed Henry knocks it out of the park! *42 Faith: The Rest of the Jackie Robinson Story* is a home run. Baseball, bravery, and the best of who we are as America move this electrifying, true tale of courage to the very top of your must-read list."

—BRAD THOR

#1 *NEW YORK TIMES* BESTSELLING

AUTHOR OF *FOREIGN AGENT*

"Just when you thought there was nothing left to say, hear, or tell about 42. This story gives tremendous insight, not based on assumptions or opinion, but from those who know, because they were witnesses and lived it. Faith is powerful. It was for Jackie Robinson."

—JIM GRAY

FAMED SPORTS REPORTER

"As a kid who grew up in Brooklyn idolizing Jackie Robinson, I thought I knew every last detail about his life. Then I read this magnificent book and was amazed to learn how much new information Ed Henry had dug up."

—JERRY REINSDORF

OWNER OF THE CHICAGO WHITE

SOX AND CHICAGO BULLS

"For so long, I could not even fathom how much adversity Jackie Robinson must have faced. But now I no longer have to wonder because of this magnificent new book from Ed Henry. My prayer is that I could handle my own daily challenges with a shred of the class and grace that Jackie had, characteristics which jump off the page here."

—Aaron Boone
Former major leaguer and
current ESPN baseball analyst

"As a lifelong Yankees fan and a student of history, I can state my unequivocal view that the greatest combination in all of sports was not Ruth and Gehrig, or Mantle and Maris, or Jeter and Rivera. It was Branch Rickey and Jackie Robinson. By their extraordinary personal courage, Rickey and Robinson changed race relations in the United States more effectively and permanently that any legislation or litigation has—and produced fabulous baseball at the same time. In *42 Faith*, Ed Henry has told the story of that remarkable courage and those happy changes and that exciting baseball with charm, brilliance, and page-turning joy."

—Hon. Andrew P. Napolitano
Senior judicial analyst, Fox News
Channel and author of *Dred
Scott's Revenge: A History of
Race and Freedom in America*

42 FAITH

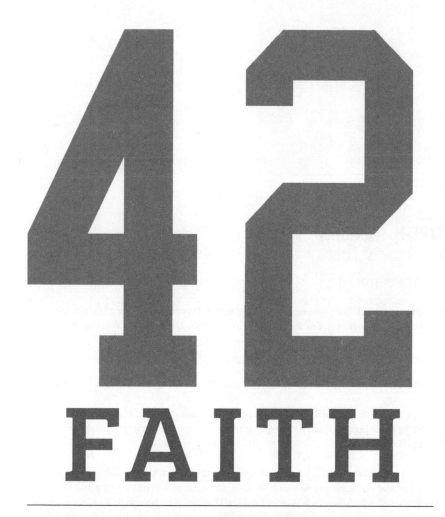

42
FAITH

THE REST OF THE JACKIE ROBINSON STORY

ED HENRY

W PUBLISHING GROUP

An Imprint of Thomas Nelson

Published in Nashville, Tennessee, by W Publishing, an imprint of Thomas Nelson.

Thomas Nelson titles may be purchased in bulk for educational, business, fundraising, or sales promotional use. For information, please e-mail SpecialMarkets@ ThomasNelson.com.

Any Internet addresses, phone numbers, or company or product information printed in this book are offered as a resource and are not intended in any way to be or to imply an endorsement by Thomas Nelson, nor does Thomas Nelson vouch for the existence, content, or services of these sites, phone numbers, companies, or products beyond the life of this book.

Unless otherwise noted, Scripture quotations are taken from the King James Version. Public domain.

ISBN 978-0-7180-8880-4 (HC)
ISBN 978-0-7180-8905-4 (eBook)

Library of Congress Cataloging-in-Publication Data
Library of Congress Control Number: 2017930376

Printed in the United States of America
17 18 19 20 21 LSC 10 9 8 7 6 5 4 3 2

This book simply would not have been possible without the love and faith of my wife, Shirley. I wrote it for her and my children, Patrick and Mila, so they will be inspired by Jackie Robinson, who said simply, "Life is not a spectator sport."

CONTENTS

CONTENTS

FOREWORD

Larry King

When I interviewed Dr. Martin Luther King Jr., I introduced him as the founder of the American civil rights movement. He immediately corrected me, saying the true founder of the movement was Jackie Robinson.

When I was but a lad of thirteen, Jackie played his first major league game. I had been thrilled, as were all my friends, when he was signed in 1945 and played a full season with Montreal in 1946—a season in which he was the most valuable player in the International League.

On that wonderful April afternoon in 1947, I was among the thousands of Brooklynites who were in Ebbets Field when Jackie made his major league debut. I will never forget that remarkable figure as he came out on the field. The Dodgers still have the whitest uniform in sports, and Jackie was a very dark man. So he stood out immediately among all the players on the field. That face against that uniform.

I would go on to admire him deeply. I saw many games that season in my fifty-cent bleacher seats. He became the first-ever Rookie of the Year. He led the Dodgers to a tough seven-game series loss to the Yankees in the World Series.

I saw him steal home. I saw him confound right fielders by taking long turns after a single and daring them to throw behind him. It was a joy to see him play. It was sad to read about all of the things happening to him, on and off the field.

Later in life, I would interview Pee Wee Reese, the white shortstop from Louisville, Kentucky, who had stood by Robinson through thick and thin. I would interview Red Barber, the famed Dodgers announcer from Columbus, Mississippi, who would broadcast his exploits.

And then, on two occasions, I got to interview the man himself. To know the real Jackie, compared to what he had to be for his first three years in the major leagues, was unbelievable. He was asked to turn the other cheek when he faced racial discrimination, which was the complete opposite of the man Jackie was.

He fought for every inch. He took nothing lying down. Something I'll always remember he said to me was, "Don't promise me equality for my children. Give it to me now so I'll know they'll have it."

One quick story: I was at an old-timer's game with Enos Slaughter, the Hall of Fame player who came of age in the South. Enos was maybe seventy-one years old, and we were talking about Jackie.

Enos said, "I had never played with or against a Negro my whole life. So I didn't know what to think, but I guess you could have called me a segregationist."

Anyway, the Dodgers were in St. Louis in Jackie's first season. Slaughter hit a ground ball, and as Jackie was covering first base to receive the throw, Slaughter stepped on his ankle and drew blood.

Jackie said nothing. Slaughter stood at first. Jackie said nothing.

Slaughter spit out tobacco juice and looked at him in anger. Jackie said nothing.

A few years later, the Cardinals were in Ebbets Field. Jackie had been removed from the shield that said he couldn't show his true personality. Slaughter rifled a shot off the outfield wall and slid into second, where Jackie was now playing.

Jackie took the throw and slammed the ball into Slaughter's face. Three teeth fell out. Slaughter looked up, and Jackie said, "I never forget."

In this wonderful book, by a terrific journalist, Jackie comes alive, both on and off the field, with great remembrance. Jackie was not a perfect man, but he was a man!

Enjoy this new look at a face that will live on as long as humans walk the earth.

INTRODUCTION

Juan Williams

My Aunt Annie loved the Brooklyn Dodgers. Why?

A black woman born in Panama, she arrived as an immigrant in Brooklyn the same year Jackie Robinson arrived in Brooklyn as the major league's first black baseball player.

To her eyes, Dodgers' general manager Branch Rickey's decision to put a black man on the biggest playing field in American sports was evidence of God working through Rickey. Aunt Annie viewed that historic moment as faith being rewarded.

Aunt Annie prayed to a God she knew as capable of parting the waters to let his people flee slavery in Egypt. She believed God loved the least of us, the children, the poor, and the racial minorities.

As a result of her deep faith, she believed God's will is done when all men and all women get in the big game—the game of life.

"If he made us all the same color, we'd go blind," she'd tell me. Once she explained to me that God made talented ballplayers, awesome musicians, brilliant speakers, and even beautiful women in all races as a glimpse of his heavenly kingdom.

Aunt Annie's Christian understanding of Branch Rickey, Jackie Robinson, and the Brooklyn Dodgers changed my view of the world.

She opened my eyes to one crucial ingredient that Robinson, Rickey, and much of Black America shared in 1947—something that can't be captured by names, dates, and talk of movement politics and economic growth.

It was a shared faith in God: the subject of Ed Henry's *42 Faith*.

As a child I first thought of Rickey's decision to put Robinson on the baseball field as an inspiring sports story.

Later, as the author of several books on civil rights history—including *Eyes on the Prize: America's Civil Rights Years 1954–1965*—I saw Robinson's story as a critical moment leading up to the Supreme Court's 1954 ruling that school segregation was unconstitutional. In that perspective, Rickey and Robinson achieved a civil rights triumph over the culture, the tradition of racial segregation in sports.

But Aunt Annie told me a different story. She saw the Jackie Robinson story as proof of God's wonders to adore.

And she was not alone. As I grew up in Brooklyn, New York, in the 1960s, I heard lots of faith-driven stories from black Christians who believed God's hand was at work in 1936 when Jesse Owens, a black American, beat Adolf Hitler's white supremacist theories in Germany by becoming the fastest man at the Olympics. In the 200-meter dash another black American finished second to Owens. He was Mack Robinson, the older brother of a young baseball player named Jackie.

The same sense of rewarded faith in God was at work when black Americans cheered boxer Joe Louis as he won the heavyweight championship. To Aunt Annie, only God could have allowed Louis, a black man known as the "Brown Bomber," to somehow become a hero to Americans of all races.

To Aunt Annie's delight, Owens and Louis showed excellence with a black face to the whole world. The Devil was losing, and God's light was pushing away the darkness of racism.

God was always her author of civil rights progress.

She saw God at work when civil rights leaders met with President Franklin D. Roosevelt to argue for the integration of the armed forces. Their demands were refused because, as a government press release made clear, integration would "produce situations destructive to morale and detrimental to the preparation for national defense."[1]

She believed it was God's doing when, in 1945, more than 160 black officers stationed in Indiana pushed through the lines of segregation by trying to enter a whites-only officers club.[2] And at one point, a soldier by the name of Jackie Robinson—yes, that Jackie Robinson—was court-martialed for refusing to go to the back of an army bus while traveling through Texas.

During the war years she kept the faith. Change was slow, but she believed change was coming in God's time under God's watch.

For example, President Roosevelt, acting to prevent a black-led march on Washington, issued an executive order in 1941 that barred racial discrimination in the defense industries even as the military remained segregated.

President Roosevelt's order drastically increased jobs for blacks in manufacturing cities like Chicago and Baltimore. Additionally, with so many white men gone to fight the war, a wave of black workers moved from low-paying agricultural and domestic jobs to work in factories. "The war and defense work," an African American woman later explained with emotion, "gave [black people] the opportunity to do things they had never experienced before . . . and their expectations changed."[3]

The nation was changing. Aunt Annie's life was changing.

Between 1943 and 1945, black public school teachers fought for equal pay in Tampa, Florida; Charleston, South Carolina; Columbia, South Carolina; Newport News, Virginia; Little Rock, Arkansas; and Birmingham, Alabama.[4] And between 1939 and 1950, the median income for nonwhite workers rose from 41 percent to 60 percent of the white median income, according to historian Philip S. Foner.[5]

Economic successes paralleled political ones. In 1945 a Baptist minister from Harlem named Adam Clayton Powell became the first African American from New York to serve in Congress. In 1946 more than twenty African Americans were serving in state legislatures. Between 1940 and 1947, the percentage of black Southerners registered to vote increased from 2 percent to 12 percent.[6] Future Supreme Court justice Thurgood Marshall, whose biography I wrote, was winning Supreme Court cases as the top lawyer for the NAACP during the 1940s. He won a case giving black people voting rights in the Texas Democratic primary (*Smith v. Allwright*) and would soon win cases ending restrictions on sale of property to blacks and even cases allowing blacks to go to law school. His cases would lead up to the famous *Brown v. Board of Education* case in 1954.

Aunt Annie kept her faith even after the war, as America celebrated its victory over Nazis and imperialists but still practiced racial oppression at home. Black people, Latinos, Filipinos, and other racial minorities on American military bases around the world, including in Aunt Annie's Panama, felt the same sting of segregation as blacks in the United States.

She knew the bitter reality of blacks in the back of the bus, praying in separate churches, children sent to inferior schools, and men segregated in the military even as they bled and died for the nation. And as a sports fan, she lived the reality that blacks were kept out of the nation's most popular sport—all-white major league baseball.

Sports in the mid-twentieth century was an accurate reflection of American life, including the torment of racism.

All this is to say that by April 15, 1947—the day that Jackie Robinson joined Dixie Walker and Pee Wee Reese to face the Boston Braves—Aunt Annie and other African Americans were primed for a hero, a leader to spearhead their fight to be treated as equals on the baseball field.

As you'll soon see in Ed Henry's book, faith in God gave Rickey the confidence to bring Robinson to the big leagues.

It was faith in God, too, that allowed Robinson to endure the endless racist taunts of players who didn't want an African American in their midst.

Now, it is ironic that my aunt and so many African Americans should find spiritual sustenance in a Christian God. After all, almost none of the twelve million African slaves brought to the New World between the sixteenth and nineteenth centuries were originally Christian. In fact, many of the European colonists believed that converting slaves to Christianity justified slavery.

To the slave master, Christianity was a tool. They hired preachers who taught their slaves about religion. But rather than explaining, for instance, the love of Jesus Christ, the preachers used the Bible to ensure obedience among them.

Slave masters even used scripture to legitimize slavery. Quoting Paul's letter to the Ephesians, they proclaimed: "Slaves, be obedient to your masters."[7]

But the black faithful saw a different God. They reinterpreted the story of the Jewish exodus from their enslavement in Egypt as reason to pray for their own salvation, their own freedom. In their songs, the word *Canaan* referred to the North, where slavery had been abolished. As historian Albert J. Raboteau has indicated, they were attracted to Old and New Testament figures like Mary, Thomas, Peter, Moses, Joshua, Noah, and Daniel—all of whom were tested by God or Jesus in some way. Like these biblical figures, the black people—even as slaves—saw their status as temporary, a test of their faith in God.[8]

As Quinton Dixie and I wrote more than a decade ago in a book titled *This Far by Faith*, black slaves cultivated an intense faith that God would, one day, end their struggle.

In the decades following the Civil War, former slaves and their progeny developed and were given structures through which to practice their faith.

Black churches grew rapidly. The African Methodist Episcopal (AME) Church and the African Methodist Episcopal Zion (AMEZ) Church were both created by free Northern blacks in the early nineteenth century. Black Baptists in the South formed churches, created state associations, and in 1895 established the National Baptist Convention. In 1890, one-third of African Americans belonged to a church.[9]

The black church became an American institution. As the sociologist W. E. B. Du Bois observed in his 1903 *Souls of Black Folk*, with its Sunday schools, special dinners, insurance societies, lectures, and six weekly services, the "Negro church of to-day is the social center of Negro life in the United States."[10]

One black Southerner whose faith in God helped her endure Jim Crow happened to be a young Methodist woman by the name of Mallie Robinson, Jackie's mother—which is where Ed Henry's *42 Faith* begins.

The book before you is, yes, about baseball. Ed has traveled cross-country to discuss Jackie's life and memory with, among other figures, Rachel Robinson, Jackie's widow; Carl Erskine, Jackie's friend and teammate; and Jerry Reinsdorf, a Brooklyn kid who grew up watching the Dodgers before becoming a major sports mogul in his own right. These interviews, along with a host of historical material Ed has unearthed from Robinson's personal papers, add new perspective to an already celebrated story.

But *42 Faith* is also about how faith in God allowed two men of opposite skin colors to work together to achieve a miracle in race relations.

The story of Jackie Robinson did not end when he hung up his glove in 1956. His mere presence on the baseball diamond cleared the path for countless other black baseball players: Don Newcombe, Roy Campanella, Willie Mays, Monte Irvin, Hank Aaron, and Satchel Paige—to name just a few.

Subsequently, other black athletes have used their platform as sports celebrities to fight racism. Heavyweight champion Muhammad Ali gained international fame for sacrificing years of his athletic prime to successfully win the right to stay out of the military because of his conscientious objection to the war in Vietnam.

Indeed, the image of the protesting black athlete—all modeled on Jackie Robinson—has earned a special place in American history. The photograph of black track stars Tommie C. Smith and John Carlos raising their fists in protest after receiving medals during the 1968 Olympics has become something of an icon. So has the November 2014 image of five members of the St. Louis Rams raising their hands in solidarity with the "Hands Up/Don't Shoot" rallying cry of the Black Lives Matter movement.

Colin Kaepernick's refusal throughout 2016 to stand up during the national anthem to protest police shootings of black people once again brought attention to the role athletes play in forcing social change.

These debates are unlikely to go away anytime soon.

But in 2017, a time when religious groups of all kinds are maligned as being too stuck in the past or overly political, Ed Henry's *42 Faith* teaches us what faith can and does accomplish in surprising places and with surprising people.

At a time when race-based issues have polarized Americans to unprecedented degrees, the relationship between Branch Rickey and Jackie Robinson reminds us of the value of working together across racial lines.

Aunt Annie would see God's hand in Ed Henry's book.

PROLOGUE

While I was covering President Obama for CNN in March 2011, I had a chance to attend an off-the-record cocktail party with him at the White House. From the outside, it probably appeared as if there was not much love lost between the two of us. That's why the private conversation we had that night in the historic Cross Hall of the White House about Jackie Robinson was so remarkable.

During my work hours, it was my job to press Obama with tough but fair questions, and I had grilled George W. Bush just as hard when CNN had assigned me to cover his final two years in office. (And anybody who doubts that can look no further than Bush's press secretary Dana Perino, now my colleague at Fox, who has quipped on-air several times that I was an "equal opportunity [expletive]" who gave her boss the business too.)

I took the same approach with Obama when I moved to Fox News in the summer of 2011, though the relationship certainly had some low moments where it appeared we were at odds.

Obama himself fed this narrative at one news conference, when he was pressed by Jonathan Karl of ABC News about problems with the rollout of his health-care law. "Since I'm in charge, obviously we screwed it up," Obama told Karl. "And it's not that I don't engage in a lot of self-reflection here. I promise you, I probably beat myself up even worse than you or Ed Henry does on any given day."[1]

Yet Obama was probably saying that a little tongue-in-cheek, and sharp confrontations in public can be blown way out of proportion. In our hypersensitive social media age, a legitimate question from a journalist at a presidential news conference can lead critics to charge the reporter with being disrespectful or partisan, when, actually, the criticism is often just a lot of noise.

The truth is that despite all the questions I would get from people assuming Obama was frosty toward me because I work at Fox, he was nothing but gracious to my family and me while he was in office.

At a White House Christmas party, he was especially kind to my daughter, Mila, telling her that of course he would love to buy Girl Scout cookies from her. He did it as a gentlemanly gesture that made a kid happy.

When we discussed Robinson in the spring of 2011, it was about a week before the president officially filed the paperwork to run for reelection. So his advisers had called in a select group of journalists to have off-the-record cocktails with the commander in chief.

I would never break the confidentiality of what President Obama or anyone else told me off-the-record, so I am still keeping the details of what he said about his administration that night confidential. (It was nothing earth-shattering.) But what he decided to tell me about Robinson is not a state secret—and it's simply too good not to share.

The president made his way around the cocktail party, spending a few minutes with each reporter and his or her guest. When he reached my wife, Shirley, and me, we talked about the campaign to come. But I could not resist also mentioning that a few days later, I was planning to meet with Rachel Robinson. I was interviewing the ballplayer's widow for a story that would become the early seeds of this book.

I figured Obama—a trailblazer himself as the nation's first African American president—would have at least a passing interest in my meeting with Mrs. Robinson. But he went further, stunning me by saying he had some specific instructions for my trip to New York.

"I want you to tell her something for me," the president told me. "Tell her I believe there is a straight line from what Jackie did to me being elected the first African American president. I want you to tell her that."[2]

In one sentence, the president had reminded me of the sheer gravity of Robinson's achievement in 1947, while also connecting it to the historic administration I was covering several decades later. And it convinced me that even if it took a few more years, after some earlier fits and starts, I was finally going to write this book about something much deeper than just nostalgia for the old Brooklyn Dodgers.

I planned to meet with Mrs. Robinson because I had learned some new information about Branch Rickey, the Dodgers' general manager who signed Jackie to his first contract, and how he had quietly thought about backing out.

It was a remarkable historical twist, and I wanted to find out if Mrs. Robinson had ever learned of it, especially because the details had been shared with only a small group of people for decades.

The heart and soul of this book became exploring the fact that the strength of Rickey's faith helped get him back on track. Or, as the wife of a minister who aided Rickey during his personal struggle explained it, the executive's indecision is a powerful sign that "someone cared enough to grope for wisdom beyond himself, to call upon God's guidance" to make such a momentous decision.[3]

Since Jackie died in 1972, I wanted to find out from Mrs. Robinson whether she and her husband had ever learned about the hidden hand of God in this awesome chapter of American history.

At the time of this writing, on the seventieth anniversary of Jackie's first game at Ebbets Field, it's easy to assume we already know exactly how it all played out, thanks to a pile of wonderful books about Robinson and Rickey, as well as the terrific 2013 movie *42*—named for the uniform number on Jackie's back. No player in modern times is permitted to use that number, retired forever by then-commissioner of baseball Bud Selig as a sign of deep respect for Robinson and his legacy.

But another element of the drama has largely gone unexamined: the role faith played in sustaining not only Rickey during his decision-making, but also Robinson, as the two men carried this heavy burden of making history together.

While Robinson was not outspoken about his faith, it was ingrained in him as a child by his mother, Mallie, and reinforced by Rickey, a devout

Methodist. "As I said before, I am not one of the big people in terms of faith," Robinson himself wrote. "But I would have to be pretty stupid, and certainly ungrateful, not to have some of the deep religious convictions of my mother, Mallie Robinson, and Mr. Rickey rub off on me."[4]

That faith helped give Robinson the confidence he needed to rise above not only the taunts and death threats he faced from outsiders but also the insults he faced from some of his own white teammates on the Dodgers.

One of the notable exceptions was the late pitcher Ralph Branca. As you will see throughout this book, Branca's strong faith in God clearly helped him through a gigantic struggle of his own. But I believe that Branca's faith was also a critical reason he stood up so early and often to defend Robinson.

In his memoir, *A Moment in Time: An American Story of Baseball, Heartbreak, and Grace*, Branca remembered sitting down with five teammates from the Deep South who were deeply skeptical of Jackie getting a chance to play with the Dodgers.

Branca reminded the players that at various points earlier in their lives, all of them had worked at Southern gas stations with African Americans. "What's the difference between that and having a black on your team?" he asked.

"At the gas station, they were pumping gas and we were fixing cars," one of the Southerners said. "We weren't equal."

Branca quickly shot back: "Well, you won't be equal on the ball field either. Jackie's better than you."[5]

"I'M TAKING A CHANCE HERE"

Except for a handful of families drowning their pancakes in maple syrup, most of the tables were empty at the IHOP just off of I-69 in central Indiana in the summer of 2016. So I figured it would be easy to spot one of Jackie Robinson's last surviving teammates.

But, of course, this veteran of the Brooklyn Dodgers refused to sit at a "showboating" table in the front of the restaurant, where he might be recognized by a fan. Instead he opted for a quiet booth way in the back by the restrooms.

Robinson and his teammates were romanticized as the heroic "Boys of Summer." But, in most cases, what actually made them great was that they were fairly regular guys grounded in reality. And several of them were serious about their faith in God—a striking contrast from the "me first" mantra of many of the spoiled athletic stars of the modern era.

"You must be here to see Mr. Carl," said a cheerful young woman running the restaurant, seeing me scan the room.

And then I spotted him. There, in a polo shirt in that distinctive bright Dodgers blue, was former star pitcher Carl Erskine.

I was thrilled to see him so I could hear all about Robinson. But I quickly found out that Erskine was excited to see me so he could eat up every morsel about the astonishing 2016 presidential campaign that I covered as a reporter. As I took a seat across from him in the booth, he immediately invoked the name of the late baseball player and broadcaster Joe Garagiola with a line that was prescient.

"Garagiola had that line, 'It might look great on paper. But in the grass and the dirt, it's going to play out differently,'" recalled Erskine. "And on the political scene, it's the same. The polls tell you one thing, the actual votes tell you another."[1]

After we kicked around the latest controversies surrounding Hillary Clinton and Donald Trump, the former pitcher mentally went into his windup, beginning three hours of magnificent stories with his first memories of his days with the Dodgers.

"So I first pitched against the real team, the big team, in 1948," Erskine remembered about his days pitching for a minor league club, the Fort Worth Cats. The boys from Brooklyn—including legendary Dodgers from the major league club like Robinson, Ralph Branca, Duke Snider, and Pee Wee Reese—had come to Texas for an exhibition contest.

"After the game, I'm in the dugout, and a voice says, 'Where's Erskine?'" He waved his arm to mimic a teammate frantically telling him to turn around and get a glimpse at the Dodger asking to shake his hand. "It was Jackie Robinson."

On this morning, Erskine was closing in on ninety years old and wearing sunglasses indoors to shield his sensitive eyes from the light. But his memory was razor sharp as he pronounced each syllable carefully.

"Young man, I hit against you twice today," Robinson told Erskine, "and you're not going to be here long."

Still in awe decades later, Erskine said, "Isn't that amazing? A minor league kid."

In fact, Robinson was dead-on. Erskine would be called up from the minors to the Dodgers within months, and the two men would become close friends despite their different races and backgrounds.

That same spring, in 1948, when the Dodgers stopped in Alabama for an exhibition game, Robinson had perhaps an even deeper impact on a young African American kid named Henry "Hank" Aaron. Aaron skipped school in order to race over and join a crowd that gathered outside a drug-store just to hear Robinson speak.

"I don't remember what he said," Aaron wrote in a foreword to Cal Fussman's 2007 oral history on Robinson's legacy, *After Jackie*.

"It didn't matter what he said. He was standing there."

What Aaron did recall clearly was sitting on his back porch in Mobile a few years earlier. When a plane flew overhead, he told his father he wanted to be a pilot.

"Ain't no colored pilots," his dad said.

A dream of playing major league baseball drew the same response: "Ain't no colored ballplayers."

But when that drugstore encounter was over, Aaron's dad brought him to the game to see Jackie play. "After that day, he never told me ever again that I couldn't be a ballplayer," wrote Aaron, who grew into one of the greats of the game. "I was allowed to dream after that."[2]

Those brief moments of grace, within days of each other in Fort Worth and Mobile, were important. They gave two young men, one white and one black, their first real window into Robinson's character.

A PRIVATE FAITH

The impact that Robinson had on Erskine and Aaron also helps set up the central question of this book: How much of a role did faith play in helping Robinson make history against such long odds?

One clue comes from an unpublished manuscript Robinson was work-ing on during the early 1960s. This rich new source of information suggests Jackie's faith may have played a bigger part in his ability to persevere than historians have ever considered before.

Robinson did publish a handful of books during his lifetime, some more famous than others. But, as you will see in the chapters ahead, he got more personal in the unpublished manuscript. It was supposed to be one in a series of books for children by famous people, who would write about their greatest day as a way of imparting lessons for others.

My Greatest Day was never published as a book of its own. Robinson and coauthor Alfred Duckett did revise the manuscript and publish parts of it as a book, titled *Breakthrough to the Big League*, in 1965. So many portions of *My Greatest Day*, some of which dealt explicitly with Robinson's faith, were left out.[3]

The deeply personal reflections by Robinson have been lost to the dustbin of history, until now.

My Greatest Day was included in the personal papers Robinson's wife, Rachel, donated to the Library of Congress in 2001. Those papers are now kept in the library's Manuscript Division in Washington, DC, where anyone can read the unpublished manuscript and other fascinating records from Robinson's life.

In *My Greatest Day*, Robinson wrote about a pivotal lesson he learned as a teenager. His Christian minister in Pasadena, California, Karl Downs, challenged him to accept that God was the ultimate force for good. "To seek to help others without expecting anything in return," wrote Robinson.[4]

He implied that faith in God is demonstrated not only in the things we say but also in what we actually do. Pouring through this trove of rich material reminded me of one of the most powerful sentences in the Bible: "My little children, let us not love in word, neither in tongue; but in deed and in truth" (1 John 3:18).

Robinson was a man of deed and truth at his very core. That approach enabled him to overcome the struggles summed up bluntly by Aaron, when he said that before Jackie, "There were a lot of things blacks couldn't be back then."[5]

Erskine also noted that when he signed his own first contract in 1946, "The baseballs were all white, and so were all the players."

That precedent was dramatically upended on April 15, 1947, when Dodgers general manager Branch Rickey brought Robinson up to the big leagues, and Robinson trotted out to first base at Ebbets Field for his first major league game. Robinson would lean in to the challenges of his unique situation so aggressively that genuine civil rights icons played catch-up to him. Jackie suited up for that game a full eight years before Rosa Parks was arrested for refusing to obey a bus driver's order to give up her seat in the "colored" section to a white person. The future Reverend Dr. Martin Luther King Jr. was just eighteen years old.

"He was a sit-inner before sit-ins," Dr. King would later write of Robinson, "a freedom rider before freedom rides."[6]

Aaron and other prominent African Americans have noted that if Jackie had failed at the start, his brethren from the Negro Leagues would not have gotten a second chance for years—maybe decades. (Black professional teams have been traced back to 1885, though the "Negro Leagues" typically refers to the seven shabbily treated leagues that started forming in 1920 and largely featured black and Latin American players.)

If Robinson failed at his big break, two-faced white owners of baseball teams would have tried to mask their racist intentions and declared—more in sadness than anger, they would claim—"Well, sorry, but the finest of the Negro Leagues tried to make it big and simply could not hack it."

Talk about intense pressure on one man's shoulders. To me, it's almost like a perverse twist on what Robert Thaves once said about Ginger Rogers doing everything Fred Astaire did, except "backwards and in high heels."

Jackie did what other Hall of Fame baseball players were doing—and more—but while facing an onslaught of death threats and racial slurs.

"He was physically and verbally abused, particularly when he was on the road, in certain cities," recalled Rachel Robinson, who was also personally instrumental in helping him persevere. "The taunts angered him, sometimes frightened him, but he turned away from them."[7]

EARLY FAITH INFLUENCES

Through it all, faith in God helped give Jackie the strength to calmly rise above all of that viciousness, though that part of the story has gotten little bursts of attention.

"[It's] something that has been barely touched on," said Erskine, who believes there had to be divine intervention because athletic ability and determination—while, of course, important—could take Robinson only so far.

"That's kind of hidden in all this," Erskine said of how pivotal faith turned out to be. "It would be hard to prove that. Except for the outcome."

His point was that the chances of the experiment being a success were pretty slim. "If Las Vegas had made the odds, it would've been overwhelming that it wouldn't succeed," said Erskine. "Segregation was so prevalent at the time. People today don't really know how unlikely this was."

Erskine believed that Rickey, who rarely said or did anything by accident, purposely invoked religion near the end of his first face-to-face meeting with Robinson at the Dodgers' offices in Brooklyn on August 28, 1945. Rickey had ordered up a complete scouting report on Robinson's personal life, not only his baseball abilities. And he had gleaned a lot. Despite their obvious racial and generational differences, Robinson and Rickey each had strong mothers who instilled in them a durable Christian faith at an early age.

Rickey instinctively knew he could connect with Robinson through Scripture. So he reached into his desk drawer to grab a copy of *Life of Christ* by Giovanni Papini. He began reading aloud to Robinson the section about turning the other cheek.

"I would say the spiritual strength that Rickey tweaked in Jackie in that meeting was the key to his ability to resist the attacks," Erskine told me in the interview.

Robinson's personal papers support this point of view, so Erskine was not going out on a limb. In *My Greatest Day*, Robinson credited God and Rickey with enabling him to keep his anger in check for the greater good.

The player made it clear that the greatest day of his life was when he sat in Rickey's office in 1945, a meeting we will delve into a lot deeper shortly, and learned he was going to be on the path to becoming the first African American in Major League Baseball. He stressed that he did not consider it his greatest day because of the fame he attained, or the comfortable home in Connecticut he settled into, after getting his shot.

Instead, what made it great was Robinson being pushed by Rickey to rise above the anger he had demonstrated earlier in his life over discrimination and denied opportunities. Robinson knew this was his chance to show that an entire race—not just one man—was up to the challenge.

"Somebody else might have . . . done a better job," wrote Robinson. "But God and Branch Rickey made it possible for me to be the one, and I just went on in and did the best I knew how."[8]

The ballplayer also explicitly cited the importance of the faith of his mother. He did this in the context of stressing that faith helped define his very being, though he did not wear religion on his sleeve during his playing career or try to hold himself up as a pious person.

"Yet, it has always impressed me that two of the people who had the greatest influence on my life—my mother and Branch Rickey—had such deep faith in the existence of a Supreme Being," Robinson wrote. "It is one thing to express faith. It is another thing to do as these two people did—to practice faith every day of one's life."[9]

Robinson explained that from an early age he learned to live by a certain code. You try to work things out and you battle back a little with your mouth, he wrote, but then maybe you simply have to settle it with your fists.[10]

Who could blame him for wanting to lash out?

A sports journalist once succinctly described Robinson as someone "born with a big mouth, a rattlesnake temper,"[11] who never took racial discrimination lightly, dating back to the slights he dealt with during his childhood in Pasadena, California, when he was banned from the local swimming pool and YMCA.

Even though he became a hero, in his writings Robinson showed himself to be human—someone who explored his faith at difficult moments like the rest of us. At the start of Rickey's experiment, Robinson honestly didn't know whether he could hold up amid all the nastiness.

He and Rickey discussed that difficult upbringing as they sat face to face. The executive pressed him about whether he could hold his temper, and Robinson admitted he was scared because he did not really know the answer.

"Could I turn the other cheek?" Robinson wrote. "Could I take insults and humiliation without fighting back? I knew what he meant—and it was frightening."[12]

"THE MAHATMA'S" DARKEST HOUR

Erskine told me he enjoyed the movie *42*, particularly because he thought actor Harrison Ford captured the mannerisms and histrionics of Rickey. But he was disappointed that the references to the Bible from that first meeting between Rickey and Robinson were downplayed in the film.

"It was omitted," Erskine said. "Why? Political correctness."

(God, of course, was mentioned several times in the movie, including when Rickey quipped, "Robinson's a Methodist. I'm a Methodist. God's a Methodist. We can't go wrong. Find him. Bring him here.")[13]

After we finally ordered our breakfast at IHOP, I told him I had a new piece of information that was also left out of the Hollywood version.

The conventional wisdom has long been that Rickey, nicknamed "The Mahatma" because of his more public pronouncements of his Christian faith, was dead certain about Robinson from the beginning. People assumed that he did not hesitate in signing Robinson to his first contract because it was the just thing to do.

This was why Rickey's push to integrate baseball variously became known as his Great Experiment, Grand Experiment, and Noble Experiment. The idea was that he felt he was morally right to hire an African American, and he never really wavered in his crusade to bring equality to the sport and, by extension, to America.

The truth, however, is more complicated.

It turns out that, as Robinson admitted in his writings, Rickey was more scared about the experiment than he let on publicly. Privately, he had second thoughts about whether he could go through with it. He was facing intense pressure from baseball's white owners and team executives, who were vehemently opposed.

At his most vulnerable moment, he sought some spiritual guidance from that minister mentioned earlier.

"He had humbled himself and sought to communicate with a Presence and a Wisdom and a Power beyond his own," the minister's wife wrote of Rickey. "For he knew that, alone, he was insufficient to the task of knowing right from wrong, as we all are."[14]

It was another sign that perhaps faith in God had a bigger role in this decision on multiple levels.

Erskine mulled over this information as he leaned back into the booth at IHOP.

"I'll be darned," he said.

And the talk of faith had stirred something else in Erskine. It was not a story directly about Robinson, but more a memory buried deep inside, about what he considers the strangest stroke of fate he saw in his long life.

It involved the 1951 Brooklyn team, on which both Erskine and Robinson played. The team suffered a heartbreaking loss to their chief rival, the New York Giants. Bobby Thomson won it with a home run that was so devastating for Brooklyn that it became known as "The Shot Heard 'Round the World," and it propelled the Giants to that year's World Series instead of the Dodgers.

"Now, I'm going to tell you a story, but you can't write it," Erskine said. "You have to give me your word. You cannot write it."

I gave Erskine my word that I wouldn't publish anything he wasn't comfortable with.

Then, as he began to tell the story, Erskine shifted course. He began cracking open the door to letting me publish the information.

"Now if you write this . . . ," Erskine said, before his voice trailed off. He was clearly still struggling over how much to share, and he noted as we sat there that he and fellow Dodgers pitcher Ralph Branca, who gave up Thomson's big home run, were the only two people still alive to know the truth. (Branca died four months after my conversation with Erskine.)

"You're the only one I've—now I'm telling it to you because I trust you."

A moment later he added, "I guess you can write it. But you have to leave out a couple of things."

Then Erskine peeled off his sunglasses and looked me dead in the eye: "I'm taking a chance here."

I poured another cup of coffee.

CHAPTER 2

JACKIE IN WINTER

As he shuffled his way to the front of the church in New Rochelle, New York, the civil rights icon's steps were heavy. It had to be difficult for some in the church to watch Jackie Robinson walk so gingerly as he labored up to the pulpit. Now stooped over, he turned to address the congregation.

"The good Lord has showered blessings upon me," Jackie said, clearly still humble and grateful, even though his body was starting to break down. "This country and its people, black and white, have been good to me."[1]

Robinson was only forty-eight years old on that Sunday in 1967, yet he carried on his back all of the stresses of a long struggle. A bright star fading away too soon, he would be dead within five years.

The legs that shakily carried him to the pulpit that day had once made him the speediest base runner of them all at another kind of house of worship—a popular baseball cathedral known as Ebbets Field—not too many years earlier.

He danced gracefully off third base, despite his pigeon-toed form, tantalizing Brooklyn Dodgers fans while terrifying fans of the opposing team.

"People say, 'Oh, Jackie was a great base runner. He must have been fast,'" recalled Carl Erskine. "No, he was *quick*. There's a big difference between fast and quick. His hands, his legs, his reactions were split-second. You could never catch Jackie in a rundown. He was so quick."[2]

At any given moment, the ballplayer who nineteen times in his career stole home plate—the most daring and exciting play in baseball—just might be about to take off from third base again like a man possessed.

"He was the most exciting player we ever saw," Larry King, the legendary broadcaster, told me.[3]

King was thirteen years old during Robinson's rookie year of 1947, and he and his friends would gladly take two different subways from the Bensonhurst section of Brooklyn to get to the ballpark in Flatbush. "To go and see him in person was a joy."

Robinson had another signature play, where he might hit a routine single to right field and then take an abnormally wide turn off first base, making the guy fielding the ball believe he just might dart to second base.

"He'd stare at the right fielder with his arms out like this," King said, jabbing his arms out wide in the shape of a T as if he were trying to balance himself. "Right fielder's got the ball, and Jackie is about a third of the way past first base."

In a split second, the right fielder had to make a decision: Should he make the easy play and throw the ball to second base? Or should he throw the ball behind Robinson to first base? That, of course, could force Robinson into a rundown—known as a "pickle" in baseball—where he would be caught between first and second base. If the other team tagged him before he reached either base, he was out.

But here is where things were different when it came to Jackie Robinson in his prime: in addition to having jet engines for legs, Robinson had eyes like lasers, spotting every little edge on the field that he could exploit.

Robinson's eyes were locked in on the right fielder, waiting for the slightest move of his body. If the fielder leaned toward first base, Robinson would bolt for second. If the fielder leaned toward second, Robinson could easily retreat back to first. Catching him in a pickle was rare, and trying was often futile.

This game of cat-and-mouse would inevitably send fans at Ebbets Field into a frenzy. Jumping to the edges of their seats, the spectators would begin goading the right fielder, telling him to throw behind Robinson to first base, knowing he'd probably wiggle out of any rundown. The fans were eager to tell the fielder he had no guts.

"And we would start chanting, '*Chick-en! Chick-en!*'" King recalled.

As you will see, though, there were many dimensions to Robinson beyond his incredible athletic skills—and make no mistake, they were remarkable. He was the first student ever at UCLA to be a "four-letter" man, dominating in four sports: baseball, basketball, football, as well as track and field.

"HE BURNED WITH A DARK FIRE"

For Branch Rickey, the first stage of integrating baseball was deciding in 1945 whether to sign Robinson to a minor league contract with one of the Dodgers' key farm teams, the Montreal Royals. If all went well, down the road he could earn a major league contract with the Dodgers, shattering the game's color barrier once and for all.

Before inking that minor league deal, Rickey studied Robinson closely. With the help of scouting reports from Clyde Sukeforth, a top adviser who would play a pivotal role in Robinson's rise, Rickey knew the so-called Negro Leagues were brimming with talented, outstanding African American players who were ready to make history with the Dodgers if only they got the call.

There was Satchel Paige, the flame-throwing pitcher. The great New York Yankees slugger Joe DiMaggio once identified Paige as "the best and fastest pitcher" he'd ever faced, though he was aging by 1945.[4]

Then there was the speedy outfielder James Thomas "Cool Papa" Bell. Legend had it he was able to run so fast that at bedtime on the road he could switch off the light and be safely under the covers before his hotel room got dark.

But Robinson was about so much more than just raw physical skill. He was crafty and cunning, he possessed guts and grit, and—oh yes—he had both brains and brawn, disproving the stereotypes about African American athletes at that time. In the 1930s, before Robinson came of age, sportswriter Grantland Rice described the Alabama-born black track-and-field star Jesse Owens's skill at the Berlin Olympics as that of "a wild Zulu running amuck."[5]

Author Roger Kahn captured this point perfectly in his famous book about the Dodgers of the 1940s and 1950s, *The Boys of Summer*, which is essentially a terrific love letter to that team of yesteryear. He noted Robinson could hit and steal bases, but a lot of players could do that. What separated Robinson from the others was something extra.

"He had intimidating skills, and he burned with a dark fire," wrote Kahn. "He wanted passionately to win. He charged at ball games. He calculated his rivals' weaknesses and measured his own strengths and knew—as only a very few have ever known—the precise move to make at precisely the moment of maximum effect."[6]

For all of their differences, these were traits Robinson and Rickey shared. The executive was a master at pushing buttons, maneuvering, and scheming to get what he wanted. Like Robinson on the base paths, Rickey in the general manager's suite knew the precise move to make at just the right moment.

To borrow Kahn's phrase about Robinson, Rickey also had a "dark fire" within him to right the wrongs of racism, which set him on a mission to bring profound change to America.

Rickey carefully plotted each step of the integration of baseball, crafting a battle plan to overcome the unofficial agreement among baseball team owners that kept African Americans out of the big leagues. And he was prepared to adjust the plan to help Robinson figure out everything from how to handle the demanding New York media to much more difficult hardships, like the white fans who would be shouting "nigger"—and even worse—from the bleachers. Inevitably, fueled by hate, violent men would threaten to kill the player and his beautiful wife, Rachel.

There were wrinkles to Rickey's plan that were kept secret from the public for decades, as we will soon explore. But somehow the executive powered through the challenges and, clearly, so did Robinson.

WINNERS' INSTINCT

Part of Robinson's strength came from his own burning desire to win at everything. This urge is perhaps best summed up by longtime baseball player and manager Leo Durocher, known as "Leo the Lip" for his blunt comments and fiery clashes with umpires. "Ya want a guy that comes to play," Durocher said of Robinson. "This guy didn't just come to play. He come to beat ya."

"He come to stuff the bat—" Durocher added of Robinson—well, you get the idea about the rest of that sentence.[7]

Yet the man who seemed as though he could stick a baseball bat where the sun didn't shine had a far gentler, more compassionate side. That side could easily be seen in Robinson's deep religious conviction. When he did embrace his role in reversing centuries of whites-only tradition, Robinson's faith became his anchor.

This comes alive in Robinson's papers at the Library of Congress. Beyond the unpublished manuscript mentioned earlier, there are also copies of dozens of sermons and speeches. Robinson delivered them after his playing days were over, in the late 1950s and throughout the 1960s.

A prime example is a speech from Robinson that was deeply personal, as he leaned heavily on the book of Job to compare Job's battle with God with the struggle of blacks in America.

The book of Job chronicles the story of an honorable man whom God, following a wager with Satan, allowed to be punished. Job lost everything but did not give up his faith and refused to wallow in self-pity, instead declaring, "Wherefore do I take my flesh in my teeth, and put my life in mine hand? Though he slay me, yet will I trust in him: but I will maintain mine own ways before him" (Job 13:14–15).

Robinson used this illustration in a speech that is undated in the archives at the Library of Congress, but other references in the speech suggest it was delivered sometime between Richard Nixon's election as president in 1968 and Robinson's death in 1972.

"As a black man I have a special affinity for Job," Robinson wrote. "It may be an exaggeration to do so, but I translate his story into the story of the black man in America."[8]

Robinson continued. "Like Job, we were suddenly bereft of our wealth (civilization, language, land)—our health (brutalized by slavery)—our family (slaves had no family rights)—kept in bondage, enduring the scornful eye of the community and the revulsion of our masters. Like Job was, we have been on our knees in this country covered not with physical sores, but with spiritual and psychological sores. Like Job we know misery. Like Job we have advisors telling us if we are so treated it must be our own fault, our natural inferiority. But like Job we answer, 'I am a man, and therefore worthy. Though you slay me, I will maintain my own ways before you.'"

It is important to point out that Robinson largely stressed a hopeful message about the plight of African Americans. Yet sometimes in his speeches and writings, he seemed to grow somewhat bitter, because change was coming too slowly. Still, he continually urged his fellow citizens of all races to pull themselves up by their own bootstraps and stand up on their own to succeed. He leaned heavily on Scripture as the road map for improving race relations in America.

"As an individual I do not pretend to [have] the status of Job, his innocence, his goodness, his courage are beyond me," Robinson declared. "But as a black man I understand him. And it was as a black man that I had to make my way, and maintain my own ways. My life is checkered with the criticism of 'friendly counselors'—the critics who thought they knew better than I what I should do, feel, and think. The acquaintance whose cheap advice I refused. The power-seeking politicians who wanted to buy my loyalty. The envious who wanted me to get on my knees in gratitude for what baseball had done for me. . . . The mentally disturbed who longed for my downfall."

Here in the speech text, Robinson added a note about "baseball fans who hated me (letters, telephone calls, etc.)."

It was clear more than a decade after he left the game he loved that the attacks still stung badly. And yet Robinson did not wallow in sorrow; in his speech, he immediately pivoted in the next line to the positive: "I had to choose early," noted Robinson. "The alternatives were these: to be owned or to own myself. I chose the latter. The only freedom . . . is the freedom to be [one's] self. Through it all I had to follow my instincts. When I made mistakes, they were my mistakes. When I succeeded they were my successes. For me there was only one choice—I had to be me. Right or wrong, good or ill, I had to be me."

Robinson revealed how this conviction played out again and again in his life: "I had to be me when black people told me to get guns and kill Whitey. That wasn't me. I had to be me when white people told me to cool it—to take all abuse and not react. That wasn't me."

This was a man who was not only prepared to face down the opposition but also determined not to lose himself in the struggle.

A DIFFERENT FACE ON THE FIELD

Robinson's personal papers reveal more hints of how faith, in ways both small and profound, helped get him through the ugly days of his time as a Dodger.

In a 1962 speech to the Southern Christian Leadership Conference (SCLC), Robinson explained to a room of pastors that "the Negro minister, North and South, was a true friend and ally to me in my early days in the game."[9]

Controversy would follow the Dodgers as they traveled with Robinson through segregated areas of the country, so ministers found creative ways to make sure the local stadiums were packed with people of color, cheering the new player on as he faced other fans trying to run him out of town.

"I guess you know that when a Baptist preacher cuts his sermon short so he can let services out early to allow the people to come out to the ball field, that's making a sacrifice," said Robinson. "Many times, this has been done by our ministers and they did it, not just to see a ball game but because they knew that, as the first Negro in the majors, I needed the support and backing of my own people. I'll never forget what ministers like you who lead [the] SCLC did for me."[10]

In another speech at a Methodist church in New York in 1966, Robinson slipped into the third person to make his point, and invoked Dr. Martin Luther King Jr.

"Well, my beloved friend Martin Luther King had a dream and Jackie Robinson has a *debt*," Robinson said, with the word *debt* underlined in his draft. "I have a debt to young people who—black and white—wanted me to make it—to succeed—back in those tough days when I was a beginner in baseball and when many people were not used to seeing [a] black face out there on the baseball field. I have a debt to Negro people who turned out to show their loyalty—NOT to me—but to the [concept] that [if] baseball was to be an All-American game, it had to include all Americans."[11]

It's a pretty simple concept: the national pastime did not begin to open up to the rest of America until Jackie Robinson played.

As Roger Kahn wrote, for decades fans had simply been conditioned to believe the baseball diamond itself was supposed to look and feel a certain way. "The grass was green, the dirt was brown and the ball players were white," declared Kahn. "Suddenly in Ebbets Field, under a white home uniform, two muscled arms extended like black hawsers. *Black.* Like the arms of a janitor. The new color jolted the consciousness, in a profound and not quite definable way."[12]

Beyond his physical gifts, there was a spiritual strength to Robinson. He saw that faith in God was woven into the very fabric of the push for civil rights. This was on display on that Sunday in 1967 for the old man in the pulpit.

The same eyes that worked so well on the baseball diamond could not see quite so clearly anymore. He was going blind, his body under assault by diabetes, which was rapidly sapping the energy of this great man. This church in New Rochelle, to the north of New York City, was only about twenty-five miles from Brooklyn. Yet Robinson was so far from his glory days. "I am not out to be anybody's martyr or hero," he said from the pulpit. "But I think we all ought to join hands and hearts and effort and whatever else is necessary to enlighten the world about us."[13]

He was taking stock of himself and of his country too. Robinson was trying to impart what he had learned, which was that belief in God could help ease racial tensions.

"If the church of the living God cannot save America in this hour of crisis," he told the congregation, "what can save us?"

Just a few months earlier, the nation had been consumed by race riots. Entire cities like Newark and Detroit were ravaged by violence and destruction.

Robinson had started his sermon by quoting from the New Testament, the gospel according to John: "He that is without sin among you, let him first cast a stone at her" (John 8:7). And here Robinson scribbled a reminder to himself: "repeat slowly," according to a notation in his personal papers. "'He that is without sin among you, let him first cast a stone at her,'" he repeated.

Then he added, "It is a fitting story to recall as we Americans turn sadly from a period of crisis and look ahead to see the almost certain development of more crisis, more danger, more riots, more bloodshed, more division and the cancerous growth of more hatred between black and white."

As this book is published, fifty years after Robinson's sermon, America is still struggling with some of the same division. So it is instructive to explore why this civil rights icon turned to God to try to answer some of these difficult questions. He had wrestled with them over and over in his life. And, at several key junctures, he leaned on the Bible and his personal faith to get him through.

This is an approach he shared with Rickey. Just as Robinson was using this church in New Rochelle to deliver his message during a tumultuous time in American history, Rickey had his own habit of slipping into churches wherever he traveled.

When he was thinking on something or felt a bit overwhelmed, Rickey would find a church to help steady himself. The denomination of the church did not matter to him.

"I like to go into a church of any faith, where the builders have had in mind a beautiful edifice. Not elaborate necessarily, but with attention to detail," Rickey explained. "Once inside, the pews, the chancel, the pulpit, the choir loft, the organ and the windows—all and everything—seeming to combine to produce a sense of worship, even without music or without a word being said to anybody."

Rickey added simply, "I like that. You can feel at once that you are in a place where you are already getting what you need—spiritual medicine."[14]

It was a clue about a little secret he appeared to have confided in just one person, a minister in Brooklyn.

CHAPTER 3

RICKEY HAD A SECRET

I first heard about Branch Rickey's secret in October 2007, from freelance journalist Donna Shor. I was sitting next to Shor at a dinner party in Washington, DC, at the luxurious home of the ambassador of Belgium to the United States.

The only other memorable parts of the dinner were that the ambassador was a delightful man with a fabulous wine cellar (that, unfortunately, had been recently raided by a now-fired employee), and he decided to serve pigeon as the main course. It was a delicacy for him back home, but it tasted pretty nasty. His other guests were politicians, and they did what they do best, giving speeches that were boring and lasted too long.

I decided to launch my early getaway, mumbling something about a World Series baseball game on television, as I said good night to Shor.

"Oh, you like baseball?" asked Shor. "My late father-in-law played a major role in baseball history, but the story has never really been told."[1]

I sat back down.

My reporter's instinct kicked in, and I suddenly could hear nothing else happening at the dinner party around me. I wanted to get every last detail from Shor.

It turns out her father-in-law was Rev. L. Wendell Fifield of what was then known as Plymouth Church of the Pilgrims, in Brooklyn, New York.

This was not just any house of worship. It was once the epicenter of the antislavery movement in America under the leadership of its first minister, Henry Ward Beecher. His sister, Harriet Beecher Stowe, wrote the anti-slavery novel *Uncle Tom's Cabin*, and the Congregationalist church became a stop on the Underground Railroad. Everyone from Abraham Lincoln to Martin Luther King Jr. preached there.

Shor revealed to me that the church was the setting for one more crucial milestone in the civil rights movement. Branch Rickey had popped into the church unannounced one day in 1945, after hesitating about whether he could really go through with integrating Major League Baseball.

My brief interaction with Shor sent me on this journey to find out how much of a role faith played not only in bringing together Rickey and Jackie Robinson but also in sustaining them through the crises that lay ahead. However, as my responsibilities at work accelerated—reporting on the historic 2008 presidential campaign for CNN and then covering the transition to power for Barack Obama from senator to the nation's first African American president—my ability to conduct the research I needed to put together the book slowed.

And I was not sure of the accuracy of the story anyway. Shor had initially described it as a story passed on within the family, but I did not have anything on paper to document it.

Then, by chance again, I ran into Shor at a charity event in Washington around the spring of 2011. She informed me her daughter, Donnali Fifield, had made a breakthrough. While rummaging through twenty-five unsorted boxes from the archives of the minister and his wife, June Fifield, she found an essay June had written about Rickey.

It suggested something magical happened at the church.

Now, more than ever, I was determined to put the story together. In April 2011, I wrote up a short version of the story for CNN with the invaluable help of my producer at the time, Jamie Crawford. We wanted to reveal our findings in time for the sixty-fourth anniversary of Robinson's first game for the Dodgers.

That is how I wound up at Plymouth Church, wandering the grounds with veteran documentary filmmaker Ken Burns. If anyone knows the intimate details of our national pastime, it is Burns. His Emmy Award–winning 1994 documentary miniseries, *Baseball*, is widely considered the definitive film on the history of the game. By now, he was working on another long documentary, this one about Robinson's life, so I invited him to join me as I tried to track down the first leg of this story. Even he had not heard about Rickey's struggle.

"We're so rarely given the opportunity to look into a moment of decision-making, and do it from a position of all the different factors that go into it," Burns told me. "It was the right thing to do. [Rickey] already understood that from his lifetime of experience. But he had to sort of square it with God, I think."[2]

AT A LOSS FOR WORDS

On this day in 1945, Rickey was bearing the pressure alone. His health was a bit shaky, and Rickey noted his wife was leery of him taking all of this upon his shoulders. "She is fearful of my health deteriorating as a result of the controversy signing a colored player is certain to generate," he said.[3] Rickey suffered from heart trouble and had been diagnosed with Meniere's disease. At times it could result in debilitating vertigo, nausea, and vomiting so bad it required hospital stays.

Rickey's grandson recalled the emotional toll. "My grandfather had riding on this a forty-year career," Branch Rickey III told me. "He had fought to come from this humble farm background and fought to become recognized as a successful businessman and a success in the sporting community. And he was faced with challenging the entire institution that he had fought hard to gain standing in, by fighting and going forward to sign Jackie."[4]

This is why Rickey thought about every nuance of the decision. He was a precise man who had privately mapped out almost every detail. This is, after all, the man who famously said, "Luck is the residue of design."[5]

Rickey had done so much planning, and yet he was not prepared for the crucial last ingredient. All the items on his checklist had been handled, but now he had gotten to his own personal part of the design. Could he go through with the last step?

He slipped out of the Dodgers' offices at 215 Montague Street in Brooklyn and headed to Plymouth Church at 75 Hicks Street. It's just about a five-minute stroll from point A to point B. Yet it was part of a much longer journey.

THE MEETING AT THE CHURCH

The intercom crackled in the office of Reverend Fifield up on the second floor of the church.

"Mr. Rickey is here and asks to come in," the secretary announced.[6]

Fifield was a scholarly man but also very informal, so he never demanded an appointment for someone with an urgent problem.

"Certainly. Show him in," said Fifield.

According to Mrs. Fifield's essay, Rickey made it clear he did not want to chat when he reached the office on the second floor of the church. Rickey said very little that day, but it is important to remember what he said about his visits to churches allowing him to "produce a sense of worship, even without music or without a word being said to anybody."[7]

This was Branch Rickey's "dark night of the soul."

That famous phrase is the title of a poem written by John of the Cross, a Catholic saint and Spanish poet from the 1500s. He described the trans-formative experience that can play out when a person struggles with a problem and seeks God's wisdom—despair can lead to illumination.

"I just want to be here," said Rickey. "Do you mind?"

Rickey began pacing the floor, clearly struggling and unable to verbal-ize his thoughts. According to Shor, the minister would later tell his wife it seemed as though the executive wore a groove into the carpet from the full forty-five minutes of pacing, interrupted by brief glances out the window at the church garden in the courtyard below. And despite Fifield's scholarly demeanor, he was the perfect sounding board, even if Rickey was not yet saying much of anything. Fifield's relatives remember him as someone who, like Rickey, was an outgoing man with a good sense of humor.

For Reverend Fifield, this was a familiar routine: a man would show up unannounced for a confession or some kind of spiritual guidance. The man would be struggling with his conscience and knew he needed to work the problem out, but maybe could not quite explain himself. So Fifield waited patiently as he went back to the paperwork on his desk.

"Don't let me interrupt," Rickey instructed the minister. "I can't talk with you."[8]

The gregarious baseball boss with the bulbous nose and bushy eyebrows, famous for being longwinded and effusive, was quite simply tongue-tied. He could not share his secret with friends, relatives, or colleagues within the Brooklyn Dodgers organization. And when it came time to confide the details of what was raging inside his soul, Rickey was so overcome with emotion he was unable to spit out what was on his mind. So he brought his problem to the church's pastor, who knew Rickey socially and had been invited to visit Ebbets Field for some games and another special occasion.

On May 13, 1945, just a few days after Victory in Europe Day, Fifield joined two other faith leaders from Brooklyn at the ballpark to help lead Dodgers fans in a "Day of Prayer" that President Harry Truman had called for to mark the end of World War II in Europe. The *New York Times* reported that Fifield, along with a Catholic priest and a rabbi, offered interfaith prayers from a microphone positioned at home plate.[9]

It was far quieter when Rickey came to visit Fifield on his turf, a meeting that appears to have occurred later in 1945, though Mrs. Fifield did not record the precise date in her essay. After Rickey entered Fifield's office, nearly an hour would pass before the executive uttered another word.

This was unlike the talkative Rickey, who looked like a lovable but slightly embarrassing uncle as he strutted around Ebbets Field in a wrinkled suit with a giant bow tie and a bright pocket square for a little flair. On the field, his floppy hat would be dangling off his head, and he would be chomping on a cigar in the corner of his mouth. He barked out orders to his associates at the Dodgers, who all referred to him quite simply as "Mr. Rickey," with no exception. He would then typically rush up to the sportswriters with a pat on the back and an avalanche of gabbing about his team and himself.

Rickey was a man who, despite his girth, was constantly in motion. He would work eighteen hours a day trying desperately to make the Dodgers a winner. He was an innovator within the national pastime. During a previous stint with the St. Louis Cardinals, he created the modern-day farm system of minor league teams. This was a place for major league teams to groom young talent, setting up a pipeline of new players—such a good idea that every other team eventually copied Rickey.

His vigorous brain activity would usually translate into nonstop chatter. Colleagues recalled that Rickey would dictate memos on cars, trains, airplanes—and, yes, even as he sat on the toilet. So many words spilled out of Rickey's mouth that the boys with the typewriters nicknamed his office the "Cave of the Winds."

In fact, Rickey earned himself several nicknames over the course of his career, beyond just "The Mahatma." Other nicknames included "El Cheapo," for slashing player contracts whenever he could, as well as "The Deacon," as a nod to his frequent sermons, formal or informal, on almost any topic.

"Mahatma" was given to him by sportswriter Tom Meany in 1942. It was a nod to John Gunther's description of Mahatma Gandhi being "an incredible combination" of Jesus Christ, a Tammany Hall leader, and your dad.[10]

"Mr. Rickey was an actor," recalled Carl Erskine. "He could have been a John Barrymore in the movies if he wanted to be—I'm not kidding you."[11]

Another side of Rickey's personality was particularly revealing as he struggled with his big secret in 1945. He was a planner, who would chew over every nuance of a problem very carefully.

Years later, Robinson would confide in Dodgers' famed broadcaster Red Barber about Rickey mapping out every last detail of the experiment. "This guy said this . . . this fellow did that . . . and I almost felt like laughing, because that is exactly how Mr. Rickey said it would be," recalled Robinson. "I haven't experienced a thing Mr. Rickey didn't tell me I would."[12]

And Rickey's relatives recall him being intense and exacting about almost anything concerning the Dodgers or within his personal life, big or small.

Every Sunday night, he would host a big family dinner at his home, sometimes with up to fifteen people around a giant table. Friends were invited to join the conversation about national issues, local politics, or the latest baseball decision he had to make. The general manager would present a series of facts, pause, and then go rapid-fire around the room to get everyone's take. He was thoughtful enough to also call on his grandson, who remembers being seven or eight years old and weighing in on the great issues of the day.

He would press each person, "What would *you* do in this situation?" Then he would carefully take in everyone's opinion before offering his summation.

"My grandfather would sit there and examine three or four more points that nobody had brought up," Branch Rickey III told me. "He needed people oftentimes to bounce ideas off of—many times members of his own family or members of his own staff. But sometimes he just needed time to resolve in his own heart how he was going to go about—and how he was going to attack—a particularly gnarly situation. And this perhaps was the gnarliest of what he encountered in his career."[13]

It's no surprise that the particularly gnarly situation the elder Rickey was mulling over on this day in 1945 was whether to sign Robinson to a minor league contract to play for the Montreal Royals and give him a shot at potentially playing for the Dodgers.

THE IMAGE OF MR. RICKEY

This meeting with Reverend Fifield was a gut check for Rickey. Could he really go through with signing Robinson? Or was it time to pull the plug?

The Hollywood version of Robinson's ascent, the movie *42*, follows the trusted narrative suggesting that Rickey's devout Christianity led him to make an unwavering, moral decision. This supported the public image of Rickey as so religious—and with the negotiating skills of a rough-and-tumble politician—that nothing could stop him from getting his way, especially when it came to his dream of integrating baseball.

And clearly, evidence suggests that he was determined. Jane Jones, one of Rickey's daughters, remembered her dad at breakfast reading from a book by Gunnar Myrdal, a famed Swedish economist and sociologist who eventually shared a Nobel Memorial Prize in Economic Sciences. The book, *An American Dilemma: The Negro Problem and Modern Democracy*, was pioneering in its study of the obstacles African Americans faced in the late 1930s and 1940s.[14] Then, following New York's passage of the 1945 Ives-Quinn Act, the first state law to bar employment discrimination, the general manager announced, "They can't stop me now."[15]

After Rickey joined the Dodgers following the 1942 season, he had settled into a house in Forest Hills Gardens, in the borough of Queens. He began attending Sunday services at a nearby house of worship, the Church in the Gardens, and sometimes he would be invited to deliver the sermon. Biographer Jimmy Breslin noted that in one of those sermons, Rickey flat-out said he came to New York "to serve the God to whom they prayed, and the Lord's work called for him to bring the first black player into Major League Baseball."[16]

Despite all that fervor, it was not just a simple baseball move that Rickey was contemplating. This was about America, not merely whether the Dodgers would sign a new slugger. The choice could have profound implications on the nation for decades. Remember that in 1945, America's military was still segregated, as were many of its schools. And even though baseball officials insisted there was no rule against African Americans playing, the game's longtime commissioner from 1920 to 1944—Kenesaw Mountain Landis—was a virulent opponent of integration. He once had the gall to claim that African American players were simply doing too well in the Negro Leagues to even desire to break into the big leagues.

When Happy Chandler became commissioner in 1945 after Landis's death, Rickey would eventually gain an ally. And a couple of years earlier, Rickey also got a boost when the board members of the Brooklyn Trust Company—which had a majority stake in the Dodgers—gave the green light on his request for more money to widen the Dodgers' scouting efforts. Rickey made it clear to the head of the bank, George V. McLaughlin, this would mean the scouts would sometimes bring back a "Negro" player for potential new talent. McLaughlin considered the consequences, including noting they could make money from the increased attendance of African Americans, and said yes.

The door had been cracked open.

Yet Rickey had enormous power in calling the shots for the Dodgers. So, as he sat there with the minister in Brooklyn, the heat was on him. The famous lunch counter sit-ins of the civil rights movement had not yet begun. *Brown v. Board of Education* had not yet been decided. In other words, Rickey "had a dream" a full eighteen years before Dr. King's March on Washington.

And as courageous as Rickey was on this day and so many other days in the years ahead, it is so critical to never forget that Robinson was the man who would soon take on the biggest burden of all. He and other pioneering African American ballplayers, like Don Newcombe and Roy Campanella, had a major impact on generations of people of all races.

Newcombe recalled, "Martin Luther King told me, in my home one night, 'You'll never know what you and Jackie and Roy did to make it possible to do my job.'"[17]

Rickey and Robinson had the guts to go first, and, eventually, they would form an incredible team. There in Reverend Fifield's office, though, the executive was groping for answers, not as sure of himself as the legend would suggest. The truth is more complicated. History is living and breathing: just as we think we know every last detail, we uncover a new layer.

As Rachel Robinson once said of Rickey in general: "I thought Mr. Rickey got stereotyped, caricatured. I saw him in different moods, so it was never just this cigar-chewing, funny-hat guy, who was Bible-thumping and always giving sermons. I saw him more as a total man and I think the legend tends to deny him that totality."[18]

A BURDEN SHARED

First and foremost, if Rickey went through with signing Robinson, he would have to excel as a baseball player. Otherwise, another African American would not get a chance for a long time.

"It might have been 50 *more* years before they'd let a black play," Buck O'Neil, a great Negro Leagues player who made it to the major leagues as a coach but not a player, would say years later. "They would have said, 'You picked the best, and he couldn't make it. So there's nobody else out there. They just can't think well enough to play major league baseball.'"[19]

That was quite a lot for Robinson to carry on his shoulders; outstanding white prospects failed in the majors all the time, and it barely registered with the public. Another white kid simply got called up from the minors and was given a chance to take the job.

Over the next few years, the death threats against Robinson would pour in at an alarming rate, racist fans warning the infielder should be careful when he jogged out to his position. As a September 1953 letter warned, he might go the way of Arnold L. Schuster, a Brooklynite shot in the eyes and groin the previous year.[20]

Yes, it was that ugly. There were times in the days ahead when Robinson would consider giving up. He later wrote in his autobiography about how he felt after a particularly awful round of abuse directed by the manager of the Philadelphia Phillies: "For one wild and rage-crazed minute I thought, 'To Hell with Mr. Rickey's "noble experiment."'" He added bluntly that he wanted to grab one of his white tormenters and "smash his teeth with my despised black fist."[21]

Yet time and again, people of faith held Jackie up in the low moments. When a local ruling in Jacksonville banned Robinson and another African American player from taking the field during spring training in 1946, a Presbyterian church in the North fired off a letter to the city leaders calling it a "great injury to democracy and brotherhood" in violation of the "Gospel of Jesus Christ."[22]

Robinson would have to try to perform under the most difficult conditions, with the vilest racial epithets shouted from the stands and with some racist players actually sharpening the spikes at the bottom of their shoes to try to injure him with an extra hard slide into a base.[23] Rickey repeatedly instructed Robinson not to fight back when spectators shouted horrific slurs at him; otherwise, the media would portray the player as belligerent.

Everyone would remember only the second punch, and it would all come undone. So why focus on the negative, when God had another path?

All of this was racing in Rickey's mind, on the second floor office of the church, when, suddenly, he had an epiphany.

"I've got it!" Rickey exclaimed, banging a fist on Fifield's desk and rattling everything from the intercom to a fountain pen.

He slammed the fist down a second time in elation: "I've got it!"

"Got what, Branch?" asked Fifield.

The minister had had enough of the silence; he pressed, "How much longer before I find out what you're up to? Pacing around here and banging on my furniture and keeping the whole thing to yourself? Come on, out with it!"

Rickey sank back into a chair.

"Wendell," he said simply. "I've decided to sign Jackie Robinson!"

Then Rickey started to cry, pulling out a handkerchief to blow his nose and collect his thoughts. Next came the moment when the gut-wrenching became glorious.

"I had to talk to God about it and be sure He wanted me to do it," declared Rickey. "I hope you don't mind."

Then Rickey straightened his bow tie and reached for his hat, preparing to leave.

"Bless you, Wendell," Rickey concluded.[24]

Had Rickey seriously been considering calling it off? Or was he certain of the path and just wanted to bring a little more clarity to it?

"We know it was a complex issue," Sharon Robinson, the late ball-player's daughter, told me in an interview. "We also know that Branch Rickey was very spiritual. So to me it makes perfect sense that he would work this through with his pastor even though in his mind he may have sort of known that was the direction he was going."[25]

Rickey's grandson says the visit to Plymouth Church is something the general manager never shared with his family. "He's seeming to come up with an answer, he's got the elation, 'I got it!'" said Branch Rickey III. "But as he stands up and leaves the office, got what? What answers? There is nothing but hard road ahead. There's no snap, the gates open and every-thing is going to be elegant."[26]

Earlier in 1945, Rickey had been ambushed at a meeting with baseball executives in Cleveland. According to his grandson, the other officials had gotten hints of Rickey's plan and decided to berate him about his efforts to change the country.

"To a man, everyone in the room condemned my grandfather," said Branch Rickey III. "No other owner, not a single one, stood up for him. Among men he thought were colleagues and friends, my grandfather found himself utterly and completely alone."

That feeling of loneliness may help explain why Rickey sought out that minister.

"If Jackie was a failure, if Jackie became something that was not acceptable, I think my grandfather's reputation could have very quickly gone down the drain," said his grandson. "And I think he would have easily been sacrificed."[27]

The elder Rickey likely felt he could trust Fifield to keep his indecision, his groping, even his tears under wraps. And that was true—to a point.

The minister fatefully shared the story with June Fifield before he died in 1964, because he wanted the world to know—after Rickey's lifetime—there was a lot more to the story of Rickey's decision to sign Robinson.

So when Rickey passed away in 1965, Mrs. Fifield acted on her husband's wishes and spilled the secret in the church bulletin in order to finally let Jackie and Rachel—and maybe someday the rest of the world—in on what she believed to be a wonderful affirmation of God's presence in our lives.

June Fifield stressed she hesitated to share the story but eventually felt it was right because she meant it as "a plea to Jackie Robinson to realize what went into the launching of his career—that someone cared enough to grope for wisdom beyond himself, to call upon God's guidance—and that the man who did this was, in common erroneous parlance, 'white.'"

In the essay she put in the church bulletin, she concluded poignantly, "I hope Jackie will see his fellow man in a new light, knowing this story. May he ever remember Branch Rickey's soul searching in the presence of the God of us all, on his own 'days of decision.'"[28]

All of us have our own "days of decision" where things may seem hopeless. We're groping for answers, not sure of where to turn. Rickey set a powerful example of turning to God for those answers, no matter how big or small the challenges faced.

I wanted to find out if Mrs. Fifield's dream of getting the message to Robinson, before he died far too young, came true. Now was the time to step up my journey to explore this story about faith in God, the glue that held Rickey and Robinson together as they changed America forever.

CHAPTER 4

JACKIE ON A TRAIN

After I had coffee with a close family friend, Susanna Quinn, an entrepreneur who was expanding her business into Chicago, it was a glorious summer day for a morning walk along South Michigan Avenue.

When I reached the Hilton Chicago, a stream of summer tourists hoping for early check-ins were wheeling their luggage through the revolving doors, blissfully unaware they were walking in the footsteps of the great Jackie Robinson. This was the spot where Brooklyn Dodgers scout Clyde Sukeforth secretly met with Jackie to start the process of seeing whether he was ready for the big leagues.

Facing Lake Michigan at 720 S. Michigan Avenue, the Hilton Chicago has been host to all kinds of amazing history. Established in 1927 by developer James W. Stevens, grandfather of future Supreme Court justice John Paul Stevens, it was named the Stevens Hotel. When built, it was the largest hotel in the world, boasting three thousand rooms. Several clues still linger on the classic edifice.

The first is easy to miss, a tiny letter "S" embossed into each of the brass revolving doors at the front entrance, a subtle nod to its origins. The second is the stunning beaux arts architectural design in the grand lobby, which helped push the original price tag for construction to $30 million, ten times what it cost a few years earlier to build the original Yankee Stadium (where Robinson would eventually play in several World Series games).

Like so many properties during the Great Depression, however, it went belly up. The US Army later purchased it and transformed it into barracks and classroom space during World War II. Conrad Hilton bought it after the war and later renamed it "The Conrad Hilton."[1]

The first guest at the Stevens was the sitting vice president of the United States under Calvin Coolidge, Charles G. Dawes. Since then, the Hilton Chicago has hosted every sitting president. John F. Kennedy was known for getting the wait staff to slip some beer into his coffee mug to help him get through never-ending dinners in the Grand Ballroom.[2]

When I entered the lobby in the summer of 2016, I quickly realized I had been there before, several times, with another president: Barack Obama. When he was rolling out new members of his cabinet as president-elect, Obama held a series of news conferences at the Hilton Chicago. And on that historic election night in November 2008, the victory party was held right across the street from the hotel in Grant Park, with hundreds of thousands of people celebrating the nation's first African American president.

"Oh, it was unbelievable," a young African American employee of the hotel told me, still in awe eight years later.

I asked if he knew Robinson had been here in 1945.

"I did not know that," he exclaimed. "Wow, something new!"

The Stevens Hotel was also the setting for part of *The Natural*, a classic baseball movie. Fake slugger Roy Hobbs (played by Robert Redford) was shot in a room at the Stevens Hotel.

The circumstances around Robinson's visit were far less nefarious. He was in Chicago in 1945, playing for the Kansas City Monarchs in a Negro Leagues game against the Lincoln Giants at old Comiskey Park.

Sukeforth was actually the second Dodgers scout to be sent to Chicago to take a measure of Robinson. In 1944, Rickey told scout Tom Greenwade—the same scout who discovered Mickey Mantle in Kansas—to surreptitiously scope out talent among black players. One of the players he followed was Robinson.

By the fifth inning of a nine-inning game in the Windy City, Greenwade had already decided Robinson was worth Rickey's time. He left the stadium and paid a cab driver two dollars to drive his scouting report to the airport to be taken to Rickey's office in New York.

In a March 1960 edition of *Sport* magazine, writer Jack Orr told the story of how Rickey called Greenwade after getting the report, and the scout said Robinson was not quite prepared to play in Brooklyn.

"Is he ready for Montreal?" Rickey added of his key minor league affiliate.

Greenwade hesitated. Rickey got impatient.

"Then Mr. Rickey, I guess remembering I'm from the South, says, 'If he was white, would he be ready for Montreal?'" recalled Greenwade. "'Yes,' I say. Then all the things happen to Jackie and he goes on to be most valuable and all that, and I still look back sometimes and feel kind of sorry that Mr. Rickey had to ask me the question, 'If he was white . . .'"[3]

Rickey let his plans for integration marinate a bit more. Then, in 1945, he ordered "Sukey," as Sukeforth was known to everyone around Brooklyn, to get to Chicago at once.

He told Sukey to keep his conversations with Robinson under wraps and not to come back from the Midwest without him: "Bring him in!"[4]

Rickey was a powerful man used to having people at his beck and call, so the next comment stuck with Sukey. "And if he can't get away to meet me," he told the scout, "I am willing to go anywhere to meet him."[5]

His biggest concern in terms of baseball skills was whether Robinson, who played shortstop, had a "gun" or not. Was his arm powerful enough to heave the ball to first base from far across the field in time to easily throw out a base runner?

The rest of Rickey's instructions belied the fact that there were much bigger issues at stake than athletics.

"Get him away from his teammates, so nobody will know what you are doing," Rickey added. "I need absolute secrecy here."[6]

Robinson, naturally, was kept in the dark about the details. All Sukeforth told him, as part of the subterfuge, was that Rickey was starting a new blacks-only league, along with Gus Greenlee, who had previously been in charge of the Negro National League. Rickey was allegedly looking to add

Robinson to a team that would be called the Brooklyn Brown Dodgers. The team would use Ebbets Field when the original Dodgers were out of town.

This was a way to throw racists off the trail of Rickey's true intention of potentially bringing Robinson to Brooklyn. Yet some African American journalists did not get the head fake, and they jumped on Rickey.

Ludlow Werner of the *New York Age* was also unimpressed with disparaging comments that Rickey had made during the press conference about communists pushing to integrate baseball. "Did you ever hear such double talk from a big pompous ass in your life?" Werner asked, calling Rickey a "big windbag" who would never put a black man in a Brooklyn uniform.[7]

Sukeforth arrived early at Comiskey Park to watch batting practice. He spotted Robinson.

"I could see the determination all over him," Sukeforth said. "He'd have impressed anybody."[8]

There was little doubt about Jackie's abilities at that time. "Duke Snider and I were roommates," Carl Erskine told me about the great Dodgers center fielder. "Duke came from Compton, California, so he saw Jackie play at UCLA. And he said, 'Shoot, Jackie would have been the greatest running back in football history'" if he had chosen that route instead.[9]

Casually leaning over a railing along the third-base line, Sukeforth began waving his arms, trying to get Robinson's attention.

"Robinson! Jackie Robinson!" yelled Sukeforth.

Robinson glanced over his shoulder to see a white man he did not know waving him toward the stands.

Robinson was rightfully cautious. Practical jokers had approached Negro Leagues players before, posing as scouts just for the sick thrill of crushing their dreams a little more. Nevertheless, Sukeforth convinced Robinson that he really was a scout. The player walked over.

"You Jack Robinson?" asked Sukeforth.

Yes, Robinson answered, but he was still puzzled.

After introducing himself, Sukey explained he was with the Dodgers.

"You know Mr. Rickey has a colored club now, the Brown Dodgers, and he's looking for top ballplayers. He's heard about you and he wanted me to watch you throw from the hole." That referred to the shortstop throwing a ball from between second and third base, out near the outfield grass, the longest toss an infielder has to make.

"Wrong time," Robinson said. "Couldn't be worse. You won't see me do any throwing from the hole tonight. I hurt my shoulder a couple of days ago and I'm not going to be playing for at least a week."

Robinson recalled that he was grinning despite the injury, perhaps because he was happy to have an excuse to tell Sukeforth to buzz off. The player had been down this same road before, and it had taken him nowhere.

But Sukeforth kept on pressing. Knowing Rickey's determination, the scout asked the player to at least do him the favor of meeting up later.

"I'd like to talk to you after the game," said Sukeforth. "I'm at the Stevens Hotel. How about meeting me there at the cigar stand in the lobby as soon as you can after the game is over?"[10]

BASEBALL'S BATTLE OF JERICHO

Robinson had already faced bitter disappointment at what essentially turned out to be a fake tryout with the Boston Red Sox a few weeks earlier. The pioneering sportswriter Wendell Smith had gotten his newspaper, the *Pittsburgh Courier*, to pay for the travel of Robinson and two of his colleagues from the Negro Leagues to Boston.

Red Sox team officials had no interest in adding African American players, but they were trying to get a local city councilman off their backs. He had been threatening to ban professional baseball in the city on Sundays unless at least one African American player was given a tryout.

Robinson rose to the occasion in his first visit to the fabled Fenway Park, and he saw it as part of God's plan for him. It seemed that on April 16, 1945, he would finally get his chance at the big leagues, along with two other players, Sam Jethroe of the Cleveland Buckeyes and Marvin Williams of the Philadelphia Stars.

"Nobody put on an exhibition like we did," Robinson recalled.

"Everything we did, it seemed like the good Lord was guiding us. Everything the pitcher threw up became a line drive someplace."

He noted they "tattooed the short left-field fence," which, of course, goes by a nickname: the Green Monster.[11]

Yet even the compliments he received offered a clue about where this was headed.

"What a ballplayer!" declared the team's top scout, Hugh Duffy. "Too bad he's the wrong color."

And truth be told, Robinson and his fellow players were talented. But they may have been playing especially well because the Red Sox had called in high school pitchers to throw balls to them—a clear sign of disrespect. And a Boston sportswriter who witnessed the tryout recounted that one Red Sox executive—either owner Tom Yawkey or general manager Eddie Collins—blurted a racial epithet.

"Get those niggers off the field!" the sportswriter heard one of them say.[12]

Yet there was a silver lining to that ugliness in Boston. It would open the door to a conversation between Smith, the African American sportswriter who helped set up the tryout, and Rickey.

Smith was mad at Rickey for holding a press conference to announce that he was starting a new team in what would essentially be a new Negro League, with that team known as the Brooklyn Brown Dodgers. Smith and other African American leaders were furious; they thought Rickey was setting back the cause of integration and keeping black players down by continuing the practice of separate leagues instead of integrating African Americans into the majors.

But it was all a con. Here was the master manipulator distracting attention from his real goal. Under the guise of recruiting for the Brown Dodgers, the general manager could deploy his top scouts to check in on African American players without anyone thinking he was actually trying to integrate the game. In fact, Rickey was filling a pool of talent to help integrate the real Dodgers and eventually other clubs.

To smooth things over with Smith, Rickey reached out to the sportswriter and asked if any of the three players from Boston were major league material. Smith mentioned Robinson, and that sparked Rickey to launch a thorough investigation of his background. Rickey sent three of his scouts to watch Robinson play at different times, including Greenwake and Sukeforth, the author Arnold Rampersad wrote, "with none knowing what the others were doing, and with Robinson unaware that he was being watched."[13]

That was until Sukeforth approached Robinson, asking him for a meeting at the Stevens Hotel. Sukey looked earnest to Robinson, so he said yes.

Sukeforth used the meeting to try a new tactic. Jumping on the fact that Robinson's sore arm would keep him out of the lineup for a few days anyway, he asked him to accept an all-expenses paid trip to New York. Robinson's chief concern was getting in trouble with the Monarchs if he disappeared.

"Suppose they fire me," said Robinson.

"I don't think they will," said Sukeforth. "Besides, I have a feeling that after you talk to Mr. Rickey the Monarchs will be unimportant to you."[14]

The last part broke through to Robinson, who stared at Sukeforth and tried to divine what he was really saying. At this point in the conversation, tellingly, Robinson thought about the Bible. He remembered the first battle of the Israelites at Jericho, when they started to seize Canaan.

"Wild fantasies crowded into my mind," Robinson noted later. "What if this was it? The big chance. Not just a job with another Negro club—the Brown Dodgers. What if the battle of Jericho in the majors was about to begin? What if the walls were about to come tumbling down?"[15]

Robinson was slowly let in on Rickey's secret plan, but only a slice of it. The executive was still trying to camouflage the next big move. All Robinson did know for sure was that something was afoot, and Rickey wanted to meet with him quickly.

Robinson tried to stop himself. He did not want to give in to silly daydreams about playing in the big leagues. But, finally, he decided there was nothing to lose. Maybe it was time to roll the dice. He was already thinking of calling it quits from the Negro Leagues anyway. At the end of the season, he was planning to return to California to marry his fiancée, Rachel, and get a job as a high school coach. He wanted to focus on his true passion, mentoring young people.

So he agreed to Sukey's suggestion.

The next step was to surreptitiously get Robinson on a train bound for

New York City. With one scheduled stop in Toledo, Ohio, this would surely be the ride of Robinson's life.

THE LONG NIGHT ON THE TRAIN

As Robinson sat on the train from Chicago to Toledo, though, he began trying to make sense of everything that was happening. If there's one thing about traveling by train, it's that passengers usually have plenty of time to think. There was no way for Robinson to know it then, but his own writings suggested he was having a "dark night of the soul" experience of his own on the train, similar to Rickey's time wrestling with his faith in Rev. Wendell Fifield's office that same year of 1945.

After scouting another player in Toledo, Sukey joined Jackie and boarded the train. On this leg of the journey, Robinson took the top bunk of a sleeper car, but he was too nervous to actually get any sleep. Was he being teased with the possibility of getting his big break? He feared he was being played again. In reality, Robinson was finally on the cusp of realizing his dream, but he couldn't be certain—and it ate at him.

"It seemed too much to hope that he intended to give me a crack at the majors . . . we would see, I told myself drowsily," recalled Robinson.[16]

Robinson confided later that he was fretting, conflicted, and confused, struggling with knots in his stomach from a wild mix of excitement and anxiousness.

"Ideas and fancies crowded my mind," Robinson would recall years later. "I wanted so badly to go to sleep."[17]

As he tossed and turned on the train, Robinson kept wondering about what the next morning would bring. It reminded him of being a kid in Pasadena anticipating what would be waiting for him under the Christmas tree. Was his mother, Mallie, the single mom who worked as a domestic helper for white families, able to afford the present of his dreams? Or would Robinson wind up being disappointed by the gift and, as he put it, "have to pretend to be satisfied" with what he received?[18]

What exactly would Mr. Rickey have waiting the next morning at the Dodgers' offices on the corner of Court and Montague streets?

Robinson's Christmas dream on this August night was a bit more complicated than unwrapping a model car from a gift box in Pasadena. Jack Roosevelt Robinson had been given his middle name to honor a president, Teddy Roosevelt, because of his public rebukes of racism. Now the namesake wanted to be the first African American to play professional baseball.

It is hard to overstate how radical of a proposition this really was for the twenty-six-year-old Robinson, whose entire early life was marked by searing experiences at every single stage. Only a few years before the train ride, Robinson suffered through a racially charged court martial while serving in the US Army.

And his early days showed the stains of racism still permeating American culture. His maternal grandparents were slaves, and Robinson was born in Georgia on the plantation where his father worked as a sharecropper. A broken home forced him to grow up in California, where a cross was burned on his lawn.

One day, when he was just a kid growing up on Pepper Street in Pasadena, a white girl living on the block taunted Jackie with a hateful little rhyme: "Soda cracker's good to eat," she declared. "Niggers only good to beat."[19]

The fact that Robinson's mother, Mallie, ordered him not to respond was instructive. And the fact that young Jackie listened was a preview of the ways he would demonstrate grace under fire when it would matter most.

How in the world did he calm himself down, when he became a player on the Dodgers and opposing players screamed across the diamond that the "jungle" was his real home? Possibly by exercising the technique he used on that lonely train ride to New York, when he struggled to get himself to sleep.

Robinson tried a memory exercise, something he called the game of recalling his yesterdays, to distract from the nervousness about his appointment with Rickey.

He starting thinking back to his youth, and one image stuck in his mind: watching his mother leave for work before sunrise. She worked so hard raising five kids alone. There on the train, the young ballplayer recalled that "if we were lucky," she would be able to come home that night with some extra clothes donated by the family she was cleaning for.[20]

That was not the only thing about his mother that left a deep impression on him. Her faith in God was real, and it stuck with her son.

"Without the belief that God was watching over her, I don't see how my mother could have made it through the difficult times she had," Robinson recalled. "She had faith and trust in God and she believed that God wants human beings to work and speak up for freedom and equality which is rightfully theirs, even if they must suffer because they do."[21]

There had been plenty of suffering for Robinson in his short baseball career before he was invited to meet Rickey. The grind of the Negro Leagues was already gnawing at him. Jim Crow laws made the living conditions horrible, starting with the lousy food at the second-rate restaurants the African American players were forced to use. As for the hotels, Robinson recalled, "the rooms were dingy and dirty, and the restrooms were in such bad condition that players were unable to use them."[22]

Above all the players simply saw no reasonable chance of making progress within the existing system. "I would have been a lot more enthusiastic, even in spite of these problems, if I could have believed there was a future for the Negro in the major leagues," Robinson wrote years later. "Oh I knew that people all over the country, the Negro press and liberal white sportswriters, were pounding away at the doors barring Negroes."

Still, Robinson could not envision positive change during his own baseball career. "We colored players weren't bitter about the situation," he wrote. "But many of us felt it was unrealistic to invest our lives in a sport where progress was limited by discrimination."[23]

A NEW DESTINATION

We know for the first time exactly what Robinson was thinking about that remarkable train ride because of a firsthand account from the man himself, gleaned from his unpublished memoir. Its pages tell us that on the train to New York, Robinson continued to focus his thoughts on Mallie as he played his memory game.

"Although she couldn't always give us enough to eat, there were three things my mother was determined about: that we get an education, attend Sunday school and church, and that the family remain together as a close unit," Robinson wrote.[24]

Mallie had taught him that he had a higher goal. Indeed, in the foreword of *My Greatest Day*, he wrote that he believed "each and every one of us was placed here on earth for a very special purpose."[25] That was the reason Robinson did not drink alcohol or go out and party with his teammates on the Monarchs: he felt that God was guiding him to something bigger than baseball.

With the wisdom of time, Robinson felt that all the opposition he faced during his career had been well documented. So, in his official autobiography that he did publish shortly before his death, he wrote that he wanted to focus on the positive. He recalled that on many days when "the going [got] rough, I could look up into those bleachers and see encouragement and friendship in the faces of young people of all races, young people of all sections of the country—and even in other lands."

Robinson saw the unpublished manuscript—if it ever got published—as a way to give back. "If this series of books helps just a few of you youngsters to understand that you are important in your family, your community, in America and in the world, it will have accomplished a wonderful thing," he wrote.

He added of the kids in the stands during his playing days: "They didn't care what color my face was or what church I attended. All they cared about was could I play the game, could I observe the rules, was I a good sport?"[26]

For Robinson, he believed the greatest day of his life was walking into Rickey's office and learning that an African American was going to finally get a chance to make history. And the faith instilled by his mother would eventually be reinforced by Rickey.

On the train, however, Robinson still did not know what was waiting for him in Brooklyn. He just could not sleep. Yet he remembered Sukeforth snoozing just fine in the bed beneath him.

"I was thinking," explained Robinson. "I was twenty-six years old and I had a dream, but I was afraid to take it out and examine it. Soon . . . soon I would know."[27]

CHAPTER 5

"GOD WILL HAVE TO KEEP HIS EYE ON YOU"

The dutiful waitress at the IHOP in Anderson, Indiana, was circling our booth on and off for an hour. Carl Erskine and I waved her off repeatedly. We were not trying to be rude. It's just that the stories about Branch Rickey, Clyde Sukeforth, and the rest of the Brooklyn gang had been flowing as easily as the coffee, so why disrupt a good thing?

"When Mr. Rickey got down to his top fifty [African American players], Sukeforth told him, 'There is a young guy named Jackie Robinson,'" recalled Erskine. "And he had some negatives in his scouting report—his temper."[1]

We paused briefly and Erskine tossed out an order. "Two eggs over easy, some crisp bacon," he said, refusing the toast.

I wanted to get back to the stories as quickly as possible. "I'll do the same. Just please give me an English muffin," I say.

"Oh, can I get an English muffin?" Erskine perked up. Then he dove back in.

"The guys in the Negro Leagues said, 'He'll never make it because of that temper,'" noted Erskine. "But Mr. Rickey began to interview Jackie, and in probing him found something that I have not seen written about a lot. He found that Jackie was raised by a strong Christian mother."

Mallie Robinson's imprint on Jackie no doubt reminded Rickey of his own mother, Emily, who also took her Christian faith seriously. Rickey believed that Jackie's faith would enable him to regulate his temper when necessary.

"You know what Mr. Rickey said in the early years, when he was trying to find a black player?" Erskine asked me. "Mr. Rickey's wisdom was to say, 'You can't win with a passive personality. You have to have a guy that's got guts, wants to fight. He'd like to kill ya! But he's got control.'"

In fact, Mallie Robinson did encourage her son to take the high road whenever possible as he faced discrimination, such as turning away when the young girl shouted epithets at him on the driveway. But make no mistake; this was a woman who also had a tough and daring side.

It was fitting that Jackie's date with destiny began on that train ride to New York. He never would have made it to Brooklyn without his mother putting him on a far more dramatic train ride at the age of one year and four months.

MALLIE'S JOURNEY

It was May 21, 1920, and Mallie Robinson had had just about enough of her husband Jerry's frequent infidelities. She decided it was time to take her five children off of a plantation in Georgia to seek a shot at attaining even a tiny sliver of the American Dream in California.

It is hard to overstate just how gutsy of a move that was. As a woman and an African American in 1920, Mallie had few rights and even less money. Yet somehow she mustered the courage and funding to leave the plantation, round up more than a dozen relatives, and pay for the indignity of segregated cars on the train.

"There were thirteen of us who went, I don't remember everyone," Jackie's sister, Willa Mae Walker, recalled years later. "Aside from my mother and her five children, there was my auntie Cora and my uncle Sam Wade, and they had two children, then there was William Wade, who was a friend not a relative, and there were a couple of others too."

Imagine trying to squeeze all of those people into the awful accommodations of the "Colored-only" cars of the train, and trying to enjoy the dozens of hours on the long journey of more than 2,200 miles from Cairo, Georgia, to Pasadena, California.

"All I can remember is that the cars were dark and crowded and the seats were very uncomfortable," added Willa Mae. "I think they were metal or something, but all I know is they were very uncomfortable."[2]

Jackie was just an infant at the time, but much later, after he had a taste of fame and some fortune, he reflected on his mother's fortitude and was left awestruck. "Of course I was too young to be affected by the hardship of the long nights and days of travel from Cairo, Georgia, to Pasadena," noted Jackie. "But when I was old enough to understand what my mother had done, the trip seemed dramatic and romantic to me. I compared it to the journeys the pioneers made when they traveled West in covered wagons, accepting discomfort and danger in order to try to establish a new life for themselves."

After they got off the train, the family boarded a bus to meet up with Mallie's half brother, Burton.

"I could just imagine what my mother had gone through, almost penniless, with five small, restless, hungry children on her hands," added Jackie. "She must have wondered if she had done the right thing . . . she must have become frightened trying to figure out whether our future would be bright or dark."[3]

How in the world did Mallie Robinson do it? First, the woman was fearless. For example, at a time when neither women nor blacks were supposed to speak up, she defied convention by telling her husband to stand up for himself and demand more from the owner of the Sasser Plantation in Cairo. Jerry Robinson, Jackie's father, worked for Jim Sasser for the grand sum of twelve dollars a month. Jackie himself called his family's life at the plantation a "newer, more sophisticated kind of slavery than the kind Mr. Lincoln struck down."[4]

Mallie Robinson pushed her husband to demand a "half crop," which would allow him to keep 50 percent of what he grew. Her husband was nervous to speak up because he had seen other workers thrown off the land after demanding more. But she put the struggle in a religious context.

"My mother finally convinced my father that he should take a chance," Jackie noted. "She believed that a human being had to stand up for his rights and that even if he suffers for it, God will look out for him in the long run."[5]

As the story was relayed to Jackie, there was a big confrontation between his parents around Christmas in 1909, when Jerry Robinson came home at the end of the work year with just fifteen dollars in his pocket. And he hadn't actually made that money. Jerry had needed to take a loan against his pay for the next year so he could give five dollars to Mallie for Christmas presents and the like.

This was the breaking point for Mallie, who pushed her husband to stand up for his rights instead of working hard all year long for a pittance. Her plan actually worked, and Jerry Robinson asked for and received a half crop. His income did jump, yet he was still earning just over $350 a year.

This meant money for the family, but less for crusty Jim Sasser, who once told Mallie bluntly, "You're about the sassiest Nigger woman ever on this place."[6] Clearly that was meant as an insult. Yet all these years later it only shows her strength. The racist plantation owner knew deep down this woman was not going to be kept down for long.

Second, Mallie Robinson mustered the strength to get her family on that train to California because she was a woman with strong religious faith who was devoted to improving her family's life. This left a deep impression on Jackie. "To my mother, I owe the shaping of my early values, the inspiration and ambition which she gave me by the courageous life she lived for her children," he wrote years later.[7]

Jackie knew full well that he never would have made it off the plantation, let alone climbed to the Dodgers, without his mother.

"I often wonder what would have happened to me and the rest of our family, if my mother had been afraid," wrote Robinson. "If it hadn't been for her faith."[8]

DEEP STRENGTH FROM A DEEP FAITH

Mallie learned about the importance of faith at an early age. Her parents, Wash and Edna McGriff, were born as slaves. They eventually had fourteen kids, including Mallie, and attended services at the Rocky Hill African Methodist Episcopal Church.

"Mallie's faith in God was linked to her keen sense of family, and both were blended with her belief that family and God were the main defense against the evils of the unjust world into which she had been born as a black in the Deep South," noted author Arnold Rampersad.[9]

Mallie's faith is illustrated in a beautiful story from her childhood. One day, when she was still a girl, her own illiterate father admitted it was his dream to gain the skills necessary to read the Bible before he passed away. So, after school, Mallie, only ten years old, started sitting on the porch to teach her dad to read so that he could appreciate the Bible on his own.[10]

Years later, Jackie wrote that faith in God is what led Mallie to urge her husband to demand more money from the plantation owner. Sadly and ironically, her push to get her husband to dream bigger—and get a half share of the land he worked on—led to the breakup of the family.

More money only led Jerry Robinson to seek a more exciting life beyond those grimy fields. Soon he was having extramarital affairs again and again. He ended up getting into a relationship with a local married woman. Mallie later confided that she had had a dream in which God told her that her husband was planning on running away for good with his new lover.

In July 1919, when Jackie was just under six months old, Jerry boarded a train of his own and left with his new girl, eventually getting a job at a sawmill. Then he ran out of money again and went back to Mallie, but this time she was less willing to forgive him for his sins.

Sasser was furious that one of his best workers was gone, and he took out his anger on the spouse who remained. At one point, Sasser tried to get the local sheriff to round up Jerry and force him back onto the plantation. Rather than shrinking amid the adversity, Mallie stood strong. She refused to let Sasser and the sheriff push her back into a marriage with the man who had repeatedly left her. And she rebuffed the plantation owner's effort to hire her as a cook.

Then Sasser brought in new tenant farmers and started pushing the Robinson family into smaller and smaller accommodations.

Finally, in May 1920, Mallie got her children to that train station. An African American woman leaving the South at the drop of a hat was no small matter. It was an insult to white Southerners who liked to keep up the myth of their perfect utopia, and black migration meant cheap labor was fleeing town. Yet somehow Mallie Robinson was not stopped from boarding that train.[11]

She boarded that train to Pasadena because of something her half brother on the West Coast, Burton Thomas, told her: "If you want to get closer to Heaven, visit California."[12] Yet, in the coming years, there would be plenty of days in Pasadena where racial attacks left the Robinsons feeling as though they had actually arrived somewhere far less divine.

But Mallie believed that God had a plan for her family and her son. Jackie recalled a story that was passed on through the family about his mother, and something she said to him shortly after he was born. Surveying the poverty around them, she whispered, "Bless you, boy. For you to survive all of this, God will have to keep his eye on you."[13]

The family never heard from Jerry Robinson again, save for the telegram years later revealing that he was dead.

In his unpublished manuscript, Jackie repeatedly mentioned that his mother's faith in God was her compass. He wrote that "this same spirit gave her the courage to take her family out of the South, even though she was almost penniless and had no guarantees" she could actually earn a living on the West Coast.[14]

In the end, though, the journey proved worth it. There on the West Coast, Jackie found himself. And, more importantly, the young man found God—with the help of his mother, of course, but also via a Methodist minister who became a father figure.

CHAPTER 6

"I RESOLVED NOT TO BE A DOORMAT"

As I walked the streets of Pasadena in January 2016, I visited spots all around town that marked critical moments in Jackie Robinson's childhood. This exercise made it easy to see how faith and family shaped him.

There was the solitude of Scott United Methodist Church, which has long had a specialty of helping troubled youth. It played a pivotal role in getting Robinson out of a gang and back on the path to greatness. A new generation of kids was playing on Pepper Street, where Jackie was nurtured by a loving single mother. It was awe-inspiring to walk the very same block, with the majestic San Gabriel Mountains in the distance, where the hero first tossed a baseball. In fact, Robinson grew up barely a mile from the Rose Bowl Stadium, in the neighborhood that plays host every New Year's Day to that perfect bit of Americana, the annual Tournament of Roses Parade and the Rose Bowl college football game.

I found perhaps the most striking tribute, however, just across from city hall: two massive, 2,700-pound sculptures depicting the heads (yes, nine-foot-by-six-foot masses) of Jackie and his brother Mack.

"I loved everyone in my family, but there was something special about my brother Mack," Jackie wrote in 1965. "A superb athlete, Mack was my boyhood hero. He was one of the swiftest track stars in our school."

Indeed, Mack was a remarkable sprinter who, despite a heart ailment, persevered and made the US Olympic team in 1936. He went on to Germany to snag the silver medal after finishing behind the legendary Jesse Owens, as his family crowded around the radio in Pasadena to listen to the race.

"Mack vindicated my faith in him one proud day in 1936 when the entire Robinson family danced and shouted with delight on learning from a radio broadcast that our Mack had finished second to Jesse Owens in Berlin in the Olympic 200-meter," added Jackie.[1]

Yet Mack grew bitter about the fact that when he came home to Pasadena from the Olympics, he was treated shabbily rather than getting a hero's welcome. Jackie said a couple of years into his Dodgers career that he had learned from his brother's troubles "to make the best of things." This offers insight into how he kept in perspective the insurmountable odds he faced over and over.[2]

On that statue in Pasadena, above Jackie's left ear, I read an engraved quote—one that shows him at his most humble: "If this can happen to a guy from a broken home, whose mother worked from sun up to sun down; if this can happen to someone who was a delinquent and who learned he had to change his life then it can happen to you out there who think life is against you."

It was a moving moment on my nostalgic tour of Jackie's childhood, until I was jarred back to reality. The statues were put up across from city hall in 1997, twenty-five long years after Jackie died, appearing to be almost a make-good because of anger the Robinson family felt about never really being embraced by Pasadena.

When he had made it big, Jackie Robinson made it clear that he wanted nothing to do with Pasadena. "If my mother, brothers, and sister weren't living there, I'd never go back," he said. "I've always felt like an intruder, even in school. People in Pasadena were less understanding, in some ways, than Southerners. And they were openly hostile."[3]

Scorching words from someone who dealt with so much discrimination in the South. Jackie's point was that while the situation in the West was arguably better than it had been in the Jim Crow South, it was still a terrible atmosphere to grow up in. There was that cross that was burned on his front lawn. The municipal swimming pool would not admit blacks, but after some protests, they relented—sort of. The city created "International Day" at the pool, one day per week when African Americans could swim. Local officials were quick to point out to whites that—not to worry—at the end of International Day, they always drained the pool and replenished it with "clean" water uncontaminated by the black children who had splashed around all day.[4]

"You don't forget these things easily," Jackie wrote later. "They create resentment in you. You are being discriminated against and segregated and you wonder why. You build, over and above the resentment, a sense of rebellion against being pushed around to one side, labeled with a racial tag. You resolve that you are only going to take as much of this kind of thing as you just have to. What you have to take today, you are going to fight against tomorrow."[5]

This shows both his determination to change America and just how difficult it must have been for him to hold his temper amid the onslaught that was coming in Brooklyn.

The last straw for the family may have come in January 1939, when even the Tournament of Roses Parade became a nightmare for the Robinsons. Jackie's eldest brother, Edgar, was beaten by two police officers. He was charged with resisting arrest and violating a city ordinance, all in a dispute over having the proper license to place chairs along the parade route.

Not so idyllic, and not so all-American, after all.

Throw into the mix that the Robinson family faced desperate poverty after fleeing Georgia. When that train first pulled into Pasadena from Cairo in June 1920, Mallie Robinson was flat broke. She arrived in her new home with only three dollars that had been sewn into her petticoat for the trip.

It's probably no surprise then that Jackie Robinson ended up joining a gang, called the "Pepper Street Gang," and was arrested a few times. But when we say *gang*, it's important not to overstate or exaggerate what being part of such a group meant for Robinson. He mostly got caught up in minor, inconsequential crimes, like stealing fruit from stands and throwing dirt at cars.

This was not a gang in the modern sense—a drug-dealing, gun-toting gang involved in violent crime. *Gang* was a word used loosely back then to describe a ragtag group—according to Robinson himself—of black, Japanese, and Mexican kids from lower-class backgrounds who had time on their hands.

Robinson readily admitted the minority kids' actions were sparked in part by a common resentment they had about the advantages that white kids had over them. Mack was blunter about it. "We just kicked some white [rear]," he told author Maury Allen. "Kids aren't so tough when you can knock them down with a punch."[6]

Mack was particularly upset that when he came home from the Olympics and applied for a city job, the best that Pasadena officials could do was give him a pushcart and broom. He became a street sweeper on the night shift. In turn, white people in Pasadena were miffed when Mack wore his leather USA Olympic jacket as he swept the streets, which was seen as a provocative move.

Was Mack showing a Jackie-style flash of temper? No, he insisted; it was just a matter of convenience. "When it was a cold day, it was the warmest thing I owned, so I wore it," he said.[7]

A FORK IN THE ROAD

The path was not easier for Jackie simply because he embraced God. He was far from perfect and had a criminal record from his days in the gang, though it is clear that at least some of the arrests were racially motivated. Jackie and some of his friends were dragged off to jail at gunpoint by a local sheriff because they had gone swimming in the reservoir. Sure, the kids were in the wrong, but it's hard to believe that a similar swim by white kids would have resulted in them being escorted to jail at all, let alone with weapons pressed to them. After all, Jackie had jumped into the reservoir to protest the ban on African Americans at the local pool. As he swam, policemen shouted, "Look there, a nigger swimming in my drinking water."[8]

All of that nastiness, plus Robinson's struggles with the law, have been chronicled before. But precious little time has been spent delving into how he got through all of it and still was able to rise to great heights. Even if his gang activity was relatively minor, it was another fork in the road where he could have veered off course and never made history without some kind of intervention. Jackie's own daughter, Sharon, would note many years later, "You see these points in his teenage years when he could have gone in either direction."[9]

Mallie Robinson was Jackie's core. She believed there was destiny from God for her son, and she continued that laserlike focus in Pasadena. "She brought us up believing in God, knowing there was a God and also a true hell," recalled Jessie Maxwell Wills, Mallie's niece.[10]

Mallie also taught her kids to get down on their knees and pray each night before bed, a habit Jackie would continue right through his days as a famous baseball player. "Prayer is belief," she told her kids, who attended church every Sunday at Scott United Methodist Church.[11]

REVEREND DOWNS

At that church, they met another critical person in Jackie's early life: Rev. Karl Downs, a young African American minister. Downs was only twenty-five years old when he took the helm of the church in 1938, so he could relate to young people. This was like manna from heaven for Robinson, who around this time had a mounting police record.

One day Robinson and his buddies were hanging out on a street corner, when suddenly Downs pulled up in a car.

"Is Jack Robinson here?" he asked.

Nobody answered, including Robinson, perhaps fearing he was in further trouble.

Downs cut a distinct impression. He was a wiry guy, tall and thin, usually dressed in a tailored suit with a white shirt and necktie.

"Tell him I want to see him at junior church," Downs said before departing.[12]

Did Mallie send him? Nobody knew for sure. The key is that Downs got Robinson's attention, and he was soon bonding with the man who became more than just a minister.

"He really was a sort of psychiatrist," said a childhood friend of Jackie. "I'm not sure what would have happened to Jack if he had never met Reverend Downs."[13]

Downs led nothing short of a spiritual awakening for Robinson. Suddenly, all the lessons Mallie had instilled in the boy were morphing into concrete steps to help him get out of the gang in the short term and figure out how to persevere over Jim Crow long term.

"Faith in God then began to register in him as both a mysterious force, beyond his comprehension, and as a pragmatic way to negotiate the world," wrote author Arnold Rampersad. "A measure of emotional and spiritual poise such as he had never known at last entered his life."[14]

This was manifested in ways both big and small. Given Downs's age, he had decided to make Sunday school more fun and church more relatable to the young adults. That seemed to appeal to Robinson. "Those of us who had been indifferent church members began to feel an excitement in belonging," he recalled.[15]

Youngsters started planning dances at the church, and the new badminton court installed by Downs gave them an alternative to the streets after church or during the week. Older members of the church, though, objected to some of the changes, since Downs ruffled feathers over some of their traditions. Maybe observing this early lesson in bumping against the establishment and not giving in would also help Robinson down the road, when the barons of baseball threw temper tantrums about the possibility of the first African American player.

As Jackie would observe later, "I had a lot of faith in God . . . there's nothing like faith in God to help a fellow who gets booted around once in a while."[16]

Jackie credited Downs with listening to him when he was feeling down about Mallie's financial difficulties. And the minister would get out of the pulpit and bond with Robinson in other settings, like the golf course.

Robinson's mother was a living example of the virtues she had been trying to teach him. And now the young man had another male to relate to and bond over sports, a father figure.

"Often he would find a way of applying a story in the Bible to something that happened in real life," noted Robinson. "He didn't preach and he didn't talk down like so many adults or view you from some holy distance. He was in there with you."[17]

So when Robinson was plucked away to play four sports at UCLA, he did not forget his roots. Even though he starred as a running back on Saturdays, Jackie would still teach at the Sunday school he used to attend. "On Sunday mornings, when I woke up sore and aching because of a football game the day before, I yearned to just stay in bed," he recalled. "But no matter how terrible I felt, I had to get up. It was impossible to shirk duty when Karl Downs was involved."[18]

Throughout his life, Robinson gave Reverend Downs great credit for his success. He wrote in his memoir, "I suppose I might have become a full-fledged juvenile delinquent" but for the intervention of key people like Downs. The kid who never really knew his dad seemed to respond to strong men, whether it was a minister like Downs or an average person in the neighborhood.

One day, as the Pepper Street Gang worked their mischief, a car mechanic named Carl Anderson watched the silliness and pulled Jackie aside. Rather than yell at Robinson, Anderson played the best possible card, telling the boy if he stayed with the gang he would not only hurt himself; he would also damage his mother.

"He told me I ought to admit to myself that I didn't belong in a gang, that I was simply following the crowd because I was afraid of being thought different, of being 'chicken,'" Jackie recalled. "He said it didn't take guts to follow the crowd, that courage and intelligence lay in being willing to be different. I was too ashamed to tell Carl how right he was, but what he said got to me."[19]

That broke through for Robinson, who remembered a line Mallie often recited to her children: "God watches what you do. You must reap what you sow, so sow well!"[20]

These early lessons helped Jackie develop character and a tough skin that he would need for the rest of his life. "From the way my mother lived and the things she told me, I became convinced, early in life, that you aren't much of a person if you [live life] like a doormat and let people walk over you," Robinson wrote in his unpublished manuscript. "Even before I went to high school and college, I resolved not to be a doormat."[21]

FORGED IN FIRE

Robinson soaked up these experiences and learned resilience at every step. *Los Angeles Times* sportswriter Shav Glick, who covered some of Robinson's early athletic accomplishments when the two men were students at Pasadena Junior College in the 1930s, believed the city shaped him.

"The Robinson the world came to know, competitive and combative, aggressive and abrasive, impatient and irascible, was tempered on the streets, the school grounds and the playing fields of Pasadena," Glick wrote in 1977.[22]

Jackie would recall going hungry throughout his childhood. Some days, his mother would have to cut the kids down to two meals a day; other days, they had to live on bread and sweet water (water with sugar); while still other times, there would have been nothing to eat but for the leftovers she brought home from her domestic job.

"My mother got up before daylight to go to her job and although she came home tired, she managed to give us the extra attention we needed," said Robinson. "She indoctrinated us with the importance of family unity, religion, and kindness toward others."[23]

At one point, Mallie lost her job, but she refused to go on welfare. She told her children that God would watch over them.

"As my mother always said, the Lord took care of us," said Willa Mae. "Because when we get to thinking back, it sure was the Lord because we couldn't get on welfare."[24]

It's no wonder then that Mallie cried with pride in 1935 when Jackie graduated from high school. Somehow she scrounged together the resources to surprise him with a graduation gift he had been hoping for: his very own dress suit.

Jackie himself cried when his mother said the credit for the suit went to God. "My mother said she always believed the Lord would take care of us," he wrote. "Right then and there, I never stopped believing that."[25]

PASSING THE TORCH

Two great mentors were about to give way to a third: Branch Rickey. Robinson himself tied his mother's faith in God directly to Rickey's own religious conviction. He believed it was the driving force behind integrating baseball: "It has always seemed to me that the spirit which inspired Mallie Robinson was like that which caused Branch Rickey to fight to bring democracy into American baseball," Robinson wrote.[26]

Indeed, when it came to the responsibility of mentoring Jackie, the torch was eventually passed from Downs and Mallie Robinson to Rickey. Downs had preached to him about honoring a God who died for his followers' sins and wanted them to turn the other cheek when confronted by enemies. It was the same message Rickey would soon preach to Robinson about enemies on the baseball diamond, which may explain why he and the general manager would connect so well in their first face-to-face meeting.

In fact, this message was reinforced in those large busts of the Robinson brothers across from city hall. Above Jackie's right ear, there's an inscription that says: "What was I doing turning the other cheek . . . in college I had a reputation as a black man who never tolerated affronts to his dignity. I had defied prejudice in the Army. How could I have thought that the barriers would fall, that my talent could triumph over bigotry?"[27]

Clearly Jackie's faith in God helped him stand firm until those barriers fell. The lessons in dignity he learned in Pasadena helped him in the battles ahead. As I looked at the bronze memorial to him in the town where the man himself was forged, I noted one last bit of symbolism. Mack Robinson's face—this 2,700-pound rendering of it, anyway—was staring directly at city hall, signifying that he never really left home. Jackie Robinson's face was staring east, toward Brooklyn, where Rickey was waiting for him.

CHAPTER 7

BRANCH FINDS GOD

There was only one place for me to meet Branch Rickey's grandson: a minor league stadium in Texas.

"A few generations now for the Rickeys, yep," he said with a smile. "I've spent a few years around baseball parks."[1]

It's been decades, in fact. Branch Rickey III today serves as president of the Pacific Coast League. It's one of two minor leagues playing at the Triple-A level, just a notch below the major leagues.

He immediately told me a story from when he was around four years old, when his grandfather brought him to Philadelphia in the late 1940s for a road trip with the Brooklyn Dodgers. After coming down to the hotel lobby, the elder Rickey realized he had left his wallet on the dresser up in the hotel room. He asked a couple of guys, who were tossing a baseball around the outside steps of the hotel, to watch his grandson while he rushed back upstairs. And that was the day Jackie Robinson and Pee Wee Reese—one of the great double-play combinations in baseball history—became babysitters.

Not a bad little nugget to have on your résumé. But Branch Rickey III knows that while he is immensely proud of his grandfather's legacy, it is important to chart your own course. In a family business like his, that takes a little more doing than most.

His father, Branch Rickey Jr., was credited with doing a good job running the farm system for the Brooklyn Dodgers. Yet he always lived under a long shadow cast by the "Top Branch," as sportswriter Arthur Daley used to call Rickey Sr.[2] After that, others in baseball would call him "Twig," which could not have been too pleasant.

Sadly, Branch Rickey Jr. died at the age of forty-seven, so Branch III was largely raised by his grandfather, though the silver lining was an amazing education at his grandfather's knee.

"He was dangerous—he was dangerous," the grandson repeated, meaning it in a good way. "He was so full of energy, so full of ideas, creativity, constantly challenging, and just contagious to be around. You couldn't wait for tomorrow to be around him."

The youngest Branch was born in 1945, the year Robinson was signed to his first minor league contract. He thinks of the two men as two very powerful individuals, neither of whom could have solved the problem independently. So they left the world a powerful example by coming together to achieve something far larger than what they could have done alone.

"I don't think that Jackie broke the color barrier as much as I have been fond of thinking of him as having shattered a myth—a myth that you can predict the person's potential on the basis of the color of their skin or whatever other false prejudices we might have," said Rickey III. "And I think that's the memorial that these individuals should have."

Faith was at the center of the lessons imparted from Rickey, whether to his grandson or a Dodgers player like Carl Erskine.

Erskine recalled sitting down with the elder Rickey for his first one-on-one after signing a contract with the Dodgers. "He had this gruff voice and he would say, 'Well, son, what do you do at night after supper?'" he told me. "He'd probe for these inside things about players, what made you tick. And then he said, 'Do you go to church?' I never expected to hear that."[3]

The elder Rickey was deeply interested in the faith of all his players, according to Erskine, because he believed it would make them stronger on the field.

Rickey was also very open about his own faith, according to his grandson. I asked Rickey III how much that faith informed his grandfather's quest to integrate baseball—and if he knew about his meeting with the Reverend Wendell Fifield.

"It tested everyone's souls," he said of the move to integrate baseball, adding he was not surprised his grandfather sat down with a minister to work through it.

"I never heard it, never heard of it," he said. "My grandfather never referenced it, but it rings—there is a ring of genuineness that I have to admit. . . . There is a genuineness to it because it really reflects the intensity with which he went about" his decision-making. "It certainly would not be a surprise to anybody who lived around my grandfather that he would have sought that kind of guidance for any kind of significant decision that he was pursuing," he added.

While his grandfather may have been a little embarrassed about the indecision, or the tears that flowed in Fifield's office, his grandson made a clear point. Rickey was very proud of his faith and would have acknowledged that even he, baseball institution that he was, needed spiritual guidance as he made the biggest decision in the history of the game.

"Certainly I don't think had this surfaced earlier, while my grandfather was alive, he would have been in any way uncomfortable or hesitant to recognize it for what it was," he said.

THE MAKING OF BRANCH RICKEY

Indeed, faith in God was central to the life of Wesley Branch Rickey from the day he was born. His parents named him after both John Wesley, the founder of Methodism, and a passage in the Old Testament. One family Bible had a handwritten note in which the word *Branch* was specifically capitalized in a passage from Isaiah: "And there shall come forth a rod out of the stem of Jesse, and a Branch shall grow out of his roots" (11:1).[4]

This particular Branch sprouted on December 20, 1881, on a small farm in Stockdale, Ohio, the southern part of the state, about thirty miles from the Kentucky border. Emily Brown Rickey, his deeply religious mother, taught him thousands of Bible stories even before he knew how to read.

One incident with his mother, Branch would recall, had a "deep effect on me for ever after." He had gotten in trouble as a boy, but rather than punish him his mother employed a different strategy. "She asked me to kneel with her at her bedside [where] she asked for God's forgiveness," Rickey recalled. In exchange for getting that forgiveness, Rickey said, his mother made a vow. "She promised to be a better mother . . . and said she would try never again to commit the sin of letting me misbehave," he said. "I felt as though I had hit her, and I was thoroughly chastised."[5]

A strong mother who stamped him early with faith in God was just one of the important links between Jackie Robinson and Rickey. Both men also taught Sunday school at their respective churches, not content with just living the Word of God themselves but eager to pass it on to future generations.

Jackie himself saw this connection: "There was a deep religious sense in the Rickey household, stemming from the boy's parents. They were the kind of devout people who were unable to talk about the Fatherhood of God without acknowledging the brotherhood of man."[6]

Unlike Robinson, Rickey grew up with an active father, who also impressed religion upon him from the start. Jacob Frank Rickey, a farmer who was known as the most pious man in their church, said grace before each meal with a simple reminder: "The Lord is the head of this house."[7]

At church, the family followed the teachings of John Wesley, who founded the evangelical movement known as Methodism in the 1700s. Wesley was known for finding ways to bring faith closer to people, often preaching outdoors to groups and urging his followers to experience Jesus Christ personally, not just theoretically.

It is not a surprise then that Wesley called slavery "a complicated villainy." And in 1784, Methodists condemned slavery as "contrary to the golden law of God . . . and the inalienable rights of mankind."[8] In the 1840s, the slavery debate split the Methodists into Northern and Southern wings. The Rickeys were vehemently opposed to it.

All of this raises a simple question: If the general manager of the Dodgers had not been someone with this moral upbringing and fierce urgency to shake up American society, what would have happened in the mid-1940s when it came to a decision point in integrating baseball?

When Rickey was a young man, his mother nearly snuffed out his dream of getting involved in major league baseball at all. Given her strong religious convictions, Emily Rickey balked by saying all baseball players did was drink alcohol, swear, and chase women.

Rickey was always quick to formulate a plan, endlessly tinkering and scheming, even as a young boy. And that's why his mother's initial refusal did not end the conversation.

"He slept on it and the next day he came back to his parents and said, 'I would ask this: If I will give you my word not to go into a baseball park on a Sunday, will you give me your permission?'" Rickey III told me.

Rickey's mother was a hard person to convince, but she bought this pitch. Yet playing only six days a week, and never on Sunday, turned out to be a mixed blessing. Yes, it enabled Rickey to go out and chase his dream, and he eventually did make it to the major leagues as a player. Yet his mediocre career as a player was short lived. He often angered team managers with his refusal to play Sunday games.

Nonetheless, this promise made to his parents would define Rickey— and not just for the early part of his life. It became a lifelong commitment that demonstrated just how serious this man was about his faith.

Before getting his crack at the major leagues, Rickey played professional football in 1902 for the Shelby Blues, in something known as the "Ohio League." It was a precursor to the modern National Football League, and Rickey developed an important friendship. He got to know the first African American to play professional football, a Virginia-born halfback named Charles Follis. As Jackie would, Follis endured racist taunts and excessive violence on the field. Perhaps this was one of the early seeds of Rickey's interest in integrating baseball.

An even bigger seed would be planted in 1903, when Rickey was playing some minor league baseball but also serving as coach of the team at Ohio Wesleyan. Something dramatic happened, which we will explore in far more depth later, and Rickey vowed to make up for it by integrating baseball someday.

Skeptics have noted if this was such a pivotal event in Rickey's life, why did it take more than forty years for him to follow through?

Part of the answer may come from the fact that Rickey did not obtain real power in the game as a decision-making executive for many years. And in his early days as a player in the major leagues, Rickey had his own struggles to deal with before trying to impose his own imprint on the game.

MAKING A MARK IN BASEBALL

In 1905, Chicago White Sox owner Charles Comiskey expressed interest in signing Rickey to the major leagues and bought his contract from the Dallas Giants, a minor league team. Remembering his promise to his parents, Rickey demanded and received a clause in the contract spelling out that he would not play on Sunday.

Then Comiskey abruptly changed his mind and decided he didn't want a catcher getting full-time pay for essentially part-time work. He traded Rickey to the St. Louis Browns, where Rickey made his debut in a June 1905 game.

Rickey struck out twice in his first three at-bats. It was an early sign that the light-hitting catcher did not have much of a chance of becoming a big-time player. His weak throwing arm from behind the plate only sealed that fate. Nonetheless, Rickey had realized his dream. He was one of a select group of men who had made it to the major leagues.

True, offering to play on Sundays could have helped to butter up his manager and further his career, and one might forgive Rickey for wanting to backslide on his promise to his parents. But there was no softening from Rickey. When a sportswriter asked him in 1906 about not playing on Sundays, he made it clear this was not negotiable.

"Sunday to me has always been a day apart," Rickey said. "I can't help it. It was bred in me. You might almost call it a prejudice. So I won't play Sunday ball. I made them put it in my contract that I wouldn't have to.

Instead I go to church. . . . You see I'm doing the things I was brought up to believe in."[9]

Rickey went much further in a stirring letter he wrote to his parents on March 4, 1906, during spring training in Texas before the start of his second season with the Browns.

"Dear papa and mamma," Rickey began affectionately. "Well it is Sunday, I am expecting developments today. Every Sunday either helps me or hurts me. Personally I don't care how it affects my career—I mean it, honestly I'm just about ready to declare myself something besides a ball player. It is a sort of disgraceful profession."

Rickey declared he was "disgusted," and part of that frustration stemmed from the fact that his manager, Jimmy McAleer, was questioning his refusal to play on Sunday. Rickey openly wrestled with whether his sports and spiritual commitments could really coexist.

"You see—church going and ball playing don't dove-tail by any means—that's why I am feeling 'sour' on baseball," Rickey continued. "It makes one worse—worse than I really am—worse than I ought to be—worse than I would otherwise be."

In the meantime, Rickey wanted to relay to his parents how "monotonous" life on the road became as a ballplayer. And even these seemingly small details led Rickey to issue larger denunciations about the entire culture of baseball.

"This hotel is a good one—so is the Southern in St. Louis; in fact the American League teams stop at only the best," wrote Rickey. "Thus another evil in the baseball business namely—that of cultivating ease—laziness and extravagant tastes." Rickey continued, "Outside the torments of one's mind (I would have said consciences [but] only few ball players have that) there are no hardships to speak of. 'Easy comes easy goes.'"

Rickey noted in the letter that his longtime sweetheart, Jane Moulton, "will be able to persuade me very easily to do something else. I hope so—at any rate."[10]

Just how sincere he was in that wish, we cannot know. But it seems that from the moment they married in June 1906, Rickey was determined to be a baseball lifer in one form or another, his bellyaching to his parents notwithstanding.

Jane was a partner to Rickey in every way—something else the executive shared with Robinson, who never would have gone as far as he did without having his wife, Rachel, at his side. Jane Rickey's best asset may have been keeping her husband's enormous ego in check—or at least somewhat in check.

Even Rickey seemed to acknowledge that fact forty-three years into the marriage, when he sat for a long interview with *Newsweek* magazine for a cover story in the summer of 1949. This was shortly after Robinson had broken into the big leagues. When Rickey was asked to name the accomplishment that had satisfied him the most, the executive veered into more personal territory. "Gaining and holding the esteem of eight women," he said in reference to his wife, five daughters, one daughter-in-law, and mother, who had died in 1935 at the age of seventy-nine.

"They are the people who know me best at my worst," Rickey added.[11]

Perhaps it was coincidence, but Rickey played his best baseball for the St. Louis Browns the year he married Jane. He ended the 1906 season on a tear at the plate, showing off some of his best batting as he helped the Browns finish with a record over .500, but not enough to reach the World Series.

Rickey was also busy that year finishing up his bachelor of arts degree at Ohio Wesleyan, and he was set to get going on a law degree as well. As if this did not keep him busy enough, Rickey became the athletic director at Ohio Wesleyan, coaching three teams. The feeble, last-place football team soared into second place, the basketball squad won all but four games, and then the baseball team took the conference title.

Rickey knew that his days as a baseball player were numbered, given that he had promised his new wife and in-laws to play until no later than 1907, and to make a law degree his central priority.[12] It turned out the St. Louis Browns were fed up with Rickey skipping games on Sundays, so he was traded to the New York Highlanders. New York law actually banned Sunday baseball, so New York manager Clark Griffith had no problem with Rickey's part-time play.

Yet Rickey could not start the 1907 season for the Highlanders because of terrible pain in his throwing shoulder that simply would not go away. Poor throwing is unacceptable for a catcher, so Griffith sent him to Hot Springs, Arkansas, hoping the town's warm baths would revive him.

It did not work. By the time Rickey finally played for the Highlanders in the summer of 1907, his arm was in such bad shape that no fewer than thirteen successive bases were stolen on him in one game, leading the Washington Senators to beat them 16–5 on June 28, 1907. He bounced some of the throws between home plate and second base. At times he simply did not bother trying to throw the ball because he had no chance of catching the runner.

It had to have stung his pride. The *Washington Post* cracked that over the course of the game the Senators' players learned that "as a thrower Rickey was many chips shy, and they paused in their travels merely long enough to get breath."[13]

By the end of the season, Rickey had a measly .185 batting average in 101 at-bats, and when he said good-bye to Griffith, he understood that this would be the end of his baseball career—at least as a player. It was time to head back to Ohio Wesleyan for coaching and a new focus on getting that law degree. He was taking night classes at Ohio State University, which meant a forty-mile round trip on the railroad a few days a week.

On top of all this, Rickey worked with young Christian men at the local YMCA, became active in the 1908 presidential campaign supporting Ohio's own William Howard Taft, and leaned on his Methodist roots to jump into the anti-alcohol initiative known as the Anti-Saloon League.

The travel and juggling caught up to Rickey, who tried to ignore the warning signs when he lost thirty pounds. Finally he went to the doctor when he started coughing up blood. He was diagnosed with tuberculosis, which was a horrifying scourge at the time that often led to an untimely death. In response, Rickey and his wife set out for Saranac Lake, New York, in 1909 because of evidence suggesting that breathing in the fresh air of the Adirondack Mountains could help him beat the disease. His immediate treatment was to rest completely for six weeks, and worst of all for Rickey, he was not even allowed to talk.

RICKEY BOUNCES BACK

His wife, Jane, saw the irony of a prescription of silence for the famously talkative man. She sent a postcard to friends quipping, "Branch was behaving fine—had to keep absolutely quiet. The blessed day. Think of Branch Rickey keeping quiet!"[14]

Instead Rickey jumped into the treatment with gusto, learning for the first time to hold his tongue. And as he gained strength in the summer of 1909, he was encouraged to further destroy the disease by putting on weight instead of wasting away. Rickey, known for his corpulence later in life, did not need to be told twice to eat more. The religious man who swore off the bottle at an early age even agreed to have some beer with dinner in order to put on weight.

He was eventually discharged with the warning that one was never fully cured of tuberculosis, so rest and outdoor air would still be necessary. But nothing could stop Rickey's joy of getting out of the sanatorium—and learning he had been accepted to the University of Michigan Law School.

Slowing down was simply not in Rickey's vocabulary. He won the right to take twenty credits in the spring term of 1910 at one of the nation's toughest law schools, and set his sights on becoming the baseball coach at Michigan. To get the job, the master manipulator showed himself to be back in fine form. Rickey meticulously wrote letters to dozens of his colleagues in college and major league baseball asking for recommendations, and he maneuvered to have a couple of letters arrive each day on the desk of the university's athletic director.

Rickey first had to convince the law school dean he could really handle the workload. Then he was called into the athletic director's office to learn he could have the coaching post on one condition: he had to tell his friends to stop sending all those letters!

It was a lighthearted moment, no doubt, but in a very touching letter that Rickey sent to his parents about the new gig, he gave great credit to his friends for rallying around him. And Rickey made it clear just how important character was to him.

"It was really their victory for the odds were against me and I counted very little," Rickey wrote. "My greatest joy is not the paltry job . . . but the fact of being known by men of such standing and character that their commendation places me above the pull and push of the other fellow."

Despite that expressed joy, Rickey was clearly feeling blue about his illness taking him off track for a bit. He was still in school and waiting to get both a permanent job and a broader purpose. He was taking it all very hard. "I want to get out and do something—some one thing and bend every effort," Rickey wrote to his parents. "I may fizzle around for a while, but if I get a good grip on some one thing—and have a purpose . . . I guess I'll do my best not to make God as ashamed of me as he has been these last few years."[15]

Rickey was being pretty harsh on himself, or at least he wanted to appear so for his parents. Yet by June 1911, he fulfilled his goal of getting his law degree with honors a year early. And on the baseball diamond he was already an innovator.

As Michigan's coach, Rickey created the "daylight play," a defensive strategy still used in the major leagues decades later as a way of preventing runners from leading too far off second base. When a pitcher sees "daylight" between the base runner and the shortstop racing to cover the base, the pitcher is supposed to turn sharply and then try to throw the runner out.

At a time when the great Ty Cobb was playing for the Detroit Tigers, word was getting around that the new coach was an up-and-comer. "Occasionally, on days off from the American League pennant race, Detroit Tigers players, scouts, and coaches came to Ann Arbor to sit in on Branch Rickey's practices and listen to his practical and inspirational instruction," noted author Lee Lowenfish.[16]

People in baseball were taking notice, and by 1913 Rickey was back in the big leagues, now as an executive for the St. Louis Browns. His biggest early accomplishment was signing George Sisler, an outstanding first baseman who in 1922 racked up one of the most impressive single seasons for any hitter in history: a .420 batting average, thanks to a whopping 246 hits, including 18 triples.

One of Sisler's most important achievements, however, came after his playing days. Rickey tapped Sisler to serve as one of the scouts he would send around the United States, Mexico, and Latin America to step up the recruitment of new talent for the Dodgers. Sisler and other scouts like Clyde Sukeforth, the man who first met up with Robinson in Chicago, were told to also keep an eye out for "Negro" players. Early on Sisler identified Robinson in scouting reports as someone who could run extremely well and was a skilled hitter. He did also highlight a sour point—the shortstop's arm was not much to write home about, which was a red flag for Rickey.

Sisler was prescient in his belief that Robinson's destiny was to be switched over to a position on the right side of the infield. The throws to first base would be much shorter. Indeed, Robinson would end up excelling for most of his time with the Dodgers at second base, where the toss to first base to get a batter out was much easier.

Just as Robinson had to find the right spot that played to his strengths on the field, Rickey went back and forth on which facet of management was best for him. He left the Browns' front office and headed to the field to manage the final twelve games of the 1913 season. He continued in that role for two more years, but the team lost more games than it won in all three seasons. While he stayed with the Browns in 1916, a change in ownership had forced him out of his position as field manager. Then, in 1917, he took a new job as president of the other big league team playing in St. Louis: the Cardinals.

He stayed with the Cardinals until announcing he would be enlisting to fight in World War I. Major Rickey set sail for France that fall on a boat named *President Grant*. Despite a brief but scary bout of pneumonia on the boat, he believed deeply in the cause of serving his country.

Even while he was serving in France, baseball was never too far away. He led a chemical training unit that included stars of the diamond like Cobb and pitcher Christy Mathewson. According to Lowenfish, their unit provided soldiers and tanks with proper chemical support in more than 150 operations.[17]

After the war, in December 1918, Rickey returned to the Cardinals, but he gave up the president title to the team's new majority owner, Sam

Breadon, and focused on his duties as field manager for the next six years. The Cards finished third in the National League in 1921 and 1922, and fifth in the NL in 1923. Rickey was eventually fired as manager in 1925.

Breadon still respected his abilities as an innovator and offered to let him stay on in the front office, but Rickey was furious that at the age of forty-three his career might be finished.

"You can't do this to me, Sam," Rickey thundered. "You are ruining me."

"No," Breadon shot back. "I am doing you the greatest favor one man has ever done to another."[18]

Breadon was right. When Rickey began his remarkable run as the front office boss of the Cardinals, several World Series championships followed. Not to mention the fact that Rickey's firing as manager put him on the path to eventually run the Dodgers and sign Robinson.

With the Cardinals, Rickey invented the modern-day concept of a farm system, as noted earlier. And his legendary major league team, which eventually became known as the "Gashouse Gang," won the World Series in 1926 and again in 1931 thanks to the exploits of rookie Pepper Martin, one of the many young stars cultivated in the farm system.

Then the floodgates of the farm system opened, and a slew of young stars streamed into the Cardinals organization over the next few years, including future Hall of Famers Dizzy Dean and Joe Medwick, who helped the Cardinals to another World Series victory in 1934.

In 1942, his last year with the Cardinals, Rickey oversaw the best season in franchise history as they won 106 games in the regular season and another World Series title. That came after Rickey's farm system tutored three more future Hall of Famers—Johnny Mize, Stan Musial, and Enos Slaughter—who helped make them the class of the National League.

Even as he rose to great heights, Rickey remained thankful for his parents' influence on him. Their letters back and forth continued, and they can be found in Rickey's own personal papers at the Library of Congress.

Rickey's parents were still in the Buckeye State after the great Ohio River flood of 1937, which killed almost four hundred people. Rickey's father, Frank, showed his Christian compassion by taking in several families who had lost their homes, and his faith was evident in the closing of the letter: "God bless you all, and keep you true to (Him). Father . . . Please let me hear from you at once."[19]

Branch also stayed true to John Wesley's famous command to "give all you can" after you have "gained all you can," as he regularly sent money back to his parents.[20]

In one November 25, 1936, letter to his father, Branch wrote, "Here is my check for $200. I am going to try to get down to you Saturday, but I am sending this check in case I do not come."[21]

On January 3, 1938, Branch fired off another note to his father: "I am sending you herewith my check for one hundred ($100.00) dollars, because I am sure with any current expenses that you have had, you will need it."[22]

On the other hand, their correspondence also suggests that despite his generosity with his parents in other areas, Branch was not just "El Cheapo" when it came to being stingy with the contracts of Dodgers players. He also pinched pennies around the house.

He wrote at least two letters in 1937 urging his father to come to St. Louis to help fix a fence at the executive's home. "It may be that you can get the wire over in Portsmouth cheaper than any place else, and have it shipped," Branch wrote at one point.[23]

It is no wonder then that one of the executive's players, Gene Hermanski, once said of him: "Mr. Rickey has a heart of gold. And he keeps it."[24]

Still, the letters back and forth with his parents show that Rickey did have a heart when it came to nurturing a close bond with them through their entire lives. And he kept the promise to never visit the ballpark on Sundays as a player long after his actual playing days were over—and long after his parents had passed on.

The pious man, however, was tempted over the years to at least skirt the rule a bit. When he was an executive with the Cardinals, Rickey would not go to the ballpark on Sundays. But he did seem to have a workaround in order to keep tabs on the team.

Veteran sportswriter George Vecsey, author of *Stan Musial: An American Life*, told me that he found in his own research of those Cardinals years that Rickey used to quietly show up at a local YMCA in St. Louis on Sunday afternoon when the Cardinals had a game.[25] The YMCA was across from the Cardinals' stadium, and Rickey found a way to keep up with what was happening in the ballpark without technically setting foot inside.

The younger Rickey noted his grandfather easily could have started going to the ballpark on Sundays during his years with the Cardinals and Dodgers. The executive's mother and father died in the 1930s.

"Even after his parents were gone, you'd think he would say it was just a pledge to his parents," said Rickey III. "But he never went into a ballpark on a Sunday. It was a commitment to his parents, respect to their religion. He was a devout person. I think it was not so much the pledge to a 'religious thing' that allowed him to keep his word to his parents. It was respecting their religion in the same way he respected his own religion."

On Sundays when he was running the Dodgers in the 1940s, Rickey would stay home with his wife, Jane, to play either some bridge or chess. He continued to keep the promise, at least most of the time, according to his grandson.

"I remember he told me, 'I did go one time but it was an exception. It was 1945 and it was a war bond drive. I went in to [Ebbets Field] to help in the spirit of raising money for war bonds,'" recounted Rickey III.[26]

Robinson saw Rickey's deep respect for religion when the ballplayer finally arrived in Brooklyn to meet with the executive, after that long train ride from Chicago, in the summer of 1945.

Rickey's faith left a deep impression on Robinson, who was still marveling about it when he sat down decades later to write his unpublished manuscript.

"Some people have laughed at this grand old man because he is so dramatic and outspoken in his religious convictions," wrote Robinson. "Others have insinuated that he is not sincere because he speaks so frequently and so emotionally about the Fatherhood of God and the brotherhood of man. It is the way of some people to make light of sincerity of this kind, because they themselves are too small to speak, think, and live big."[27]

Both Rickey and Robinson lived big and dreamed big. Especially on that hot August day when the nervous young African American player arrived at the Dodgers' offices at 215 Montague Street and was finally let in on the secret details of Rickey's experiment.

CHAPTER 8

JACKIE MEETS MR. RICKEY

After grabbing a quick dinner at a Brooklyn diner just a couple of blocks from Hillary Clinton's presidential campaign headquarters, I hopped in an Uber car to get in place for another night of primary coverage for Fox News Channel.

It was April 5, 2016, and Clinton was still "feeling the Bern" on what was supposed to be an easy route to becoming the first female president in American history.

As the Democratic presidential race continued to unexpectedly heat up, my reporting and writing for this book on Jackie Robinson went on the back burner. But ten days before the sixty-ninth anniversary of his first game, I was about to run smack into one of the landmark sites of Robinson's rise.

Brooklyn-born Bernie Sanders was stunning Clinton yet again with a victory in that night's Wisconsin primary. She did not want to stay in Wisconsin to hold a rally explaining away another defeat, so she was already in New York gearing up for what she hoped would be the comeback she needed two weeks hence, when voters in her adopted home state would go to the polls.

So my cameraman, Eric Conner, had randomly picked a pretty back-drop in Brooklyn Heights, with the Brooklyn Bridge glowing in the night sky behind me, for us to stage live shots for Fox's special coverage that night.

The driver picked me up at the diner, and he punched into his GPS the street address where Conner had set up his camera. We passed the building for Clinton's headquarters, and suddenly the GPS told him to turn right on Montague Street.

"Montague Street?" I repeated.

It immediately clicked in my mind: I knew from my research that the Brooklyn Dodgers had their offices at 215 Montague Street. It's where Branch Rickey was waiting for Robinson when he arrived in New York in 1945.

I was covering a history-making campaign based just around the corner from another remarkable piece of history.

Unfortunately, the historic spot is now a bank. And while a plaque marks the fact that it is sacred ground, sadly, the marker spends just as much time trying to remind locals that there actually used to be a team based here before it was abruptly moved to Los Angeles.

"Once upon a time (1890–1957), there was a major league baseball team in Brooklyn—the Dodgers," reads the plaque, with the visage of Robinson at the top right. "They played their games at Ebbets Field (1913–1957) in Flatbush, where fans and players dodged trolley cars to get to the ballpark."

Hence the team name, *Dodgers*, boys and girls.

The inscription continues that on August 28, 1945, Robinson and Rickey met for the first time and ended up signing a contract for him to start in the minor leagues, "thus initiating the process of becoming the first African American player on a major league baseball team—integrating the major leagues and making baseball truly the pastime of all the nation."

That is all true. Yet it only begins to scratch the surface of how intense the situation must have been after Robinson arrived at these offices at 10:00 a.m. sharp. Clyde Sukeforth was waiting in the lobby and recalled later that it was steaming in Brooklyn that summer morning.

Sukeforth's shirt was stuck to his chest with sweat as the elevator brought them up to the fourth floor to see Branch Rickey.

"Hot day," muttered Sukeforth.

The *Farmers Almanac* suggests on that date in history the high temperature in New York was only about 81 degrees. Maybe Sukeforth was suffering more from nerves than some kind of heat stroke.[1]

Either way, Rickey was calm and cool, going through his normal routine despite the heavy stakes.

One of Robinson's takeaways from this historic meeting was the rather mundane fact that he was initially overwhelmed by a "smokescreen" from Rickey's cigar when he got his very first glimpse of the executive sitting behind his desk that morning.

They didn't call him "El Cheapo" for nothing. He spent only about twenty-two cents on each of the several cigars he might smoke on any given day in 1945, even though by now he owned a 25 percent share of the Dodgers, a team that was worth more than $8 million by the end of the decade.[2]

Robinson immediately took note of something else. The office was big yet not ostentatious, and there were four framed pictures on the wall. There was a snapshot of Leo Durocher, the manager of the Dodgers, who would soon be sidelined. The second was a portrait of the late Charley Barrett, a talented scout who worked with Rickey in St. Louis and signed sixty-six players over the course of his career, a nod to the Dodgers executive's own roots in the game. The third framed picture was of Air Force Lieutenant General Claire Lee Chennault, a legendary hero who commanded the Flying Tigers, an impressive group of pilots who helped defend China from the Japanese during World War II.[3]

Robinson would recall that he felt less nervous as he noticed the last picture. "And the fourth and largest smiled down on me with calm reassurance, the portrait of the sad, trusting Abraham Lincoln who had pleaded for malice toward none," he noted.[4]

Lincoln, of course, also freed the slaves with the Emancipation Proclamation. And in the office where he was staring down at Robinson, something of great import was about to take place again.

Lincoln was a hero to Rickey, who had books stacked atop one another in his office—especially ones focused on the Great Emancipator. He collected every single book that had been published about Lincoln in the previous couple of decades. Rickey always had a collection of Lincoln's speeches handy, plus a copy of the Bible, of course. "I like the Old Testament best, for sheer reading interest," he would note.

He especially loved to read in bed, because he was known as the hardest-working executive in baseball, getting just two or three hours of sleep.

"Judas Priest!" Rickey liked to say. "Who wants to sleep anyhow—what's it good for outside of 'knitting up the raveled sleave of care?'"[5]

The veritable cottage industry of books, articles, and films that document Robinson's career—all of which at least touch on the meeting that was about to commence—all provide slightly different accounts of what exactly was said over the next few hours.[6]

Yet one thing is for sure: neither the calming fish tank nor the heavy venetian blinds blocking the hot sun from coming into Rickey's fourth-floor office could cut through the heavy cloud of stress hanging over them.

Rickey stood up to greet the player, offering a handshake and a respectful greeting. "Good to meet you, Mr. Robinson."

"Mr. Rickey," Robinson said simply.[7]

Then the two men sat down and seemed to be sizing each other up from across Rickey's desk, according to Sukeforth.

"As if they were trying to get inside each other," he said. "The air was electric in there. They just stared and stared at each other. Oh, what a pair, these two!"[8]

Finally, after the long pause, Rickey offered a bit of a curveball. It seemed to have nothing to do with the matter at hand, when in reality it was everything.

"Do you have a girl, Jackie?" Rickey asked.

Robinson started to open his mouth but seemed surprised by the question as he struggled to formulate words. "I don't know," he said.

"What do you mean, you don't know?" the boss pressed.

Rickey had carefully done his homework with a full background check on Robinson's entire life and knew full well that during his senior year at UCLA, Jackie had met a beautiful nursing student named Rachel Isum, who was now his companion.

Robinson was stuttering to explain: "Well, the way I've been traveling around the country and not writing as I should—well, I don't know if I have a girl or not."

Rickey was not satisfied with that answer, knowing all about Rachel from his background research.

"Is she a fine girl?" he asked. "Does she come from a good family background? Is she an educated girl?"

Jackie jumped in and fessed up. "They don't come any finer, Mr. Rickey," he said.

"Then you know doggone well that you have a girl," interjected Rickey. "And you need one. You ought to marry her quick as you can. . . . But sit down. Make yourself comfortable. We have a lot of things to talk about, and we've got plenty of time to do it."[9]

Robinson sat back in a leather chair and settled in for the start of hours of rapid-fire questions from Rickey that would get increasingly intense—and racially charged.

"Are you under contract to the Kansas City Monarchs?" Rickey demanded.

"No sir," said Robinson. "We don't have contracts."

Rickey dove back in for more. "Do you know why you were brought here?" he asked.

"Not exactly," Robinson struggled. "I heard something about a colored ball team at Ebbets Field. That it?"

He was referring to the fake Brooklyn Brown Dodgers of the United States League. Rickey decided to finally come clean.

"No, that isn't it," Rickey said. "You were brought here, Jackie, to play for the Brooklyn organization. Perhaps on Montreal to start with and—"

Robinson jumped in, knowing that Brooklyn's minor league squad was just one step from the major leagues.

"Me? Play for Montreal?" he said, confused.

"If you can make it, yes," Rickey said with a simple nod, before delivering his real pitch. "Later on—also if you can make it—you'll have a chance with the Brooklyn Dodgers."[10]

Robinson remembered Rickey smoking those cheap cigars throughout the meeting. Rather than act cavalier, though, the executive was trying to be accommodating.

"Do you think you are capable enough to play baseball in the major leagues?" Rickey began.

"I don't know," admitted Robinson. "I've only played professional baseball for one year. I don't know how the Negro Leagues stack up against the minors, let alone the majors."

Rickey was confident in the research he'd done and had faith in Robinson, so he raced to the point.

"I am willing to offer you a contract in organized baseball," said Rickey. "Are you willing to sign it?"[11]

TROUBLE AHEAD

This is what Robinson had so desperately been yearning for, yet he hesitated.

"Mr. Rickey, it sounds like a dream come true, not only for me but for my race," Robinson said. "For seventy years, there has been racial exclusion in big league baseball."

Robinson was elated. But he was also scared. Was he good enough to make the Dodgers? And what if he failed? Would it just be a blow to Robinson—or would it also set back the cause of civil rights? In an instant, an enormous weight fell on Robinson. He was taking it all in fast. Yet he was reassured as he stared at the bushy-browed Rickey.

For the first time in his life, Jackie Robinson saw a boss and a father rolled into one. So he felt comfortable going out on a limb.

"There will be trouble ahead," Robinson said. "For you, for me, for my people."

That phrase—"trouble ahead"—lit a fire inside Rickey.

"Trouble ahead," Rickey repeated, lingering on each and every syllable. "You know, Jackie, I was a small boy when I took my first train ride," he said.

Of course, Robinson had taken a few important train rides himself.

"On the same train was an old couple, also riding for the first time," said Rickey. "We were going through the Rocky Mountains." Looking out the window, the old man suddenly got worried the train was about to flip.

"Trouble ahead, Ma!" the old man said to his wife. "We're high off a preci-pice and we're gonna run right off."

Rickey was now in full preacher mode, talking about how his boyish ears kept hearing the noise of the train wheels repeating in his mind, "Trouble ahead . . . trouble ahead." Decades later, Rickey still flinched whenever he heard train wheels screeching. But on that initial ride, the train reached a tunnel and came out the other side just fine, which brought him to the end of his homily for Robinson.

"That's the way it is with most trouble ahead in the world, Jackie, if we use the common sense and courage God gave us," Rickey said. "But you've got to study the hazards and build wisely." That reference to God also enabled Rickey to connect with Robinson. When it came to the Bible, these two men were speaking the same language.

Then, without warning, Rickey delivered the most important line in a meeting full of pivotal moments.

"God is with us in this, Jackie," he said quietly. "You know your Bible. It's good simple Christianity for us to face realities and to recognize what we're up against. We can't go out and preach and bust our heads against a wall. We've got to fight out our problems together with tact and common-sense."[12]

Rickey would soon talk a lot more about faith, but first he wanted to map out a plan. He started slow, laying out his dream of the Dodgers lock-ing up the National League pennant, so they could then try to win their first World Series over the best in the American League.

"I want to win the pennant, Jackie, and we need ballplayers to do it," said Rickey. "Do you think you can do it?"

Robinson knew it would be more authentic to not just rush into the answer, so he mulled it over a moment, before finally saying simply, "Yes."[13]

Rickey added that Robinson would need more than hitting or fielding—it would take courage. Sukeforth was still there witnessing all of this. He mused aloud that it might take even more courage by Brooklyn manage-ment to not cave when the pressure got intense, and he wondered if the player had thought all of this through.

"I haven't thought of anything," Robinson said. "It's all so sudden. It kinda hits me between the eyes."

Rickey jumped in, "Do you think he can take it, Clyde?"

"He can run," said Sukeforth. "He can field. He can hit."[14]

All of that was true, but Sukeforth was either stalling or just missing the broader point altogether. Rickey knew Robinson could play ball. But could he take a punch—literally and figuratively—without swinging back?

TESTING THE LIMITS

This was where Rickey sprung into action as an actor, ripping off his suit jacket, revealing white suspenders wrapped around his ample girth. He loved to perform, and suddenly he was playing the role of all kinds of angry white people who would try to deny Robinson things in the days ahead.

First Rickey became the nasty hotel clerk who would greet Robinson when the Dodgers came to town. *Sorry, Mr. Robinson, no rooms for your kind. You'll have to get your own room at the "Nigger" hotel across town.*

Then Rickey was a white waiter, telling the player he would not be getting a meal. *You know we do not serve your kind here, "Boy!"* Rickey added nasty buzzwords for emphasis.

Sweat was pouring down Robinson's forehead as Rickey pounded the table and acted out the vicious slurs that were about to come the ballplayer's way.[15]

"They'll call you 'dirty Nigger!'" Rickey thundered. "Can you take it? Will you take it?"[16]

At another point, Rickey tried to test how Robinson would balance being a devout Christian and an intense competitor. If tensions grew on the field, would Robinson's Christianity kick in and enable him to hold back, or would his intense competitiveness lead him to throw a punch or kick someone at second base on a tough play?

Having seen Rickey up close for several years, Carl Erskine believed this was the point in the meeting where the executive was using his acting skills with aplomb. "He keeps piling this on Jackie," said Erskine. "And knowing Mr. Rickey, his inflection, all of it is very powerful."[17]

Since Erskine would eventually spend nine full seasons as Robinson's teammate, he had a good idea of what was going through his head too.

"Mr. Rickey had Jackie in a fever pitch," said Erskine. "This temper that his teammates in the Negro Leagues said he can't control—he was bringing that to a fever pitch. And Mr. Rickey finally says, 'If a fight breaks out, you can win it. But here's the question—are you strong enough *not* to fight back?'"

While he was not in the room, Erskine instinctively believes Robinson must not have answered immediately. The kid knew deep down he would have a hard time controlling his temper.

"His life must have flashed through his eyes," Erskine told me. "He was a sharecropper's kid from Cairo, Georgia. Then he went to Pasadena and suffered all of those indignities; blacks in those days could not go here, could not swim there."

But Robinson could sense the gravity. "His better sense was to see this was bigger than his own feelings," said Erskine, "and he finally told Mr. Rickey, 'I can do it.'"

Rickey soothed Robinson by dipping into that vintage copy of Giovanni Papini's *Life of Christ* he had in the office.

"Ye have heard that it hath been said," Rickey began reading aloud. "An eye for an eye, and a tooth for a tooth. But I say unto you, that ye resist not evil. But whosoever shall smite thee on thy right cheek, turn to him the other also."[18]

Rickey's musings may have fallen on deaf ears with another player. But the boss knew full well that was not the case with Robinson.

Rickey would later confide that the concerns he had about Robinson's possible "deeper racial resentment" were eased by the fact that he knew the player was "Christian by inheritance and practice."[19] In fact, when Rickey sent Sukeforth and other scouts on the secret mission to find the first African American major leaguer, the notoriously chintzy executive shelled out $25,000 to get it done right.[20]

"He must be a superlative man," Rickey instructed his aides. "An outstanding player on the field and a thorough gentleman off it."[21]

That meant background checks about personal lives that went far beyond what scouts normally measure—much more than finding out how quickly a runner can race down the first-base line. Rickey, the devout Methodist, wanted to know if the player also had a strong faith in God as well as a good support network. That's why he had started the meeting with Robinson with the abrupt question about whether he was getting married soon: the player would need all the support he could get.

At one point in the meeting, Rickey swung his fist through the air and just missed Robinson's face as he played out an imaginary scene in a World Series game.

"I'm a hotheaded player!" Rickey shouted. "I want to win that game, so I go into you, spikes first. But you don't give ground. You stand there and you jab the ball into my ribs and the umpire yells, 'Out!'"

Rickey got more intense, now pretending to be a white player writhing on the ground ready to jump up and fight Robinson at second base.

"I flare—all I see is your face—that black face right on top of me," he declared. "So I haul off and I punch you right in the cheek!"

This is when Rickey's fists began flying.

"What do you do?!" he screamed about Robinson getting smacked in the cheek.

"Mr. Rickey," Robinson said softly, "I've got two cheeks."[22]

THE FAITH CONNECTION

Robinson instinctively got that reference to the Bible. His mother and Rev. Karl Downs had prepared him well.

"I have another cheek," Robinson repeated matter-of-factly.

Rickey still was not convinced. He had more questions, which would keep the already-long meeting going for a couple more hours.

"I want to be honest with you, Jackie," Rickey said. "I've heard all the stories of racial resentment toward you. They told me out in Pasadena that you're a racial agitator."

Before becoming a four-letter star at UCLA, Robinson had also excelled at several sports at Pasadena Community College. The basketball team was in an almost all-white conference, and the referees were white. Robinson and his black teammates were fouled more than anyone and felt they were being racially targeted for injury.

In one game, Robinson fought back by slamming a white player, and blood actually splattered. On the positive side, the hard fouls against Robinson slowed, because the message had been sent.

The tension boiled over in a game at Long Beach Junior College, where black spectators were not exactly welcome. Jack's brother Frank came anyway, packing a tire iron in case there was trouble.

Sure enough, at the end of the game, an opposing player punched Robinson. Jackie pounded the player relentlessly, and pandemonium ensued. It was described as a "riot," though perhaps it was more like a melee between about fifty players and spectators throwing punches. So there was trouble. There were incidents. But was Robinson really an "agitator," or was he just defending himself?

Another time at the junior college, a white student tossed out a racial slur at a picnic, and Robinson immediately challenged him to a fistfight. Yet when the white student quickly backpedaled and insisted he could not break the habit of using the slur and meant no harm, Robinson accepted his apology and shook hands to defuse the situation.[23]

To his credit, Rickey had, in fact, done his homework. He found out the context to these stories at the junior college, as well as at UCLA. This became clear in the Brooklyn Dodgers' offices as he spilled more details.

"They told me at UCLA that, in basketball, you had trouble with coaches, players and officials," Rickey told him. "I just want to tell you that my thorough investigation convinced me that the criticisms are unjustified, that if you'd been white it would have been nothing."[24]

Finally a white man with authority was hearing Robinson out, giving his side of the story some weight, which must have built credibility in their relationship. Rickey clearly understood there had been hardships for Robinson, but the challenges were just about to expand.

"I need someone, Jackie, who can carry that load," said Rickey. "Above all, you cannot fight back. That's the only way this experiment will succeed, and others will follow in your footsteps."[25]

Again this connected with Robinson, who had lived by the code of using his fists. "Whoever told Branch Rickey that I believed in fighting back told him the truth," Robinson admitted in his unpublished manuscript.[26]

Now it had to be different, and, of course, Rickey came to the meeting prepared with a choice quote from "Essay on Man" by Alexander Pope. "We first endure," Rickey told Robinson. "Then pity, then embrace."[27]

His first contract would be worth $5,000—$600 a month plus a $3,500 signing bonus—paltry by today's standards but decent money back then.

After Jackie's marathon meeting with Branch Rickey, it is really not surprising that one of the first things he did was place a call to his mother, Mallie, in Pasadena. What his mother told him to do next, though, has never been reported in the many books about Robinson.

Robinson revealed the details of his August 1945 phone call with his mother in a little-noticed interview more than a decade later with *Viewpoint*, a widely popular syndicated interview show hosted by Rev. Dana F. Kennedy.

Asked about his "inner reaction" when Rickey first told him he had the chance to play for the Dodgers, Robinson did not hesitate.

"Well, I naturally wanted to talk it over with my mother," Robinson said. "We've all been very close."

Robinson added he had an idea that the first thing she'd tell him to do was square the situation with God. Jackie said the challenges he discussed with Rickey needed to be chewed over with someone, so his mother "felt that because I was so far away from home at the time that the person should be a minister."

This instinct appears to be something else special that the Robinson family shared with Rickey, since he also wanted to talk to Rev. Wendell Fifield in his own time of need.

Robinson did not specify which minister he went to see to discuss his meeting with Rickey, and the interviewer did not follow up.

Though Robinson did again mention the importance of Rev. Karl Downs, the minister who had such a big impact on his childhood in Pasadena but died unexpectedly at an early age in the 1950s.

"He had a great deal of influence," said Robinson. "As a matter of fact, I had played football for UCLA on Saturday afternoon and would come limping in to teach Sunday school on Sunday morning just because of this wonderful influence."[28]

Now Robinson would be giving his all for Rickey, and he was impressed with the old man's stamina. "When he offered me a contract he was sixty-five years old," said Robinson. "Isn't that when most people are retiring?"[29]

Robinson felt wanted, understood, and he said many times later that he felt determined not to let Rickey down.

But what gave Rickey his determination to see all of this through? He gave Robinson a little hint during their meeting, suggesting there was divine inspiration for his push to integrate baseball.

In his unpublished manuscript, Robinson wrote he remembered "Mr. Rickey talking to me about the promise he made to God and to himself when he was teaching sports at college."[30]

It turns out Robinson was not the first African American player whom Rickey had gone to bat for. The first was Charles "Tommy" Thomas.

CHAPTER 9

NO DOUBTING THOMAS

It was right around dinnertime in the heartland of America on a Sunday night, and I was trying to make the two-and-a-half-hour drive north from Indianapolis to South Bend before it got too dark to see something important. I was about to visit the setting of one of the most important moments in Branch Rickey's life.

The road gave me the incredible vantage point to watch the sun beginning to set over one farm and cornfield after another in beautiful Indiana towns like Kokomo. It was a truly all-American vista along the side of the road.

I was rushing to South Bend on I-31 in order to get to the very spot where Rickey decided back in 1903—or 1904, by some accounts—that he had a burning desire to integrate America's national pastime. "He had decades and decades of awareness of the size, and the monumental character, of this problem of discrimination in our society," Rickey's grandson, Branch Rickey III, had told me.[1]

But that problem smacked the elder Rickey in the face when he was coaching baseball at Ohio Wesleyan University at the start of the twentieth century. He brought his team to South Bend to face the University of Notre Dame, and they tried to check in to the Oliver Hotel. A special "Throwback" piece published by the *South Bend Tribune* noted it had been "the fanciest place to stay in town and the finest place to dine" for decades.[2]

The best place to stay and eat, of course, if you were white. But the team's star catcher, Charles Thomas, was African American.

"The clerk said, 'We can house the rest of the baseball team, but your black athlete cannot stay here,'" Branch Rickey III told me in our interview.

This would infuriate the coach, who was just starting his long career in the game, and he resolved to actually do something about it.

So the Oliver Hotel, like Plymouth Church, was another stop on my tour of Branch Rickey's own personal civil rights sites. Of course, when I visited South Bend, the hotel was long gone. It was renamed in 1957, shut down in 1967, and then torn down to make room for an office building. By the time I got a glimpse at the corner of Main and Washington streets, there was not much more to see than an eyesore of a construction site.

But when I grabbed a slice of pizza at a place down the street, I spotted something interesting. Over at Bruno's Pizza, in a state that is still 80 percent white, students of all races from Notre Dame were eating together with not much of a care in the world.

It was a sharp contrast to the anger burning inside of Rickey as he sat down for a meal of his own in March 1945. The story of Charles Thomas was still seared into his memory. The executive was huddling with someone absolutely crucial to his experiment: Walter "Red" Barber.

A RHUBARB FOR RED

Rickey invited Barber, the Dodgers' famed radio broadcaster, to lunch at Joe's Restaurant on Fulton Street. A Southern boy from Columbus, Mississippi, Barber was critical to getting Dodgers fans behind Robinson and, by extension, the bigger cause.

"The Ol' Redhead" was beloved for sprinkling his radio broadcasts with all kinds of syrupy phrases in his Southern drawl, as he spoke from "here at Ebbets Field, Brooklyn, USA."

A player doing well was "sittin' in the catbird seat," while a late-inning rally or a winning streak by the Dodgers was known as "tearin' up the old pea patch." An early inning rally was merely described as "the pot is bubbling" a bit. If a fielder could not get his hands on a tough ground ball, the ball was "slicker than boiled okra," while any kind of dispute on the field was simply called a "rhubarb" by Red.[3]

If this good ol' boy could be heard on the radio embracing the new African American ballplayer, it would be far easier for Brooklyn fans to do the same. The inverse was true as well, of course. If Barber could not bring himself to cheer on a black man, it would be devastating. This is why, Rickey's grandson told me, the executive gave the broadcaster a chance to bow out gracefully and avoid a messy episode. If Barber wanted no part of this experiment, the boss was giving him an early heads-up to go seek another broadcasting gig, with no hard feelings, before Robinson was signed.[4]

At lunch, Rickey swore Barber to secrecy—with the exception of his wife—about what he was about to tell him. The radio man reflected in his memoir, titled *1947: When All Hell Broke Loose in Baseball*, "The place was empty. The lunch hour was over. Rickey led the way to a table in the back corner. There was no one near us."[5]

Once they were completely alone, the executive declared flatly he was going to sign an African American player—not that he was *thinking* about it or hedging on whether he could put all the pieces together.

"I don't know who he is or where he is," Rickey said of which player would be selected, noting he had sent Clyde Sukeforth and other scouts around the country searching for the right one.

As for the scouting reports, Rickey added: "I study them, narrow them down. I'm doing that now. When the time is ripe for a decision on the one man, I'll make it."

Then Rickey said the words that hit the broadcaster the hardest: "As I said, I don't know who he is or where he is, but he is coming."[6]

Barber marveled at how excited the executive was to lay out his plan as the meal played out. "He wanted to know if I would come aboard," recalled Barber. "I can still see those strong catcher's hands of his, trembling with intensity as he began to break a hard roll."[7]

THE CHARLIE THOMAS STORY

Rickey's hands were shaking because he was still full of rage as he told Barber about his days as coach at Ohio Wesleyan University and that trip to South Bend. One player after another checked in at the Oliver Hotel without incident, except for Thomas.

"As Charlie picked up the pen, the clerk jerked the register back and said in a loud voice, 'We do not register Negroes here,'" Rickey told Barber.

The coach jumped in to help Thomas, who was close to Rickey.

"You don't understand," Rickey told the clerk. "This is the Ohio Wesleyan baseball team. This young man is our catcher. We are the guests of the University of Notre Dame."

"I don't care who you are," shot back the clerk. "We do not register Negroes at this hotel."[8]

There was no room at the inn for Thomas, and the symbolism was not lost on author Roger Kahn. "To a devout Christian believer such as Rickey, the incident resonated with the Bible story of the first Christmas in Bethlehem," noted Kahn.[9]

While accounts differ on what exactly happened in South Bend, and in what order, what is clear is that Rickey, as stubborn as he was quick on his feet, would not allow his catcher to be treated unfairly. He gave Barney Russell, the team's equipment manager, orders to see whether there was space open for the night at a nearby YMCA.[10] In the meantime, Rickey quickly came up with a scheme. Until he could find a place for Thomas to stay the night, he convinced hotel management to let the young man stay in his own room.

Rickey had no intention of letting Thomas stay anywhere but the hotel in which they were currently standing, so he finagled his way into getting a cot placed in his room for the catcher. "I handed Charlie the key to my room, told him to go there and wait for me, that I'd be up just as soon as I got the rest of the team settled," recalled Rickey.[11]

All was well—at least until Rickey made it upstairs. Rickey found Thomas sitting at the end of the cot sobbing, in almost a trance.

"Black skin," Thomas said, scratching at the skin on his hands. "Black skin. If only I could make them white."[12]

If only he could pull the skin off, Thomas told Rickey, "I'd be just as good as any other man."

The scene offers a window into the fact that decades before Robinson burst onto the scene, Rickey had at least some understanding of the depth of this national problem. "Come on, Tommy, snap out of it, buck up," Rickey said. "We'll lick this one day, but we can't if you feel sorry for yourself."[13]

As it was recounted to me by Rickey's grandson Branch Rickey III, this story can be seen as a touching American tableau: the tears of a catcher inspiring Rickey to integrate baseball. But some historians have another take on it: Was the story overblown to make Rickey sound a bit more heroic? As author Jules Tygiel noted, "The Charlie Thomas story, although based in fact, is vintage Rickey. The allegory is almost biblical and the sermon-like quality of the tale invites skepticism."[14]

Similarly, biographer Lee Lowenfish conceded that "the South Bend encounter between Rickey and Thomas has been retold innumerable times and was undoubtedly embellished over the years by the master storyteller Branch Rickey."[15]

Skeptics have suggested the story was tweaked to sound more dramatic. One of their supporting arguments is that if it was such a searing moment for Rickey in 1903 (or 1904), it seems curious he did not start talking about the Thomas incident publicly until 1945.

In a long 2013 essay, historian Chris Lamb went beyond only wondering why it took about forty-two years for Rickey to start *talking* about it. More importantly, if Thomas's struggles had such a profound impact on Rickey, why did the executive wait several decades to actually start *doing* something about it? In the essay, Lamb raised the possibility that Rickey used the Thomas incident to suggest he had long been planning to integrate baseball, in part to steal the thunder from sportswriters and progressive activists who were pushing hard for change in the 1930s.[16]

In a 1998 essay, Bill Mardo, former sportswriter for the *Daily Worker*, a newspaper published in New York City by the Communist Party, lashed out at the executive by writing, "There was the pre-Robinson Rickey who stayed shamefully silent for much of his baseball life."[17]

In part, Mardo was echoing a charge of other critics of Rickey over the years, who believe his real motivation in signing Robinson was more about new revenue than justice.

The criticism has been that rather than being Lincolnesque, Rickey simply realized before others that bringing in African American players was important for the future health of the Dodgers franchise. It would not only improve the stream of talent to make the team better but would also bring a new stream of revenue from black spectators rushing to Ebbets Field.

There was the post-Robinson Rickey, Mardo wrote, "whose extraordinary business and baseball sense helped him seize the moment, jump aboard the Freedom Train as it was getting ready to pull out of Times Square, catch social protest at its apex, and then do just about everything right once he signed Robinson."[18]

After exhaustive research, Lamb concluded that while the heartache in South Bend should not be exaggerated, the significance of Rickey seeing Thomas try to peel off his skin should not be diminished either.

Lamb urged his readers to move away from the language of "inspiration," arguing that while it may be historically impossible to definitively know whether the famous hotel scene directly led Rickey to integrate baseball, we can certainly say that Charles Thomas helped shape the executive's feelings about racial injustice.

Thomas and Rickey were close, and the coach felt badly about his catcher being cheated out of more than just a hotel room. Thomas was considered a spectacular player who "could have perhaps played in the big leagues, if his skin had not been so black," noted Lamb.[19]

The South Bend incident was hardly the only time Rickey saw him being treated poorly. As Thomas later recalled, "On several occasions, he talked the management [of hotels] into allowing me to occupy a double room" with another member of the team.[20]

"Yes, Rickey realized the economic opportunity that came with desegregating baseball," noted Lamb. "But it's important to acknowledge that for

Rickey, the breaking of baseball's color barrier was less a business decision than a personal one, based on a friendship with Charlie Thomas that helped shape his belief that blacks should have the same opportunities as whites."[21]

And more research, made possible by the detailed footnotes in Lowenfish's biography of Rickey, suggests the friendship between Rickey and Thomas continued for years and included reaching out to one another when times got tough.[22] In an October 26, 1921, letter to Rickey, Thomas wrote in despair that he had become very ill several months earlier. He was so sick with an unspecified illness that he had to break up his dentist practice and leave his home in St. Louis, decamping to Albuquerque to try to recuperate.

"My wife remained behind to sell the house, which I hope will be soon," wrote Thomas. "I am in need of some money for her and some for my expenses . . . would you advance me $100, to be paid back immediately upon the sale of my home, and if we don't sell it immediately, give me time to pay it back."[23]

It is worth noting that in the exchange of letters, kept with Rickey's papers at the Library of Congress, the executive promised to help only after doing one of his classic "Cave of the Winds" sermons about the difficulty of his own finances. "It is a long story to recount to you [about] my personal affairs of the last two years and I shall not undertake it," Rickey began, before undertaking the details after all.

"I wish to say that my losses here have been so large that I have simply had to practice the strictest economy to meet my necessary current expenses," wrote Rickey. "We have not repaired and improved our house for two years simply because we were not able to do so. I am driving the same Ford Sedan I had a year ago although it is not nearly large enough for my family which will shortly number five children."

Despite that windup, Rickey added he would be in touch with Mrs. Thomas: "I want you to know that any assistance I can render to you will be most gladly rendered."[24]

Rickey was there for Thomas throughout most of their lives; the South Bend incident was just the tip of the iceberg.

"From the very first day I entered Ohio Wesleyan, Branch Rickey took special interest in my welfare," Thomas said.[25] At one game in Kentucky, opposing players and fans started chanting a racial slur in order to try to get Thomas to leave the field. Rickey was having none of it. "We won't play without him!" he shouted, even running to the Kentucky dugout to make his point clear.[26]

TEARS FOR THOMAS

Many years later, with the Dodgers, Rickey still had Thomas on his mind. During World War II, a lot of baseball teams skipped the traditional trip to Florida for spring training because train travel was harder to come by. So the Dodgers worked out at the Bear Mountain resort, near the US Military Academy at West Point in upstate New York. In the spring of 1945, the African American sports journalist Joe Bostic, from the self-described "militant" newspaper the *People's Voice*, visited unannounced with two athletes from the Negro Leagues and demanded tryouts for them.

This was clearly a stunt. Given there had not been any kind of a heads-up, Dodgers officials did not allow the players onto the field for a tryout. Ever the politician, Rickey tried to diffuse any tension by inviting Bostic and the players to lunch.

And then—*bam*—Rickey launched into the Charlie Thomas story with great emotion, bursting into tears as he got to the point about the catcher ripping at his own skin. Bostic did not have a good response to the fact that the executive he was trying to embarrass actually had a heart, so the journalist tried to avert his gaze and stare down at his meal. Rickey did not let him off the hook.

Rickey saw right through Bostic's plan, calling the forced tryouts "pretty cute."

"No, I'm not cute," shot back Bostic. "I'm not concerned with being cute. I brought you two ballplayers."

"Yes, but if I give these men a tryout, you've got the greatest sports story of the century. And if I don't give them a tryout, you've got the greatest sports story because it's an absolute showdown. I don't appreciate being backed into this kind of corner."[27]

For the record, Rickey did end up giving both men tryouts, though he never followed up with either of them. He was ready to integrate baseball, but on his own timetable.

Lamb did concede that the Thomas incident had a major impact on the executive. "The sight of a sobbing Charlie Thomas became both a reminder and a metaphor for the cruelty of segregation," concluded the historian. "But more than this, Rickey's friendship with Thomas gave the baseball executive a perspective of racism that no other baseball executive had. Indeed, perhaps relatively few white Americans had had it."[28]

At least it woke up Rickey, who was determined to right a wrong when he eventually signed Robinson.

"That seed must have been there for all those years from 1903 until 1945," Carl Erskine told me. "I think that lingered in Mr. Rickey's heart. It must have never left the back of Mr. Rickey's mind, and he said, 'Someday and somehow I'm going to confront this bigotry.'"

Erskine added, "Who knows whether, when Charles Thomas was denied that room, that that didn't prick Mr. Rickey's Christian faith as he was taught to dignify anyone and everyone?"[29]

DECIDING OVER A MARTINI

Red Barber was stunned by Rickey's directness, and he stayed mostly silent during the lunch, telling himself he was struggling with the idea. The broadcaster did not consider himself a racist. Yet he had been born in Mississippi and grew up in central Florida, deep in the Jim Crow South, a place where, by Barber's own admission, "I saw black men tarred and feathered by the Ku Klux Klan and forced to walk the street. I had grown up in a completely segregated world."[30]

Barber did not give Rickey an answer at Joe's, instead quietly shuffling off to the subway in Brooklyn, stopping at Grand Central Station in Manhattan, and grabbing a commuter train home.

When he reached his house in Scarsdale, New York, Barber told his wife, Lylah, that he was done.

"I'm going to quit," said Barber.[31]

It would be a big blow to Rickey if the man who spoke directly to the people of Brooklyn walked away rather than broadcast games with Robinson. At a time when television sets were not yet the norm, in the days when Americans crowded around the radio for news and entertainment, broadcasters like Red Barber held major places in the social lives of everyday Americans. He had more listeners for his games than all of the readers of the many New York City newspapers combined.[32]

Mrs. Barber came up with a clever idea, telling her husband he did not have to decide on quitting that night. She counseled him to sleep on it after they had a nightcap. "Let's have a martini," she said.[33]

Barber's own faith in God helped him see the light as he started to look inside himself. He noted a sentence in the Book of Common Prayer that he kept falling back on: "and hast opened the eyes of the mind to behold things invisible and unseen."[34]

Barber made it clear that after some contemplation, he realized he had no business running away from the Dodgers and shunning Robinson. He told Rickey this Southern boy was staying.

"I made myself realize that I had had no choice in the parents I was born to, no choice in the place of my birth or the time of it," noted Barber. "I was born white just as a Negro was born black. I had been given a fortunate set of circumstances, none of which I had done anything to merit, and therefore I had best be careful about being puffed up over my color. Chance, sheer chance."

CHAPTER 10

"ALL HEAVEN WILL REJOICE"

The breakfast dishes had been cleared at the IHOP, but the coffee was still going strong—and so was Carl Erskine.

"You know, timing is everything," he told me. "When you're kissing your girl, or making a sale, or calling the right pitch."

Erskine declared it was unfair for people to criticize Branch Rickey for not pushing sooner to make good on his vow to right the wrong against Charlie Thomas. The nation was still not quite ready for Jackie Robinson in 1945, and if Rickey had tried to do it in St. Louis in the 1920s and 1930s, integration would have been an even tougher sell.

"But Brooklyn was a different story," Erskine said. "Two million people, an ethnic mix, lots of culture. . . . All of those things kind of came together, and Mr. Rickey must have said in his gut, *Now is the right time.*"[1]

While Rickey and Robinson had unofficially agreed to the terms on his minor league contract at their meeting in August 1945, the deal still had not been made public by autumn. The boss was putting the pieces in place, but various politicians were hearing whispers about Rickey's plan and itching to get ahead of him and snag the credit.

In late September, a commission led by New York governor Thomas Dewey demanded that the three bosses of the Empire State's three big league teams—the Dodgers, Giants, and Yankees—sign a pledge that they would not discriminate on the basis of race, color, or creed when hiring and firing employees in the state. The Giants in particular balked at giving in to what they saw as coercion.

Legendary New York City mayor Fiorello La Guardia had heard whispers that the question was moot since Rickey was already sitting on a signed contract with Robinson.

La Guardia stood at only five feet two inches, but he was a giant when it came to many areas, especially securing publicity for himself. So the mayor sent word to Rickey that he would like to announce the Robinson signing on his radio program, and he wanted to tell voters it was a direct result of his own special committee on antidiscrimination.

Rickey stalled La Guardia and dispatched Robinson to Canada at once. It was there that he formally signed his first contract to play for the Montreal Royals on October 23, 1945.

After all, the many boxes on Rickey's carefully crafted list had been checked. He had spent hours behind closed doors with Robinson, prepping him for all of the racial nastiness he was about to face, while trying to balance that ugliness with the uplifting nature of their noble experiment by reading Scripture aloud.

Rickey had dined with broadcaster Red Barber and gotten him on board. He had also squared the situation with God in his private meeting with Rev. Wendell Fifield, and now faith was on his mind again as new signs of trouble flared up.

The executive called another broadcasting friend, Lowell Thomas, to give him a heads-up that Robinson would be unveiled the next day as the newest member of the Montreal Royals.

"Branch, tomorrow all hell is going to break loose," Thomas warned Rickey.

The boss would not budge. He was convinced all the struggle was part of God's plan.

"Lowell, I believe tomorrow all heaven will rejoice," insisted Rickey.[2]

Rickey was supremely confident that over the long haul, he and Robinson would survive the storm. Yet Thomas was looking out for his friend in the short-term, and he was right. As soon as Robinson attended a news conference in Montreal the next day, he and Rickey walked into a buzz saw of criticism and controversy.

Clark Griffith, president of the Washington Senators, had been ignoring the push to hire African Americans. He accused Rickey of trying to become "dictator of Negroes in baseball!"[3]

And white baseball stars immediately started lashing out at Robinson and his abilities. "He couldn't hit an inside pitch to save his neck," declared Cleveland Indians pitcher Bob Feller. "If he were a white man, I doubt if they would even consider him as big league material."[4]

Jimmy Powers, sports editor at the *New York Daily News*, predicted the newcomer "will not make the grade in big leagues next year or the next . . . Robinson is a thousand-to-one shot."[5]

These were brutal attacks on Robinson, one of the great athletes of any generation. Rickey did not want him to face further fire at the Montreal news conference, so he basically told Robinson to stick to their talking points and move on without taking questions.

"Just be yourself," said Rickey. "Simply say that you are going to do the best you can and let it go at that."[6]

Robinson went off script by taking a dozen questions at the news conference with Branch Rickey Jr., who ran the Dodgers' minor league teams, and Hector Racine, president of the Royals. Yet Robinson was poised, and he managed to perfectly deliver his message.

"Of course," Robinson told reporters, "I can't begin to tell you how happy I am that I am the first member of my race in organized baseball. I realize how much it means to me, my race, and to baseball. I can only say I will do my very best to come through in every manner."[7]

Rickey Jr. declared his father and Racine were "not inviting trouble," but would be ready if it came. And that trouble was coming fast.[8]

It is hard to imagine in the modern age, when players make so much money and sometimes get to hold their teams hostage in contract negotiations, but back in the day "El Cheapo" held most of the cards. Rickey had his son deliver a threat to Dodgers players who might think they could balk at playing with a black man.

"Some players with us may even quit," Rickey Jr. told reporters. "But they'll be back in baseball after they work a year or two in a cotton mill."[9]

It was a not-so-subtle reference to how the world was changing. Now, the many white ballplayers from the South might be the ones working in a cotton mill if they were kicked off the team, and they would have to come crawling back for less money in a year or two for the privilege of playing for Rickey.

PERCEIVED THREATS

The threat of potentially losing a job came not only from Rickey and his refusal to put up with racism on the team. Some players were afraid Jackie's abilities would make them obsolete. This threat was real for Dodgers stars like shortstop Pee Wee Reese, who would eventually become one of the African American player's closest friends on the team.[10]

As Robinson signed with Montreal in late 1945, Reese was serving in the US Navy and was on a ship headed home from Guam.

A petty officer kicked up a lot of noise as he came rushing up a flight of steel stairs to deliver Reese some urgent news about the Dodgers signing an African American to a minor league contract.[11]

Harold Henry Reese was a tiny kid whose first brush with greatness was becoming the best marbles player on the streets of Louisville, Kentucky. Any kid worth his or her salt knows the key marble is the biggest marble that you can use to knock all the other marbles around. Broadcaster Larry King told me that Reese noted to him that he flipped that assumption on its head, figuring out a way to use a small marble to blast all the others. So "Pee Wee"—the name for the tiniest marble—became the perfect nickname, even though he had grown to a respectable five feet ten inches by the time he made it to Brooklyn.

On that navy ship, the petty officer had another detail that was a gut punch to Reese.

"The colored guy is a shortstop," the officer said.[12]

Resentment quickly built up inside Reese; baseball had sent some of their stars off to fight in World War II with the vow that their jobs would still be there when they made it back to the ballpark, as author Scott Simon explained in his 2002 book on Robinson.

Simon put it this way: "If a sixteen-year-old kid, or a Mennonite pacifist, or someone rejected by the armed forces for having hammertoes, played well in the absence of a major leaguer who had been taken away to defend his country, Reese felt, then a veteran—whether he was a steamfitter, bank clerk, or shortstop—should not have to worry about returning home to find his job filled."[13]

It was a reasonable proposition: if you were sent off to war with a wave of the American flag and a parade, you deserved to get your job back upon finishing your service to the nation. But lurking beneath that justifiable explanation was the real thing that was eating away at Reese aboard that ship. Decades later, Reese bluntly leveled with author Roger Kahn.

"I go back to Louisville," Reese said. "The people say, 'Reese, you weren't man enough to protect your job from a nigger.'"[14]

Keep in mind that Reese grew into one of Robinson's strongest allies. The shortstop was merely reflecting the reality of the times.

Dixie Walker was a popular Dodger who was born in Georgia and lived in Alabama during the offseason. He would soon lead a formal effort to block Robinson from joining the team. And he did not keep his initial disgust about the minor league contract under wraps.

"As long as he isn't with the Dodgers, I'm not worried," Walker said.[15]

Players on opposing teams, like Bob Feller of the Indians, also offered withering criticism. And Feller tried to mask the idea that race motivated the critique. "Jackie will be in a tough spot," he said. "I'm not prejudiced against him, either. I hope he makes good, but, frankly, I don't think he will."[16]

Feller tried to claim Robinson had previously failed to get a hit against him in a 1945 exhibition game on the West Coast, though his memory seemed to be a bit hazy about what really happened.

"As a matter of fact, I hit a double off him, down the right-field foul line," countered Robinson.

Even the immortal baseball star Rogers Hornsby took his shots. "The way things are, it will be tough for a Negro player to become a part of a closely knit group such as an organized ball club. I think Branch Rickey was wrong in signing Jackie Robinson to play with Montreal and it just won't work out."[17]

Such was the pessimism about what turned out to be one of the most triumphant moments in American history.

What all of the baseball greats who criticized Robinson and Rickey did not know then—but we learned later thanks to poring through thousands of pages of Rickey's papers held at the Library of Congress—is that average Americans were sending the executive telegrams brimming with optimism.

In a telegram dated October 24, 1945, an African American from Schenectady, New York, identifying himself simply as "Smokey," told Rickey, "Congratulations it was a brave move will make a big difference to our race."[18]

Another telegram declared: "Congratulations to you Branch Rickey for [breaking down the] longtime discrimination against Negro athletes in professional baseball. May your leadership be followed."[19]

Not all of the telegrams were positive, and the nasty ones show how divided the nation was on race. One friend of Rickey's in Texas actually wrote in to claim that he was trying to convince some buddies that the executive's move was an effort to somehow continue white supremacy by picking a player who was going to do terribly and set back the cause of African Americans.

Rickey wrote back to this fellow, "The signing of Jackie Robinson has caused considerable furor but most of the comment we have received has been favorable. While the path may not be easy it seems straight to me. I need good ball players, my reports are that Robinson is a good ball player, and it is my belief that every American citizen should have the opportunity of earning a living at the job he can do best."[20]

It was a novel concept that Rickey was laying out—that all Americans deserve the opportunity to earn a living, regardless of their background.

SECRET MEETING

It was a simple concept that was not yet grasped or accepted by the other team owners and top executives in baseball. They had been actively trying to prevent the integration of the game, and they didn't even have the guts to do it in public. This may give more context for why Rickey did not act sooner to right the wrong he saw up close with Charles Thomas.

Within a few months of the news conference in Montreal, Rickey's contemporaries held a secret meeting at the Blackstone Hotel in Chicago on August 28, 1946.[21] Rickey had signed Robinson to only a minor league contract. So the other leaders in the American and National Leagues saw an opening to try to strangle integration before Robinson was signed to a major league contract.

Rickey recounted later that behind closed doors, fifteen of the sixteen teams approved a secret report declaring "however well intentioned, the use of Negro players would hazard all the physical properties of baseball."[22]

All copies of that report, passed around at the meeting in Chicago, were given back to baseball officials so they could be shredded, never to be revealed.

"I sat silent while the other fifteen clubs approved it," said Rickey. "I've tried to get a copy of the report, but league officials tell me all were destroyed."[23]

One of the only reasons we know about the secret meeting is that Rickey blew the whistle on it with a speech in 1948, as Robinson got ready for his second season with the Dodgers. And Rickey chose a venue for the speech, Wilberforce University in his home state of Ohio, that had clear religious connotations.

Like Rickey and Robinson, William Wilberforce was Methodist. He became an influential nineteenth-century abolitionist who crusaded against Britain's slave trade. The university in Ohio was founded in 1856 by the African Methodist Episcopal Church and is one of the oldest predominantly black colleges in America.

In his February 17, 1948, speech, Rickey was at his best in terms of showmanship, declaring that baseball officials could "deny they adopted such a report, if they dare. I'd like to see the color of the man's eyes who would deny it."

The baseball establishment was rattled by the speech because an Associated Press reporter was there, and he wrote it up for publication in newspapers all across the country. The reporter noted Rickey grew more passionate with each paragraph.

"I believe that racial extractions and color hues and forms of worship become secondary to what a man can do," said Rickey. "The American public is not as concerned with a first baseman's pigmentation as it is with the power of his swing, the dexterity of his slide, the gracefulness of his fielding or the speed of his legs."

Rickey was far from finished.

"Who thinks of the inconsequential when great matters of common challenge and national interest confront us?" Rickey asked. "It is not strange that Robinson should be given a chance in America to feed and clothe and shelter his wife and child and mother in a job he can do better than most. It is not strange that a drop of water seeks the ocean."[24]

While the executive believed he had finally broken through on his argument and would win adulation for the speech, condemnations came fast and furious. Larry MacPhail, Rickey's former deputy who was now with the New York Yankees, insisted there was no secret report and that the actual report that was distributed dealt with more mundane matters. He claimed it was only destroyed because it said some unflattering things about the commissioner of baseball. "Rickey was lying if and when he said the committee recommended that Negro players be barred from major league baseball," he declared.[25]

Rickey never spoke to MacPhail again.

ALLIES IN THE PRESS

To be sure, Rickey was far from the only person who wanted integration. Chris Lamb, the historian, devoted a scrupulously researched chapter of the book *Blackout* to sportswriters—black and white—who pushed to open up baseball years before Robinson promised Rickey he would turn the other cheek.[26]

In February 1933, the *New York World-Telegram* sportswriter Heywood Broun declared in a speech at the New York Baseball Writers Association dinner that he could "see no reason why Negroes should not come into the National and American Leagues. Why, in the name of fair play and gate receipts, should professional baseball be exclusive?"[27]

Leaving African Americans out of the game was not only inherently unfair. It deprived the game of loyal fans—and talented players—of all races. After Robinson integrated the game in April 1947, eleven of the next sixteen Most Valuable Player awards in the National League would go to African Americans—an incredible run.

Not surprisingly, the African American press was particularly vocal in its frustration with baseball's color line—especially the *Pittsburgh Courier*, a black newspaper that grew increasingly popular in the 1930s and 1940s. In response to Broun's speech, the paper published a series of articles detailing various officials' opinions on segregated baseball.

Later that month, National League president John Heydler actually told the *Courier* that "beyond the fundamental requirement that a Major League player must have unique ability and good character and habits[,] I do not recall one instance where baseball has allowed either race, creed, or color to enter into the question of the selection of players."[28]

Leslie M. O'Connor, secretary to the commissioner of baseball, told the *Courier* the next month that "there isn't any rule which keeps colored players out . . . If a club owner wanted to place a colored player on the team, he could do so far as the rules go."[29]

Rickey knew all of this was nonsense, and he was outmaneuvering all of the apologists of the old system to get Robinson to the big leagues. And now that the door was ajar with Robinson in Montreal, Rickey decided to push it wide open. Within weeks, he signed four more African American players. In addition to Roy Campanella and Don Newcombe, there were two more pitchers, Roy Partlow and John Wright.

Neither Partlow nor Wright ever made it to the big leagues. In fairness, they had both labored a long time in the Negro Leagues and were each thirty-seven years old at the time of their signing and on the downward slope of their careers.

Campanella, affectionately known as "Campy," was short and stocky with tree trunks for arms that generated enormous home run power. He eventually won three Most Valuable Player awards just in the span of 1948 to 1957, when his career was cut short by a terrible car accident that left him paralyzed.

Newcombe, known simply as "Newk," was the first African American pitcher to start a World Series game and the first to reach the coveted milestone of twenty games in one season. At this writing, he was ninety years old and still doing work for the Dodgers. He is just one of two pitchers in history to win three big awards: Rookie of the Year, Most Valuable Player, and Cy Young. (Modern star Justin Verlander is the other.)

"El Cheapo" got Newcombe for a $1,000 cash bonus and a $350 monthly salary. Campanella snagged a bigger bonus of $2,400, but settled for a measly monthly salary of $185.

Rickey also had a chance before anyone else to sign another terrific African American ballplayer, Larry Doby, who eventually would break the color barrier in the American League in July 1947, a few months after Robinson in the National League. Rickey instead urged Bill Veeck, the owner of the Cleveland Indians, to sign Doby to a contract.

Why did he give up a chance to snag such a talented player? Carl Erskine, who had told me timing is everything, cited this as another example of Rickey's wisdom.

If Doby joined Jackie immediately, then the Dodgers could have been marginalized as "the black team," and the National League could similarly be considered a black league. That also made it more likely the American League could stay all white, creating a new form of segregation.

Rickey's belief was that integration would be more durable if the wealth of new players was spread around to both leagues and multiple teams. Though Erskine told me he couldn't help but think that if the Dodgers had signed

Doby right after Robinson, they would have given the New York Yankees—and slugger Yogi Berra, who got ten World Series rings—a better run for their money.

"I would have gotten all of those rings instead of Yogi," Erskine said with a smile.[30]

JACKIE'S ODYSSEY

Campanella, Newcombe, and Doby were all great men who blazed the trail for so many others. Yet Robinson still came first, which meant he faced unique pressures.

Forget World Series rings—Robinson could not even get a hotel room in some cities during his first minor league season with the Montreal Royals. It led the sharp-tongued New York sportswriter Dick Young to crack that in 1946, "Jackie Robinson led the league in everything except hotel reservations."[31]

A funny joke, but it was no laughing matter for Robinson, who also had trouble getting plane and dinner reservations. Rickey's insistence that he not fight back as he faced indignities would be immediately tested.

As he headed to meet the Royals and Dodgers at their joint spring training facilities in Florida before the 1946 season, Robinson could not even make it to the field.

Jackie had just married his longtime sweetheart, Rachel, and they cut short their honeymoon to make the long journey from California to Florida for spring workouts and practice before the official regular season started.

The couple had met at UCLA when she was a freshman and he was a senior, and they were engaged the following year. But she still had four more years of college and nursing school to finish, so they did not marry until 1946.

During that senior year at UCLA in the spring of 1941, Jackie abruptly left school because he became convinced that it did not matter whether or not he received a degree—it would not help an African American man get a job. He was torn because his mother's dream was for him to finish college, but he also felt pressure to help relieve her financial troubles and felt guilty about the expenses associated with college.

"I picked up odd jobs here and there, hawking candy and hot dogs at the Rose Bowl, working as a bus boy in a restaurant and a part-time janitor at the college," he noted. "Despite all this, I was unable to help my mother the way I thought I should."[32]

UCLA begged him to stay, offering more financial aid and whatever they needed to do to keep this young man on the field. His girlfriend, his mother—even his minister, Karl Downs—begged him to stay in school too.

"I can get along fine without your money," Mallie insisted. "I did it when you boys couldn't wipe your noses and I can still do it."[33]

That unselfishness settled it for Jackie. He felt he simply could not continue to be the recipient of his mother's generosity, and he expressed the desire to devote more of his time to teaching sports to young people. A man who basically never knew his father had resolved to always give back.

Robinson got a gig with the National Youth Administration, a government program, working with kids from poor or broken homes. He had plenty of experience with both, but the job did not last long because World War II broke out and the government closed down some of the projects.

African American kids were still locked out of playing professional baseball or football, so Robinson had to go all the way to Hawaii to play football for the semi-pro Honolulu Bears, which was integrated. Yet it paid very little, so he took a job on the side with a construction company that was near Pearl Harbor.

Robinson would work construction during the day and play football at night. But Jackie grew disenchanted with the Bears and was missing home. So he boarded a ship heading back to California two days before the Japanese attack on December 7, 1941—yet another near miss for the integration of baseball.

Now in the spring of 1946, as they headed from the West Coast to the East Coast for what was supposed to be a triumphant moment, Jackie and Rachel were about to face a series of indignities.

RUDE AWAKENING IN FLORIDA

Unlike Jackie, Rachel had never been to the South before. She described herself as a "bewildered and disturbed bride" when they finally arrived in Daytona Beach, Florida.

They had planned to fly all the way from California to Florida, with a stop in New Orleans on the way. Upon arrival in Louisiana, they were told the next plane was going to be very late. "There was no place at the airfield where Negroes could lie down and rest, so we went into town and rented a hotel room, asking the airport to notify us when the plane was due," recalled Rachel.[34]

They were starving in the hotel room and remembered that before they left California, Jackie's mother, Mallie, had packed them a shoe box full of fried chicken. The always-wise old woman knew her son and new daughter-in-law needed to be prepared for anything in the South.

"That evening we sat on the side of the bed and pulled out Mallie's chicken," Rachel recalled in the 1996 book *Jackie Robinson: An Intimate Portrait*. "As we quietly ate, I could feel humiliation and a sense of powerlessness overpowering me. More importantly, I appreciated Mallie's wisdom as never before."[35]

Nearly a dozen hours after they had touched down in New Orleans, Jackie called the airport and was told to rush in to catch the plane. But when the plane landed in Pensacola, Florida—the next stop on their increasingly long trip to Daytona Beach—the Robinsons were told, without explanation, to get off the plane.

That sort of thing might happen during wartime to make way for servicemen who needed the seats, but it was now 1946. There were all kinds of other explanations tossed around by airport personnel, from bad weather to the need to refuel. Yet the only passengers bumped off were the two African Americans, plus a Hispanic. The rest of the passengers were allowed to stay on the plane.

Suddenly, as Jackie and Rachel stood at the airport, their bags now tossed at their feet, they saw some white passengers led onto the plane to take their seats. Clearly, the minorities had all been abruptly kicked off because a few white people needed the seats. The airline tried to cover it up by providing Jack and Rachel a limousine to take them to a hotel.

One problem: there was no "Negro" hotel in Pensacola.

The limo driver thought quickly and popped into a restaurant to find a few African American waiters. It was a smart way to figure out what was the closest town where the Robinsons would be allowed to stay. One of the waiters did them one better by offering to let the couple stay at his own personal residence.

"But when we drove out there at 11:00 at night, we found he just had a tiny place with only one bedroom, where the children were already asleep," recalled Rachel. "These people were very nice, and offered us the bedroom, saying the rest of them would sleep in the living room. But we couldn't do that. We decided to go to the bus station."[36]

At the station, they had to wait a lot longer for the next bus to Daytona Beach. They were both hungry because they had never had a chance to stop for dinner.

"But my pride rebelled against accepting food shoved through a little opening into the Jim Crow waiting room, so Jack went out and bought sandwiches and candy bars," said Rachel.

As the sun started coming up over Florida while they were aboard the bus, more and more men on their way to work started getting on. Suddenly the "colored" section got so crowded that Jackie and Rachel took turns standing and sitting.

They noticed several empty seats in the "white" section, but they were not allowed there for the ride to Jacksonville.

Rachel, who was expecting to be on a couple of clean planes from California to Florida, was dolled up in a new trousseau suit and a three-quarter-length ermine coat that her new husband had bought after saving up for three years.

No surprise that the workers were in laborers' clothes, and the dirt from the previous day was all over the seats. Soon Rachel was distraught over her new coat getting filthy.

Once they made it to Jacksonville, the Robinsons were led to another tiny Jim Crow waiting room to get ready for the last leg of this disaster, a bus to Daytona Beach.

"I was tired, dirty, depressed—and hungry again," recalled Rachel. "But I hung on to my pride. Again I refused to eat the food shoved through the Jim Crow opening. Jack went out and found some apples."[37]

Mrs. Robinson also detailed this painful journey in a personal essay she wrote in the March 1951 issue of *McCall's* magazine, titled "I Live with a Hero" and billed as a "true story so warm, so human, so full of courage, that it is almost certain to make you cry."[38]

Rickey waived the long-standing "no wives" rule at spring training, instituted because players were at least ostensibly supposed to focus on baseball there, in order to give Robinson a companion. He was not allowed to bunk with his white colleagues, and the hotels in Florida were not hospitable, so he and Rachel stayed at the home of an African American family.[39]

"Jack was overanxious and tense all through training and, as a result, was not hitting well," noted Rachel. "Later, when I began to absorb baseball terms, I learned to refer to that as a 'slump'—and, like all players' wives, to shiver at the idea. When this happened, I found out in Florida—and I still know no better way to help my husband—that the best thing I can do is urge him to get away from it a little more, to think of things besides baseball."

Except about the only thing the couple was able to do in Florida was go to the movies.

"Night after night we would go to the same old Negro theater, seeing the same old movies over and over," she recalled. "And day after day I would go out to the ball park and sit in the Jim Crow section to watch."

Rachel admitted she really did not understand much about baseball strategy, and she was not as rabid as those fans from Brooklyn who loved "Dem Bums" season after season. "But I don't see how any wife of a baseball player could help being vitally interested in her husband's team and particularly in what her husband does," she declared.[40]

She was a strong woman backing up her husband amid extraordinary adversity. Over the next few years their marriage would get stronger because they were a team.

"We're very close," Jackie would say ten years into the experiment. "Probably it's because of the importance of what I've had to do. We've just gotten closer and closer. A problem comes up for me, I ask Rae. A problem for her, she asks me."[41]

Rickey had clearly thought of this when putting together his carefully orchestrated plan. His very first question at that August 1945 meeting in Brooklyn had been that brusque, "Do you have a girl?"

In his private moments, Jackie was not really sure if he could follow Rickey's orders not to fight back against injustice, especially after that horrific cross-country journey and the indignities his wife had suffered.

"Turn the other cheek, he was pleading," Robinson reflected later in his unpublished memoir. "But then I started wondering again whether I could."[42]

Robinson felt a duty to hold back—for the black ballplayers who would be coming up behind him, for Rachel, and for Rickey. "Because when a man like Branch Rickey invests faith in you, you want to be decent enough to strive to help the gamble pay off for him," wrote Robinson.[43]

After this disastrous trip with his wife, Robinson must have looked back to that August 1945 meeting with Rickey, when the boss had acted out all of the potential slights Robinson would face. It had come to pass in Florida, and the executive's words were still ringing in his head. "As I kept listening, I knew I had to do this thing for myself and for my race and then I began to feel I had to do it for this spellbinder . . . Branch Rickey," Robinson said later.[44]

But even after he finally made it to spring training in 1946, Robinson would be tested again. His new manager with the Royals was a man who openly declared that African Americans were not human beings.

CHAPTER 11

THE CONVERSION OF CLAY HOPPER

The defining moment in Carl Erskine's friendship with Jackie Robinson came a few years after the Indiana native joined the team, when the two men reached across the racial divide that still existed on the Brooklyn Dodgers. This was three full years into Branch Rickey's "Great Experiment," and yet there were still white fans—and even some of Robinson's teammates—who had not yet embraced the history maker.

Erskine told me he noticed this particularly after a 1950 game at Ebbets Field, when he emerged from the clubhouse to see a big group of fans waiting on the street to get autographs.

Jackie's wife, Rachel, and their young son, Jackie Jr., were waiting all alone in one corner with nobody talking to them. So Erskine went out of his way to engage them in front of the mostly white fans.

The next day Jackie wanted to have a word with Erskine. Robinson said, "I want to thank you, Carl, for what you did out there in front of all those fans yesterday."

"Jackie, you can thank me for a well-pitched game, but don't ever thank me for what just came naturally," Erskine replied.[1]

What may be most remarkable is that Robinson thought it was out of the ordinary for Erskine to even talk to African Americans in public. But that was America, even after Robinson had "broken" the color barrier. And to think that times had allegedly improved for Jackie and Rachel since 1946, when they traversed the country with planes, buses, and automobiles just to get to spring training.

SAVING FACE AT SPRING TRAINING

All told, it had taken Jackie and Rachel at least thirty-six hours to get from California to Florida. The delay came in large part from the uncomfortable stops in New Orleans and Pensacola, not to mention the long time on the bus.

Some brave African American sportswriters who had pushed for integration since the 1930s, including Wendell Smith and Sam Lacy, were waiting for the Robinsons in the Sunshine State. And waiting.

"History is to be made here this week," Lacy wrote in the *Baltimore Afro-American*. Lacy told his audience that Robinson and another African American player, Johnny Wright, were about to make their marks "deep in the heart of the traditionally fascist Southland."[2]

Smith, writing in the *Pittsburgh Courier*, added, "the atmosphere in this beautiful Southern city is tense with excitement."[3]

That drama only kept on building when Robinson did not show up on time for spring training. "*Jackie Robinson Fails To Attend Montreal Drill!*" blared a headline in the *Chicago Daily Tribune* a day before he and Rachel arrived in Daytona Beach.[4]

Smith used one of Robinson's many nicknames to reveal something had gone awry. "Jack (The Rabbit) Robinson, the mercury-hoofed shortstop who leaped from the demoralized ranks of Negro baseball to the blue-blooded Royals of Montreal in less than one year, was expected to arrive here today by plane," he wrote.[5]

Branch Rickey was desperately trying to keep the real reason for the delay under wraps. Now that the Great Experiment was in motion, he did not want it to be derailed by stories about the despicable Jim Crow bus rides that would only inflame the already combustible situation.

So Rickey told reporters that Robinson reported late to camp because of some "bad weather" along the way.

Yet there was no disguising that more racism was waiting for Robinson in Florida. After two days of practice in Sanford with teammates, he and African American pitcher Johnny Wright, who had also been recently signed to a minor league contract, were forced to head back to Daytona Beach. They were run out of town by local civic groups in Sanford that declared, "We don't want no niggers mixing with no whites here."[6]

Even Clay Hopper, the manager of the Montreal Royals, who would be overseeing Jackie's debut, was blunt about how he believed African Americans were inferior.

Hopper was a native of Mississippi, and his family still owned a plantation there in 1946. He had not attended the big news conference in Montreal unveiling his new player the previous October, and when he eventually met Robinson, the manager barely shook his hand, doing so only out of respect for Rickey.

In an early exhibition game that spring training, Robinson made a spectacular defensive play. A line shot forced Robinson to dive to get the ball, stretching the glove across his body to knock it down and recover in time to get the out.

"My gosh, Clay, did you see that?" Rickey, sitting behind the Royals' dugout, shouted to Hopper. "No other human being alive could make that play."

Hopper was unconvinced.

"Mr. Rickey," Hopper said, "do you really think a Nigger is a human being?"[7]

Hopper immediately started to cry, a sign to Rickey that the manager simply had racism ingrained in him early and was not acting out of hate.

"Regarding a Negro as subhuman was part of his heritage," Rickey said later. "Here was a man who had practically nursed racial prejudice from his mother's breast. So I decided to ignore the comment."[8]

Maybe that was his reason. But perhaps he also wanted to protect his experiment by not pouring gasoline on the fire.

Local officials forced the Royals to cancel games in a long string of Southern cities from Savannah to Richmond. The city of DeLand, Florida, blocked a Robinson game because they said the stadium lights were not working properly. A reasonable excuse, but for the fact it was a day game.[9]

In Jacksonville, a game against the Jersey City Giants was called off because of a law in the city that actually stated that blacks and whites were not allowed to compete against one another on public playgrounds, though Robinson would soon get his shot at that team in the regular season.

Another time in Sanford, Florida, Robinson was even threatened with arrest. After Robinson got a base hit, he stole second base and then raced home on a teammate's single. Waiting for Robinson in the dugout was a sheriff with handcuffs, ready to enforce another local law that banned the mixing of races on a sports field. The Royals were winning, so Hopper did not want to forfeit the game. Instead, he diffused the sheriff's concerns by getting Robinson to bow out of the game.

Before a game in Jacksonville, Robinson would recall to a group of students years later, local officials padlocked the stadium to make sure an African American would not play there. He felt depressed about the attacks, which undoubtedly affected his play, so he started to seriously think about giving up.

Rickey, like the second father he was for Robinson, pulled him out of the slump by sheer force. The executive would lurk down the first-base line so he could clap and cheer and try to will Robinson out of his malaise.

Robinson would confess later in speeches and magazine articles that he felt as if the other players were all staring at him and wondering what the Dodgers were waiting for. If he had been white, Robinson imagined his teammates muttering, he would have been cut from the minor league team already and never have gotten a shot at playing for the Dodgers.

Feeling desperate, Robinson decided to jump off first base late in one Florida spring training game to try to steal second base, and at least prove he could run—if not throw or bat well. The pitcher tossed for home plate but it was low and hit the dirt, skipping past the catcher—a wild pitch. That enabled Robinson to touch second base, and then immediately race for third base.

The catcher was still struggling to retrieve the ball, so Hopper told Robinson to keep on digging for home plate. But he was thrown out.

After being just a few seconds from the ecstasy of scoring a run and proving his worth, Robinson instead faced a torrent of boos from the crowd. And when he returned to the bench, his Royals' teammates said not a word of encouragement.

"They've made up their minds already," thought Robinson, "that I can't make it."

Except a moment later, a boy stood up in the front row near the Royals' bench, and he declared, loud enough for Robinson to hear, "Attaboy, Jackie! Nice try, Jackie."

More important than the words, as Robinson looked up he noticed the boy happened to be white. "It wasn't much of a voice, but you'll never know how it lifted me inside," noted Robinson. "I was hungry for a few words like those. Outside of my wife, Rachel, and Mr. Rickey, and a few friends I had made among the colored people of Florida, nobody was saying them."[10]

Still, the pressure on Robinson was building—and not just off the field. Scouts were whispering that he simply did not have a strong enough arm to make it in the big leagues as a shortstop, an issue that had first popped up when Dodgers scout Clyde Sukeforth reviewed the player for Rickey in 1945. Those whisperers simply did not know how fiercely competitive Robinson was—at everything.

Years later, when Robinson was playing with the Dodgers in the 1950s, sportswriter Roger Kahn saw the ballplayer's determination up close. During a break in the action at spring training, some players started playing ping-pong. Kahn joined in and started beating one player after another, until Robinson ambled by to check things out. Suddenly, and without warning, he crushed Kahn. He held the paddle like a world-class player from China and slapped the tiny ball ferociously, his face focused in almost a catatonic state.

Kahn's winning streak was snapped, yet Robinson was still not quite finished with him.

"Now," Robinson said, staring directly at Kahn. "Would you like to take me on in gin rummy? For dough?"[11] Kahn politely declined, not wanting to pick another battle with Robinson.

The otherwise-astute sportswriter had apparently not heard about one of the legendary Robinson stories from Pasadena. At the age of fifteen, already a standout in several sports, Robinson popped into a local YMCA and noticed a funny-looking paddle. He started playing a little ping-pong in Pasadena, and a few months later he won the city championship. It was the first of many times he would get written up in a newspaper.

As he struggled during that first spring training in 1946, that competitive fire propped Robinson up. He answered his critics by putting extra heat on every single throw he had to make, when players should be pacing themselves rather than going through full exertion. And after a week of flame-throwing balls to first base from shortstop, Robinson's arm was throbbing. Rachel would apply cold compresses to no avail. A doctor in Florida tried hot compresses, and that did not work either.

"I played as best as I could through all that pain," Robinson said later. "On top of which I simply was not hitting. Pressure? Maybe. Whatever. I specialized in pop flies to shortstop."[12]

Then the Royals played Indianapolis, which had a pitcher, Paul Derringer, who was a friend of Hopper. Before the game the two men discussed Robinson's hitting trouble. "Tell you what I'm going to do, Clay," said Derringer. "I'm going to knock him down a couple of times and see what makes him tick."

When Robinson came to bat the first time, Derringer threw a pitch high and tight that forced Jackie to the ground. He got back up to face the next pitch and slapped a line drive for a single. Then the second time up, Derringer threw a pitch even closer to Robinson's head. The next pitch was a curveball and Jackie, unbothered, slammed the ball to deep center for a triple.

Robinson was rising to the occasion, and Derringer told Hopper he had a star in the making.[13]

HOPPER GETS ON BOARD

As spring training wrapped up in 1946 and Robinson's first official minor league season got underway, Hopper, like Derringer, became a convert. Just weeks after Hopper had questioned whether African Americans were even human beings, the skipper had seen enough of Robinson's talent to render a whole new judgment.

"Mr. Rickey, those words I said in Florida about Robinson not being human," Hopper said, "Mr. Rickey, sir, right here and now I want to apologize."[14]

Rickey stayed in Robinson's corner, becoming his biggest cheerleader, and all but skipping the Dodgers' camp in order to pour all his energy and attention into the Royals camp and keep an eye on him. Robinson recalled that Rickey kept him going through the pain, and when he reached first base after a hit, he tried to block out the noise of the crowd and yet heard the executive's voice break through.

"He'd get a seat near first base and shout to me over and over again. 'Be daring. Run it out. Take a bigger lead. Worry that pitcher into a sweat. Adventure! Adventure!'"[15]

Adventure would be a charitable way to process the hate that was still being spewed at both these men.

Robinson never forgot a white newspaperman in Florida that spring who wrote something the ballplayer remembered as, "It's do-gooders like Rickey who hurt the Negro. They try to force inferior Negroes on whites and everybody loses. Take this guy Robinson. If he was white the Royals would long ago have booted him out of camp."[16]

Rickey ignored the haters. He had carefully put together his plan and was sticking with it.

"Try not to be perturbed, Jack," Mr. Rickey said. "We have scouted you most carefully. We know you're going to make a great success."

Robinson would reflect later, "I did my best to tune out the hate. Mr. Rickey's words kept me going."[17]

Like the biblical Job, who would inspire one of Jackie's later sermons, the player stood tall. He knew that he was "a man, and therefore worthy."[18]

And when the Royals finally played their first real game of the season on April 18, 1946, Robinson would get an unexpected assist from another member of the Dodgers family motivated by his Christian faith.

"ROBINSON AT SECOND BASE"

The morning of the game there was actually some snow on the ground before the sun rose over Jersey City, New Jersey, just outside New York City, where Robinson would finally get to square off with those Jersey City Giants. It was not just any road game; it was Jackie's first official minor league game for the Montreal Royals.

Jersey City was a minor league team that fed future stars, like Bobby Thomson, to the New York Giants. Jersey City had a stadium that seated only 25,000 fans, and yet the team sold 51,872 tickets for Robinson's first game.[19] Maybe Rickey's gambit was going to pay off in at least one respect: it would eventually provide a financial boost to Brooklyn as Ebbets Field swelled with larger crowds from an influx of African American fans.

"The pressure was on and I was very nervous," Robinson said later.[20]

Ironically it may have been Hopper who settled the new guy down after the "Star-Spangled Banner" played. The manager offered a pregame pep talk that ended with him doing something that seemed obvious—reading out the starting lineup; yet it was anything but typical this time. "You know the lineup," Hopper said. "Breard at shortstop. Robinson at second base . . ."

But this was not a simple "you know the deal" kind of announcement. This was an African American batting second in the lineup. In that moment, Robinson realized integration was no longer a gleam in Rickey's eye. It was happening.

"I finally knew that it was real," said Robinson. "Some said that this project was a phony attempt to please Negroes. I wasn't really a ballplayer, just window dressing. The hell with that. Right then in Jersey City I knew I was within reach of the dream of every boy who ever went to a sandlot carrying a ball glove."

He added simply, "The major leagues."[21]

It was a storybook beginning for Robinson, as he smacked four hits, including a home run.

"I couldn't have dreamed up a better start," he said.[22]

Nor could he have dreamed up what happened right after he hit that first home run: another moment inspired by faith in God.

The next batter up was a white player, George Shuba, known as "Shotgun" for the way he smashed line drives. While it is common for the on-deck hitter to congratulate the guy who just hit a homer, people actually wondered whether a "Shotgun" snub was coming.

Instead Shuba waited at home plate and shook the hand of a smiling Robinson. An Associated Press photograph of that moment became an iconic image, even though Shuba tried to downplay it.

"I couldn't care less if Jackie was Technicolor," Shuba said many years later. "We'd spent 30 days at spring training, and we all knew that Jackie had been a great athlete at UCLA. As far as I was concerned, he was a great ballplayer—our best. I had no problem going to the plate to shake his hand instead of waiting for him to come by me in the on-deck circle."[23]

It was a profound approach to have at the height of Jim Crow, though Shuba's upbringing in Youngstown, Ohio, clearly had an impact. He was taught to be welcoming by a father who was an immigrant from Czechoslovakia and worked in a steel mill.

As a Catholic who was once an altar boy, George Shuba passed that Christian approach on to his own son, Michael, when he told his father of bullying at school. "Look up at that photo," Shuba would tell his son, pointing at the only baseball memento on his living room wall decades later. "I want you to remember what that stands for. You treat all people equally."[24]

It was a simple gesture to Shuba, but it was a monumental boost to his teammate and the cause of civil rights.

Robinson said that first home run (and possibly the handshake) helped "burst the dam between me and my teammates. Northerners, Southerners both let me know they appreciated the way I had come through. I began really to believe one of Mr. Rickey's predictions: Color won't matter if the black man is a winner."[25]

Rickey skipped the game in Jersey City because, in a thoughtful gesture, he did not want to be there and put more pressure on Robinson. Instead the boss was hosting a small dinner party that night at Mama Leone's Restaurant on West Forty-Eighth Street in Manhattan.

Suddenly a Rickey assistant, who had been dispatched to Jersey City to watch the game, burst into the restaurant as the executive prepared to take his table.

"Mr. Rickey," he said excitedly, struggling to spit it out. "Mr. Rickey! Jackie Robinson . . ."

Broadcaster Red Barber was at the dinner and watched the eager young assistant struggle to catch his breath.

"Mr. Rickey, Jackie came up in the third inning with two men on and hit a home run!"

"He did?" Rickey responded, in the days before game highlights came in by text message in real time.

"Yes, he did, Mr. Rickey," said the assistant. "And, Mr. Rickey, he got three singles and he stole two bases!"

Rickey squeezed Red Barber's elbow as he took his table and said proudly, "That's a pretty good way to break into organized baseball."[26]

Unfortunately the storybook start did not last long. A catcher named Dixie Howell would tell Dodgers teammates years later that pitchers were constantly throwing pitches at Robinson's head. Howell played on that Royals team with Robinson and point-blank said that practically every time the kid came to bat there would be at least one pitch aimed squarely at him.[27]

A player from Syracuse's team actually held up a black cat and shouted, "Hey, Robinson! Here's one of your relatives!"[28]

Robinson got his revenge against Syracuse by smacking a double that led Montreal to win the game. And despite all the distractions, Robinson's batting average that season was a sensational .349, though there were stretches of time when he struggled in the face of all that pressure.

"I was trying too hard," he confessed later. "I knew I had to keep my temper bridled at every turn. Guarding so carefully against outbursts can put a damper on one's competitive spirit."

Robinson wished he could just "blow his top" every now and then, ripping off his hat and yelling at an umpire to help stop a slump and vent a little rage.

"But I didn't dare let loose this way," Robinson said. "Many would have dubbed me a 'hothead' and pointed to my outburst as a reason why Negroes should not play in organized baseball. This was one of the hardest problems I had to face."[29]

Throughout the season, Rickey would trek to Montreal to encourage Robinson and try to keep him calm. "Always for as long as you are in baseball, you must conduct yourself as you are doing now," Rickey said during one of those face-to-face conversations. "Always you will be on trial. That is the cross you must bear."[30]

When Rickey had first issued those instructions, Robinson nodded, but later admitted he was not really sure he could comply. "How could I turn the other cheek if I met the same kind of abuse not only in the South, but also in the 'enlightened' North? I didn't know, sitting there in Mr. Rickey's office, how I would be able to discipline myself, to control my innate sense of rebellion at injustice."[31]

Robinson noted that whenever he reflected on this question, he would think back to his rocky days in the US Army during the early 1940s, which started with him being relegated to segregated barracks.

RACISM IN THE ARMY

At Fort Riley in Kansas in 1942, Robinson was shut out of officer training—until he griped to another star athlete stationed there, boxing champion Joe Louis. After Louis used his clout to grumble to the White House, the Pentagon intervened, and suddenly Robinson was made a lieutenant.

Robinson was shipped to Fort Hood in Texas and appointed a morale officer for African American soldiers. He was strongly encouraged to lean on his stellar UCLA background to join Fort Hood's football team, but that was small-time for him, so he refused.

He had his eyes instead on joining the baseball team but was stopped in his tracks, a white officer telling Robinson he had to "play for the colored team," even though there wasn't one.

Pete Reiser, who later played with Robinson on the Dodgers, was stationed at Ford Hood and witnessed him stalking off the field after that confrontation. Reiser later said Robinson looked like a man fighting back the urge to scream, looking furious with his glove planted firmly into his hip.[32]

It went downhill from there. Robinson used his role as morale officer for African American soldiers to get them more spots at the soda fountain, where military families hung out to grab a burger and milk shake. A white base officer did not take kindly with the new guy trying to change the fact that there were twelve prime seats reserved for whites right in front of the fountain.

The officer, mistakenly assuming that a lieutenant like Robinson had to be white, stepped in it on a phone call. "Lieutenant Robinson, let me put it this way," the officer said. "Would you like it if your wife had to sit next to a Nigger?"

Robinson exploded, showing off his famous temper.

"I am a Negro officer, and how . . . do you know that your wife hasn't already been with a Negro?"[33]

That was still nothing compared to what was coming on July 6, 1944, when Robinson was staying at a hospital thirty miles off-base so doctors could examine the bum ankle from his days as a college athlete. This exam would determine whether he was healthy enough to be deployed overseas (and maybe taken off the path to Brooklyn).

When he boarded the bus that would take him to the hospital from the officers' club, where he had been relaxing, Robinson walked to the back. But four rows from the rear, he stopped as he bumped into Virginia Jones, the wife of another officer, who happened to be African American.

The bus driver seemed to assume Jones, who was light-skinned, was white and thus Robinson should have kept walking further back in the bus.

"You got to move back, boy," said the driver.

Robinson ignored the driver, sitting next to Jones and staring defiantly out the window.

The driver brought the bus to a screeching halt, declaring it was against the law for an African American to sit so close to the front. Robinson fired back that military regulations allowed for him to sit in any open seat he wanted. Finally the driver raced the bus back to his depot and grabbed a supervisor to report Robinson, who shook a finger at them and declared, "Quit [bleeping] with me."

As a crowd of white people formed, a white woman felt confident enough to spit out awful racial epithets to Robinson.

Then the military police arrived, perhaps to defuse the situation involving one of their own officers, while also reserving the right to call him on the carpet. When Robinson arrived at MP headquarters, a private had the nerve to ask whether he was the "Nigger lieutenant" that had been on the bus.

Robinson fired back, "If you ever call me a Nigger again, I'll break you in two."

When this exchange was relayed to a captain, he told Robinson not to be "so uppity" at the MP headquarters.

A stenographer arrived to take down Robinson's account of what the bus driver had told him. "He told the people, 'This Nigger is making trouble,'" said Robinson. "I told the bus driver to stop [bleeping] with me. So he gets the rest of the men around there and starts blowing his top and someone calls the MPs. Outside of telling this lady that I didn't care if she preferred charges against me or not, I was speaking direct to that bus driver. And just as I told the captain here, if any one of you called me a Nigger, I would do the same."

Robinson was slapped with a court-martial for swearing and talking tough to the officer who questioned him, the report declaring he was "insubordinate, disrespectful, and discourteous." His refusal to move to the back of the bus was not part of the court-martial. Robinson was correct about army regulations superseding Jim Crow.

Robinson was aggressive about getting his case in the hands of the NAACP (which, unfortunately, could not help him), as well as rallying

African American sportswriters and other reporters to aid him in his cause. The army blinked and acquitted him, and then Robinson's bad ankle got him "permanent limited duty."[34]

Robinson soon received an honorable discharge—an important twist of fate on multiple levels. His unit later got deployed, so he could have been overseas risking his life in 1945. Instead, he was in Chicago playing for the Kansas City Monarchs of the Negro Leagues, where he got that tap on the shoulder from Clyde Sukeforth.

And if Robinson had been convicted with even a slap on the wrist, the author Scott Simon noted, "it seems reasonable to assume that Brooklyn's upstanding General Manager, Branch Rickey, would have ruled him out of consideration for the role he wanted to cast for a man to break baseball's color barrier."[35] In fact, Robinson's status as a military vet with a clean record put him higher on the list, ahead of other Negro Leagues stars like Satchel Paige and Josh Gibson.

Once Rickey did call Robinson's number, the ballplayer had to put that rough time in the army behind him. No more cussing people out or backtalk; otherwise, the experiment would fail.

All of this reminded me of that quote I read, engraved in the bronze monument depicting Robinson's head on the lawn outside Pasadena city hall: "I had defied prejudice in the Army. How could I have thought that the barriers would fall, that my talent could triumph over bigotry?"

MONTREAL EMBRACES JACKIE

In the summer of 1946, Robinson's talent did start winning out over bigotry. He won the batting championship and led the league in runs scored, with 113 in 124 games.

Jackie and Rachel would later marvel at how well they were treated by the people of Montreal, especially compared to the Southern part of the United States, even though the Canadian city's population was only 2 percent black at the time.

Immediately after the Royals clinched the Junior World Series, Robinson modestly headed to the clubhouse to decompress. Rowdy fans spotted Hopper in the dugout and lifted him up on their shoulders, racing him around the field in joy.

Then the fans started their chant, "Roh-been-son! Roh-been-son!"

Robinson finally emerged only to be swarmed with hugs and kisses from Canadians. He was also paraded around the field, but eventually Robinson ran through a stadium exit door, insisting he was going to miss a plane.

The fans were having none of it. They chased his car, screaming deliriously at their new hero, and tears streamed down Robinson's face as he took in the scene.

"I'll tell you what made me cry," said Robinson. "I realized here was a big white crowd chasing after a lone Negro, not with lynching in their hearts, but love."[36]

Now Robinson was ready to triumphantly march on from Montreal to Brooklyn and crack the big leagues. But the greeting from some of his white Dodgers teammates would be anything but loving.

CHAPTER 12

NO SLEEP TILL BROOKLYN

There it was in the distance: Ebbets Field, or what was left of it. I finally got a glimpse of it for the first time near Bedford Avenue and Sullivan Place in Brooklyn.

Something had been drawing me to this spot for years—a romantic vision of what baseball used to be, a voice inside that kept telling me for years that I had to write this book about Jackie Robinson's faith. But when my bike reached the bottom of the hill in the Flatbush section of Brooklyn, there was no stadium. Instead there was a giant old apartment building sitting where that bandbox of a ballpark had been.

Dodgers owner Walter O'Malley had moved the team from Brooklyn to Los Angeles in 1958. So many hearts were broken after the move, only to be broken a second time when a wrecking ball demolished Ebbets Field to make way for that apartment complex.

O'Malley was so hated in Brooklyn for the move out west that it sparked an oft-told joke in the borough: "If a Brooklyn man finds himself in a room with Hitler, Stalin, and O'Malley," went the joke, "but only has two bullets, what does he do?" Punchline: "Shoot O'Malley twice."[1]

The situation was far more tranquil decades later as I stood outside the former site of Ebbets Field, desperately searching for some kind of a sign that history was made here at Jackie Robinson's first major league game on April 15, 1947.

Sadly, the first image I found was just a mural of Robinson across the street painted on the side of a Rite Aid pharmacy. Time moves on.

Standing in front of Rite Aid, which is close to where the outfield used to be, I saw across the street the front side of a giant public housing project. There is now a simple sign that reads Ebbets Field Apartments.

The real kick to the gut came when I looked up at the apartments themselves and spotted a sign listing the no-nos for the building. No dogs allowed, no bicycle riding, and then came the sucker punch: "No Ball Playing. This Area For Tenants Of Ebbets Field Apts. Only." Yes, no more ball playing here.

At least there is something special on the back side of the apartments along McKeever Place, named after two brothers (Edward and Stephen) who helped Dodgers co-owner Charles Ebbets build Ebbets Field in exchange for half the team's shares.[2] When Ebbets died in 1925, Edward McKeever became the team's president for the grand total of only about a week until he died too. Stephen stepped in as the acting president of the club for the following few weeks, and then again in 1933 until his own death in 1938.

Decades later, along McKeever Place an elementary school was named after Robinson. The public school—PS 375 in New York City parlance—featured a beautifully painted mural in front with poses of Jackie swinging a bat and reaching for the heavens to catch a fly ball.

Several months after my visit, documentary filmmaker Ken Burns planned a stop of his own near the school, and he brought along a beautiful plaque to mark the precise spot on the street where home plate at Ebbets Field used to stand. It read, in part: AT THIS LOCATION ON APRIL 15, 1947 JACK ROOSEVELT ROBINSON INTEGRATED MAJOR LEAGUE BASEBALL.

It's a wonderful improvement; during my trip, I was disappointed to find the only other marker, out near the old center field, was a feeble sign carved into the apartment complex: THIS IS THE FORMER SITE OF EBBETS FIELD.

The bulky numbers of the address for part of the apartment complex hang right above that sign, giving it the feel of something slapped together rather than a genuine tribute to a place that was once the heart and soul of Brooklyn.

Broadcaster Larry King had a similar experience a few years ago with his young son, Chance. When they pulled up to the same site where the father started watching games in 1943, King was distraught to see the playground of his youth reduced to some apartments. Yet Chance had a far more optimistic reaction.

"Why can't we move here?" Chance demanded to know about the apartment building. "Jackie walked through those doors. Those doors."

King also walked through those doors—well, they were turnstiles back then—for Robinson's first game. He ran through the turnstiles with excitement, was more like it, as he arrived at Ebbets Field a few hours early with three friends, including a buddy that to this day he still calls "Herbie the Yankees fan." They all wanted to see history.

"We were banging on the gates, 'Open the gates!'" King recalled to me over lunch, rapping on the restaurant table in front of him, remembering what they shouted at Dodgers employees. "And there it was. 'Open the gates, you creeps!'"

Then the four boys, all roughly thirteen years old, raced to their bleacher seats. They had to run up a circular catwalk, and the first ones to the top of the bleachers could then get dibs on the first row down below, closest to the action. "Where you could lean over and feel like you could *touch* the center fielder," King said.

King has a distinct memory of Robinson from infield practice before that first game started. "I saw Jackie at first base, taking the throws [from other infielders]. That white uniform and that black face. Number 42. I was caught up in the thrill of the moment; we knew we were part of history."[3]

Indeed, Robinson played first base at his inaugural game because it was the only position open on the Dodgers' infield. Second base, the position Robinson would eventually take, was filled at the time. And Pee Wee Reese was still a fixture at shortstop, despite his initial nervousness about Jackie taking his job. This meant Robinson, who played shortstop in the Negro Leagues, had to learn a new position on the field on top of all the other challenges he faced in his first season.

With Robinson manning first base, rough-and-tumble players like

Enos "Country" Slaughter of the St. Louis Cardinals had a free shot at trying to injure him with their cleats as they ran past him on a ground out or
a base hit. Slaughter was dubbed "Country"—as in a country boy—when
he showed up as a rookie wearing a uniform that was clearly too big for
him. The saggy socks with some sad-looking shoes completed the image of
someone who had just gotten off the turnip truck. He was not too keen on
the idea of sharing the field with an African American.

In the early 1980s, King caught up with Slaughter in Washington, DC,
at the Cracker Jack Old-Timers Baseball Classic, a game played annually for
a few years to raise money for retired ballplayers who had fallen on hard
times.

"Can I talk to you honestly?" Slaughter asked King, in an anecdote the
broadcaster alluded to in the foreword to this book. "Jackie has meant a
great deal in my life."

"In what way?" asked King.

"In a cruel way, he taught me understanding, he taught me forgiveness,"
said Slaughter. "In a cruel way."

Slaughter explained that later during that first season of 1947, the
Dodgers came to St. Louis, and he was eager to leave his mark on Robinson.

"I beat out a grounder to first and stepped on his ankle, and I drew
blood," said Slaughter. "And he's wiping the blood off. And I'm standing
next to him at first."

Slaughter had grown up in segregated North Carolina and had never
played with or against an African American on a field. He decided to test
Robinson some more, knowing that Rickey had publicly said the new guy
wasn't going to fight back.

"I just looked him in the face and spit out my tobacco juice, put my
hands on my hips, and just stared him down," said Slaughter. "He didn't do
nothing. He didn't say nothing. I knew he couldn't say nothing cause he was
ordered to say nothing."

Robinson indeed could say nothing or do nothing. But this hot-
tempered, ultracompetitive man took it all in.

Fast-forward a couple of seasons to when the Cardinals were visiting

Ebbets Field, where Robinson had moved to second base. And he had been given a green light from Rickey to fight back when he wanted.

Slaughter smacked a double and came sliding into second base like a freight train.

"Jackie tags me in the mouth and knocks out some of my teeth," recalled Slaughter. "He looks at me and says, 'I never forget.'"

Slaughter was floored: "That he could have the joy to remember an act of forgiveness, but still knock out my teeth!"[4]

Robinson was in a constant balancing act of forgiving some things while fighting back over others. He faced yet another obstacle that nearly derailed that first game on April 15, 1947, when some of his fellow Dodgers—not players from opposing teams like Slaughter—tried to stop him during the spring of 1947.

PETITION IN PANAMA

Rickey was working toward finally getting Robinson from Montreal to the big league club in Brooklyn, so the executive moved a big chunk of the spring training operations out of Florida to Cuba. The Dodgers would have fewer distractions and remain insulated from Jim Crow racism, or at least so they thought.

The trouble started in Havana, when Rickey forced Robinson and other African American players—like Roy Campanella, Don Newcombe, and Roy Partlow—to stay in a much less glamorous hotel than the one where the white players were staying. What galled Robinson is that the owner of the first hotel had not forced the African Americans to stay elsewhere. It was a decision Rickey made himself because he did not want fights to break out in the first hotel.

As author Jonathan Eig noted, the "dingy hotel felt like an insult . . . Until that moment, [Robinson] had thought he could trust Rickey to do the right thing. Now some doubt crept in."[5]

In his unpublished memoir, Robinson seemed to give Rickey more of a pass on this incident, writing that they had to live Jim Crow in Havana "because Mr. Rickey felt sure we were on the brink of cracking the opposition to Negroes in the majors. He didn't want to take any chance of inciting incidents at this crucial point."[6]

It's unclear whether the player wrote these words with the benefit of hindsight and wanted to smooth over a tough moment, or if he genuinely thought his boss was focused on the greater good.

Yet when it came to incidents, the master planner had miscalculated on at least one point—big time. Rickey thought the white players would be motivated by greed to accept Robinson as a teammate if he was promoted to the major leagues in 1947. He believed the prospect of money flowing in from bonus checks would lead the white players to say they could care less about Robinson's race. "After all," Rickey said, "Robinson could mean a pennant, and ball players are not averse to cashing World Series checks."[7]

Rickey had planned a nearly two-week stop in Panama for his players, and he decided to give Robinson a pep talk in the meantime. He told him his phenomenal year in the minor leagues in 1946 meant nothing. This was the time to really step up as Montreal played the big boys from Brooklyn over the course of seven games head-to-head.

"You'll have to make the grade on the field against major-league pitching and major-league defense, so I want you to be a whirling demon against the Dodgers," said Rickey. "I want you to concentrate, to hit that ball, to bunt, to get on base by any and every means, I want you to run wild, to steal the pants off the Dodgers."

Rickey emphasized that this would both earn him the respect of the Dodgers players and open the eyes of sportswriters following the teams in Panama. Reporters would then type up stories for newspapers back in New York touting how this new kid just had to be called up to the big leagues.

"I'll do my best," Robinson said.[8]

Maybe he simply did not need to elaborate beyond that. He just about tore the cover off the ball, racking up a scorching .515 batting average.

Yet heeding Rickey's advice did not help Robinson with the Dodgers' veterans, many of whom clearly felt their own star status was being threatened. Here again, Clyde Sukeforth, the scout who brought Robinson from Chicago to Brooklyn for the original Rickey meeting, was in the middle of the action.

Sukeforth was now a coach for fiery manager Leo Durocher. In Panama, Sukeforth started hearing about a petition circulated among some of the Dodgers. It said if Robinson was promoted to the big leagues for the start of the regular season, they would bolt.

Durocher did not have the best reputation for moral rectitude or doing the right thing. He was in hot water for consorting with gamblers and being a womanizer. But when it came to Robinson, he had been paying attention during the spring, and the skipper was not going to go along with the old-boy network.

"You could see he was a really good hitter," noted Durocher. "And that nothing in the world scared him."[9]

While the story varies from book to book, by most accounts, the surreptitious petition was organized by Dixie Walker, a slugging outfielder who hailed from Georgia and was not quite ready for change.[10]

As Durocher described in his 1975 memoir, *Nice Guys Finish Last*, he initially decided he should wait for Rickey to arrive in Panama a few days later and let him handle the insurrection. As Durocher reflected, in an age when players had few—if any—rights, what were they going to do about it? Organize a strike?

As he waited for Rickey, Durocher decided to mess with some of the veterans. Pretending he knew nothing about the petition, the manager would go out of his way to bring up Robinson in conversation to see if any of the players would give up their allegiances by overreacting. "Doesn't bother me any," Durocher would say about the prospect of an African American joining the Dodgers at the end of spring training.

It seemed as though Durocher was also trying to gauge which guys could have signed such a petition, jibing to players, "If this kid can play ball, boy, I want him on the ball club."

In the early interactions, many of the players were fumbling over their words in their chats with Durocher—a sign to him that his suspicions had been justified. It seemed as though a growing number of guys had signed the petition and were now nervous about being confronted.

When Durocher went to bed one night, he seemed to experience a pang of conscience and started to toss and turn. Maybe, deep inside, the man who was a bit of a troublemaker—but was raised a Catholic and grew up serving as an altar boy—felt it was simply time to do the right thing. He thought to himself, *Why am I waiting on Rickey to arrive and take charge of the situation?*

"Once the battle lines were drawn, it was going to become a very messy situation," Durocher wrote later in his memoir. It was time to nip the revolution in the bud. "And while they couldn't possibly win, the club couldn't possibly come out of it without being ripped apart, either."

Not to mention that baseball's Great Experiment could be annihilated. Yet an unlikely hero was about to ride to its rescue.

Still in his pajamas, Durocher woke up his coaches and ordered them to gather the entire Dodgers squad. There was to be an emergency middle-of-the-night meeting in an empty kitchen where the team was staying in Panama, the US Army barracks at Fort Gulick.

Players piled into the kitchen, clad in their underwear or PJs, some sitting on chopping blocks while others leaned against an industrial refrigerator.

"Well, boys, you know what you can do with that petition," declared Durocher, before getting more graphic.

Then Durocher trained his fire on Walker, revealing he heard the player was also preparing a separate petition to Rickey demanding a trade.

"Just hand him the letter, Dixie, and you're gone. *Gone!*" barked Durocher. "If this fellow [Robinson] is good enough to play on this ball club—and from what I've seen and heard, he is—he is going to play on this ball club and he is going to play for me."

Then Durocher could not resist mentioning that there were other great African American players—like Campanella and Newcombe—coming up right behind Robinson. He told the players to chew on that as their heads went back on the pillow later that night. "From everything I hear he's only the first. *Only the first, boys,*" Durocher was shouting now. "There's many more coming right behind him and they have the talent and they're gonna come to play. These fellows are hungry. . . . Unless you fellows look out and wake up, they're going to run you right out of the ball park."[11]

This was a remarkable moment. Durocher was a free spirit willing to say whatever he wanted at any given time; but, mostly, he was usually too busy partying to focus on taking a grand moral stand.

Pitcher Ralph Branca described Durocher as a "pool-hustlin' dead-end kid from West Springfield, Massachusetts, a poor town west of Boston," who grew up to be a manager. He cursed like a sailor and lived a playboy life of gambling and carousing through a series of marriages.[12] Durocher was known for loving the limelight when he made it big in New York first as a shortstop and then as a manager, peacocking in new suits for the paparazzi waiting outside Jack Dempsey's restaurant after he enjoyed a few highballs or a meal with Frank Sinatra or some other star.[13]

Yet there was also a sense of righteousness burning inside Durocher; he thought the game of baseball was to be played by a certain code among men. During an earlier spring training, Durocher flipped out when an aggressive baserunner for the Yankees, Johnny Lindell, decided to slide into second base spikes high, even though it was just an exhibition.

Durocher immediately called Branca over to him in the dugout, fuming over Lindell's targeting a Dodgers infielder in a game that wouldn't even count toward the Yankees' record. "I'm putting you in there, Branca, 'cause next time he comes up I wanna see him on his [rear]," Durocher said, signaling the pitcher needed to drill Lindell with the baseball.

Branca, too young to disobey a direct order, did what he was told. He fired a pitch between Lindell's shoulder blades so that he had no time to react and wound up sprawled in the dirt.

"Never have I seen Leo so happy," recalled Branca.[14]

There were many other times down the road when Durocher wanted to send a message to the opposing team, and he instructed Branca, "Stick it in his ear!"[15]

Back in that kitchen in Panama, Durocher brushed back some of his own Dodgers players, all out of a sense of decency and fairness for Robinson.

"I don't give a [bleep] if his skin is blue and his [rear] is green, he's a great player!" Durocher screamed at his players, adding that if the Dodgers signed Robinson, they could "like it or lump it."[16]

When Rickey arrived in Panama the next morning, Durocher recalled he had never seen him so furious upon learning his own players had tried to turn on him. The executive called the ringleaders in, one by one, to set them straight on the fact that it was not going to be other players who stopped his integration plan.

Walker, allegedly one of the masterminds of that petition, fired off a separate note to Rickey demanding to be traded. It was no light matter since Walker, while not a household name or Hall of Famer, was a star player and fan favorite in his day. He had won the National League batting title in 1944 with an impressive .357 average.

"For reasons I don't care to go into, I feel my decision is best for all concerned," Walker wrote to Rickey.[17] The reason clearly was race. But ironically, the botched effort to stop Robinson actually ended up helping him because it drew Pee Wee Reese in as one of his closest allies.

PEE WEE STEPS UP

Walker had slyly tried to recruit Reese, a key team leader from Kentucky, figuring there would be a Deep South alliance. Reese refused. And while his decision was at least partially motivated by raw dollars, his insistence that he would not sign on the dotted line was a turning point.

"I can't sign this thing," said Reese. "I don't know about you guys, but this is my living. I got a wife and a child. I have to play ball."[18]

Reese was not named the captain of the team until 1950, but long before getting that title, he was already showing the kind of character that clearly helped Robinson get through this monumental challenge.

One day down the road, Al Gionfriddo, an outfielder who robbed Joe DiMaggio of a home run with a nifty catch in the 1947 World Series, organized a game of hearts that included Robinson. Reese was asked to join.

"How can you sit and play cards with that guy?" another player said in reference to Robinson.

"What in the world is wrong," Reese fired back, "with playing with a guy on your own team?"[19]

The future captain could also defuse the tension with a dose of humor for Robinson, who would tell Reese about the death threats he received. Robinson got one letter during a stop in Atlanta from the Ku Klux Klan, saying they would shoot him if he played. So during warm-ups before the game, Reese pretended to be nervous beside Robinson: "Jack, don't stand so close to me today. Move away, will ya?"[20]

In truth, many death threats poured in for Robinson, and it was no laughing matter. Rickey publicly discussed these threats without ever getting the player's permission to do so—an attempt to further build the narrative that Robinson was, in Eig's words, a "Christ-like figure" turning the other cheek, despite the onslaught.[21]

DECISIVE COURAGE

Robinson was surely headed to the big leagues now, thanks to an unexpected assist from Durocher, on top of the unshakable support of Rickey. "With all the other opposition Mr. Rickey anticipated, he wasn't having any revolt on his own home court," Robinson wrote in his unpublished memoir. "The revolt crumbled as revolts usually do when met with firmness and decisive courage."[22]

Rickey stood up to Walker in Panama, and he eventually traded him—but not immediately. The executive could not initially get much for a thirty-six-year-old outfielder, so he held on to him and let Walker stew about the trouble. Then the master wheeler-dealer got the upper hand when he waited long enough to trade Walker to the Pittsburgh Pirates after the 1947 season was done.

In exchange for Walker and two forgotten pitchers, Rickey snagged two key players that became pillars of several more stellar teams that would keep the Dodgers in contention for the World Series: left-handed pitcher Preacher Roe and star third baseman Billy Cox. The Dodgers also got Gene Mauch, who was not much of a player but eventually became a top-flight big league manager.

Meanwhile, Walker became a has-been, banished to Pittsburgh and locked out from the epic Brooklyn battles with the New York Yankees for the World Series.

To his credit, Walker later admitted his mistake and tried to atone for it by befriending Robinson.

"I organized that petition in 1947 not because I had anything against Robinson personally or against Negroes generally," Walker told author Roger Kahn in 1976. "I had a wholesale hardware business in Birmingham and people told me I'd lose my business if I played ball with a black man. That's why I started the petition. It was the dumbest thing I did in all my life and . . . I am deeply sorry."[23]

Robinson believed in forgiveness and was always careful to not hold himself up as being perfect.

"I am not the most religious person in the world," Robinson wrote in his unpublished memoir. "I believe in God, in the Bible and in trying to do the right thing as I understand it. I am certain there are many, many better Christians than I."[24]

CHAPTER 13

"GOOSE PIMPLES" AT EBBETS FIELD

I was asking for big favors from Jerry Reinsdorf, owner of the Chicago Bulls and Chicago White Sox, and yet in the summer of 2016 he kept on going out of his way to accommodate me. Maybe it had something to do with the fact that Reinsdorf grew up in a lower-middle-class family from Brooklyn. And no matter how many championship rings he won in the Windy City with stars like Michael Jordan—or how much money had piled up in his bank accounts—he was still a lot like that humble, eleven-year-old kid who will never forget the joy he felt attending Jackie Robinson's first game in a Dodgers uniform at Ebbets Field.

"Oh, there was a lot of pressure on him, but you could see from the beginning what an exciting player he was," Reinsdorf told me, cigar wafting above him at a private club in Chicago. "One year he stole home seven times!"[1]

When my trusted friend Mark Sullivan first brought us together a couple of years earlier, Reinsdorf and I realized we had a common interest in Robinson. So he quickly gave me his direct cell number and e-mail address without a fuss. Reinsdorf never once asked me to go through a personal assistant, despite the fact that my frequent phone calls probably got annoying as I set up multiple interviews in Chicago and Phoenix, where he has a second home near the spring training facilities for the White Sox.

Then, once I was on his home turf in Chicago, he insisted on picking me up himself. He had no chauffeur or fancy car, despite the fact that *Forbes* has estimated his net worth to be a cool $1.35 billion.

"A seven-year-old Cadillac," Reinsdorf said proudly as I took my seat on the passenger side, when he picked me up at my hotel. "I've got the same exact Cadillac in Arizona—when I get to the airport I don't even want to think."

He was deferential and straightforward, just like many of the Brooklyn Dodgers he came to revere. Like Reinsdorf, Carl Erskine exuded humility too. When Erskine first arrived in Brooklyn in 1948, he stayed at the Hanson Place YMCA. "It had a cot, a desk," Erskine told me. "Everything else was down the hall—the shower, the phone—a pay phone that cost five cents a call."[2] When Erskine needed to get to Ebbets Field, there was no black sedan to pick him up at the YMCA. He took the subway with the fans, who in their unique Brooklyn accent affectionately dubbed him "Oisk," as in, "There's *Oisk-Ine!* Da guy from the Dodgers! I love dos guys, dem Bums!"

Erskine wasn't the only one. First baseman Gil Hodges owned a bowling alley in Brooklyn and would mingle with fans. Center fielder Duke Snider lived about a block from the Reinsdorf family's one-bedroom apartment, and he would actually play stickball with the kids in the neighborhood.

"They were part of us," Reinsdorf said simply. "It was like family. We just worshipped them."

Reinsdorf recalled people in Brooklyn still having chips on their shoulders about why it had stopped being its own city in the late 1800s. Once it became one of New York City's five boroughs, Brooklyn was overshadowed by the glitz and glamour of Manhattan. Plus, in the 1940s and 1950s, when baseball was the dominant sport in America, Brooklyn fans were the underdogs—they were tired of hearing all about the New York Giants (in Manhattan) and the dominant New York Yankees (in the Bronx).

"What else was there to be interested in back in those days?" said Reinsdorf. "The NBA didn't even start until 1946. Football was nothing. The only sport was baseball. And the Dodgers—they were the unifying thing. It was the one thing that everyone was interested in."

This is why Reinsdorf never tires of recounting how many balls and strikes a specific batter had and which pitcher he was facing, in a precise inning of a game in a World Series played decades ago. "Ask me about yesterday. I don't know anything about yesterday if I don't write it down," said Reinsdorf. "If it's fifty or sixty years ago, I have instant recall."

And total recall, especially when it comes to his fascination with the Dodgers.

It began innocently enough when he knocked on his friend Norman Ricken's door to see if he could come out to play.

"He's listening to the ballgame," Ricken's mother said.

Reinsdorf thought to himself: *He's listening to the ballgame. Who does that?*

Well, Norman Ricken grew up to be the president of Toys "R" Us, and he turned out to be one of a whole lot of people who listened to the radio broadcasts by Red Barber.

"Everything happens in Ebbets Field, so it's worth coming out, but still, there are no fans anywhere like the Brooklyn fans," Barber said in his drawl, over and over. "Anywhere. No suh."

Reinsdorf wanted to check out this Ebbets Field, so he and Ricken saw the Dodgers play the St. Louis Cardinals in 1946, and he was hooked. The boys would take the subway to the game so they could get there as early as possible. "The subway was a nickel," he said. "But we would walk home—save the nickel."

Even though Ebbets Field itself was so gray, there seemed to be something magical about the place when Reinsdorf stepped off the subway platform and walked onto the giant ramp that led to the park. "Everything was gray and drab going to the park and going up the ramp, it was all drab," recalled Reinsdorf. "And all of a sudden this green just burst upon you."

Reinsdorf added, "I still get goose pimples thinking about it. I still—just talking about it I get excited. I remember it so clearly."

Ebbets Field was so small—with a capacity of about 32,000, compared to 67,000-seat monsters like the original Yankee Stadium—that fans felt closer to players. Plus the ballpark was full of character—and characters.

At the bottom of the scoreboard in right field was a sign declaring, HIT SIGN, WIN SUIT. This was the creation of a guy named Abe Stark, a politician and tailor who owned a clothing store in Brooklyn. There was another sign advertising a soap company, Lifebuoy, but after a series of Brooklyn losses, an angry fan brought some paint and defaced it: "The Dodgers Use Lifebuoy, and they still stink."[3]

Then there was the organist, Gladys Gooding, who seemed to have a wicked sense of humor. She would play "Three Blind Mice" when the umpires made a bad call. At the final game ever played at Ebbets Field in 1957, Gooding felt sad about the Dodgers moving to Los Angeles, so she brought a brown bag of booze to work. Then Gooding played a series of increasingly more depressing songs as the night wore on. When officials tried to get into the organ room to change the tunes, they were rebuffed. Gooding had locked herself in.[4]

Vin Scully, the legendary broadcaster who started as an understudy to Barber, may have put it best when he noted that in other ballparks, the crowd was merely wallpaper. "All the faces merge together into an anonymous landscape," said Scully. "Ebbets was radically different. Because the facility itself was so small, the minute you stepped inside you felt an intimacy. You didn't see a crowd, you saw individuals. The distance between the playing field and the stands was negligible. The fans were practically on the field. The players smelled the breath of the fans, and the fans smelled the breath of the players."[5]

RETURNING STARS

Fans in Ebbets Field were anxious to get their beloved Bums back to Brooklyn in early 1947. The team had dashed all over Latin America. That had given Robinson the time and space away from the United States to get ready to make history if Rickey called him up to the Dodgers. But now the fans wanted the players to come back home to see if they could finally succeed this season after so much failure.

They had come up just short of reaching the World Series at the end of the 1946 season, and optimism was running high because of the squad being beefed up with the possible addition of Robinson and a slew of other budding stars.

With the slugging Snider also emerging at the start of the 1947 season—and pitcher Ralph Branca still a newcomer, and only getting better—the long-suffering Brooklyn fans felt as though they might finally be on the cusp of a historic run of World Series championships.

After their long travels through Cuba, Panama, and Venezuela, the Dodgers returned home to the friendly confines of Brooklyn on April 9, 1947. The players were greeted with a humorous column by writer Arthur Daley in that morning's edition of the *New York Times* that jokingly referred to them as refugees from Latin America.[6]

That afternoon the Dodgers were playing an exhibition game against their minor league team, the Montreal Royals. Robinson would be playing in the uniform of the Royals; the reporters who had followed the Dodgers around Latin America still were in the dark about whether he would be promoted to the big league club or spend another season with Montreal in the minors.

A clue, though, had come when Rickey instructed the Royals' manager, Clay Hopper, to give him some practice at first base in the waning days of spring training. The Dodgers just so happened to have an open spot at first base as they closed in on the start of the regular season, April 15, at Ebbets Field.

It was all up to Rickey, and while he was not quite tipping his hand yet, the betting was that he was about to promote Robinson. Except, suddenly, yet another wrinkle nearly derailed the Mahatma's plan.

DUROCHER THROWN OUT

On the morning of April 9, 1947, the Dodgers' offices at 215 Montague Street, scene of the remarkable first meeting between Robinson and Rickey, were at the center of the action again.

Rickey was presiding over an intense meeting among eight men, including manager Leo Durocher and longtime scout Clyde Sukeforth, about who would be on the Dodgers' roster for opening day. One entire wall was covered by a blackboard with the names of players who would miss the cut and be assigned to various minor league teams around the country.

The secretary had been told to block all calls unless there was an extreme emergency. But, suddenly, the private phone on Rickey's desk started to ring.

"You can't do that!" Rickey yelled into the phone.[7]

Happy Chandler, the commissioner of baseball, was on the other end of the call. He suspended Durocher from baseball for a year for associating with gamblers. Sukeforth was elevated to manager of the team, though he would take over for only a couple of games. Then Rickey tapped Burt Shotton to manage the club for the rest of the 1947 season.

This was a blow to Rickey's Great Experiment, to be sure. If he were to call Robinson up to the Dodgers, he would need a strong manager to take charge of the situation. Now that he no longer had the gutsy Durocher, who had stood up for the African American player in that middle-of-the-night meeting in the Panama kitchen, could the general manager go through with promoting Robinson?

"Abruptly the meeting was over," declared Barber, phrasing it as only he could. "Reporters began swarming like bees on a busted honey barrel on a hot afternoon."

Rickey was pounded with question after question about Durocher from the press. Then he kicked everyone out and started mulling a final decision on Robinson.

"Rickey had the strength of being quiet and looking into himself," noted Barber. "He had learned that during the long year he spent at Saranac Lake getting over tuberculosis, knowing that when he left the sanitarium he had a young wife and no job."[8]

Rickey also had the capacity to take bold action—once he had done his homework. In this case, though, losing Durocher created a quandary. The executive had wanted to insulate himself from the charge that he was imposing his personal crusade on baseball. He wanted to use Durocher to legitimize the claim that Robinson's promotion was being demanded from within the team.

"This suspension of Durocher puts a thorn in my plans," Rickey admitted to Robinson. "I had planned to have Durocher ask for you for the Dodgers. Now I will have to make the announcement directly."

Of course, Rickey had been engaged in a long mission to integrate the game. But Barber suggested there was now another reason to elevate Robinson. It could help squash the Durocher story. Now he could use the chaos caused by the gambling story to finally move forward with his experiment. "Rickey countered the whirlwind with action," noted Barber. "He knew that the quietest place in a storm was at the very heart of it."[9]

In the sixth inning of another exhibition game between the Dodgers and Montreal, a simple press release, signed by Rickey, was distributed to the media: "The Brooklyn Dodgers today purchased the contract of Jack Roosevelt Robinson from the Montreal Royals. He will report immediately."

With one fell swoop, the color barrier was obliterated.

It left an indelible mark on far more than just baseball or civil rights. It was, as George F. Will put it, "one of the great achievements not only in the annals of sports, but of the human drama anywhere, anytime."[10]

JACKIE ROBINSON, DODGER

The next day, April 11, the Dodgers had an exhibition game against the Yankees. It would be Robinson's first game at Ebbets Field in a Dodgers uniform, though his first official regular season game that counted in the standings would come on April 15.

Reinsdorf attended the April 11 game, but he was honest about saying that as an eleven-year-old he did not immediately grasp the history of it. "I don't remember—I wish I could tell you—but I don't remember there was any particular buzz that there was a black player," Reinsdorf said.

It's easy now to romanticize Robinson's first season, as if everyone in America stood up and cheered. In reality, Robinson's first official game on April 15 was not even a sellout at Ebbets Field, proving that a lot of adults did not immediately grasp the full impact of it either.

One kid sitting in the crowd on April 15 was five-year-old Donald Graf, who contacted me by e-mail after learning about the book. Graf recalled his father, John, worked for Westinghouse, and would often take his son to weekend games at Ebbets Field to sit in the utility company's box along first base. But this time he decided the kid needed to attend a weekday game, because it was special.[11]

"He knew it was Jackie Robinson's first game," Graf remembered. "He said, 'You're going to witness history being made.'"

Instead, Graf mostly recalled six very drunk men sitting nearby and alarming him with racially charged verbal attacks on Robinson.

"They were drinking like beer after beer after beer out of cardboard cups," Graf said. "And someone had a pen knife. So they were cutting out the bottoms and making a megaphone. They rode him the whole game. It was the first time I heard the 'N-word' and a lot of other stuff."

Graf could not possibly understand the context at the time, though looking back as he closed in on seventy-five years old, he had new admiration for Robinson. He noted that because Ebbets Field was so small and intimate, Robinson, who was playing first base, must have heard the nasty words, but seemed laser focused on the task at hand. "Jackie never turned his head and looked at these guys, compared to the umpire near first base," he said. "I can still visualize the umpire looking at them. You could tell he was upset. But Jackie never turned."[12]

Robinson, of course, grasped how big this was and leaned on his faith as he geared up for his first game. "I did all my thinking last night," he said. "Before I went to bed I thanked God for all that's happened, and for the good fortune that's come my way."

Robinson did an interview with the drama critic Ward Morehouse, where he made it clear that he tried to ease the tension by remembering he had risen to the occasion when the Reverend Karl Downs gave him another tough assignment years ago. "I belong to the Methodist Church in Pasadena and I used to be a Sunday school teacher at UCLA," Robinson said. "They gave me the bad little boys, and I liked it."[13]

Well, breaking the color barrier and then surviving in the big leagues— and actually thriving—would be a bit more of a challenge. In an odd way, though, that pressure was relieved a bit by the fact that the Dodgers had raised the expectations of their fans in 1946, with some young players who jelled quicker than anticipated.

Fans like Reinsdorf, after having their hearts broken again at the end of that 1946 season, were excited about the team's chances for 1947. Robinson was not the only newcomer on the radar.

"They had Jackie and a left-handed-hitting third baseman named Spider Jorgensen," recalled Reinsdorf. "So now everybody was optimistic. That's all we cared about—are these two guys going to be good enough to put us over the top?"

Race was simply not a factor for some fans like Reinsdorf. "I don't remember thinking, 'Oh, one guy's a white guy, one guy's a black guy,'" he said. "I just wanted to see how good these guys were."[14]

Oh, the innocence of a child who simply wanted to see his team win. He did not realize it at the time, but Reinsdorf was instinctively buying into what Rickey was trying to sell with integration.

"A champion is a champion in America, black or white," Rickey had told Robinson as they prepared for the big day.[15] But let's face it: there were plenty of Americans who were not happy with an African American getting this opportunity.

On April 15, there were rumors that an assassin was lying in wait somewhere around Ebbets Field to kill Robinson with a sniper's bullet once he took the field.

Branca, who would soon play a critical role in another historic Dodgers moment, was one of the white teammates who embraced Robinson early on. Even despite rumors of an attempted assassination brewing, Branca decided to stand right next to Robinson when the team lined up on the field before the game started to kick off opening day.

There was no assassination attempt, and the Dodgers won the game, 5–3, over the Braves. Robinson did not get a hit, but he scored the winning run.

After the game, one of Branca's brothers rushed up to him.

"Ralphie, you were crazy to stand next to him," he said. "What if some sharpshooter missed him by three feet and got you instead?"

Branca did not hesitate.

"I'd die a hero," he said. "There are worse ways to go."[16]

Another person in the Dodgers organization who became a key backer of Robinson was Red Barber. Rickey was smart to get buy in from him, and Barber more than embraced Robinson; he was rooting for his success. In baseball, getting three hits for every ten at-bats is an outstanding average of .300. Yet Barber suggested he did not want Robinson to make a single out all season. "I hope," he told his listeners, "he bats 1.000."[17]

For all of Barber's previous hand-wringing, it turned out to be not that complicated for him. He planned to focus on his own work and Robinson's performance on the field, not the social impact. "There was no trouble," he said. "I got no complaints. I reported what Robinson did as a ballplayer. That was all there was to it. I reported him as I would any other player. That was all the public wanted, all Rickey wanted and all Robinson wanted."[18]

It was indeed all Reinsdorf wanted when he was a young fan. He and many others just cared about the game. Speaking of the historic broken color barrier, Reinsdorf recalled, "The first time it really hit me was when I asked my friend Lester Davis, who was black, I asked, 'Who's your favorite player?' He looked at me like I was crazy. He said, 'Jackie Robinson, of course.' That's when I realized: Jackie *is* the only black player."

Reinsdorf still shakes his head at the memory decades later.

"I was eleven years old," he said of the long-ago conversation. "I didn't know 'social significance.'"

CHAPTER 14

PRAYERS FOR JACKIE

Now it was my turn to take a train, from Washington to Philadelphia, so I could find out more about the uglier side of Jackie Robinson's first year in the major leagues.

When Robinson took his tension-filled train ride to Brooklyn in 1945 to meet Branch Rickey for the first time, it had reminded him of Christmas Eve. He wasn't sure if he would be full of joy or disappointment on the other side. The truth is that he ended up getting plenty of both.

Most of us like to focus on the poetry of Robinson fulfilling his dream and joyfully taking his position at Ebbets Field. It makes us feel better to think about limitless possibilities. The same line of thinking led the history books to conclude that, at one point during a game in 1947, either in Philadelphia or Cincinnati, shortstop Pee Wee Reese threw his arm around Robinson on the field in a poignant gesture of racial harmony.

Ken Burns asserted in his spectacular 2016 PBS documentary about Robinson's life that it never happened—at least not in 1947—even though there are statues in New York and Cincinnati of Reese and Robinson embracing.

While Burns was promoting the documentary in interviews, he said the story had become mythology because "no pun intended, we white people wanted to have skin in the game" and show that white people did wonderful things for Jackie.[1]

Burns correctly noted that in 1947, Robinson was playing first base, and it would have been highly unusual for Reese to leave the shortstop position and cross the field in the middle of a game.

It does appear, however, that some version of the embrace did in fact happen in 1948 in a game with the Boston Braves, according to a 1952 interview Robinson did with *Focus* magazine. By then, Robinson had moved over to second base and was closer on the diamond to Reese. "We were in Boston in '48 and the Braves were 'giving it' to Reese for playing shortstop alongside me," Robinson said. "Pee Wee came over from shortstop, put his arm around my shoulders, as if he had something to say. Actually, he just wanted to show where he stood. The jeers subsided."[2]

In a 1955 piece that Robinson penned for *Look* magazine, the player suggested that he and Reese actually embraced several times, not just once, starting in Boston in 1948. "He walked over to me, put his arm around me and talked to me in a warm and friendly way, smiling and laughing," wrote Robinson. "His sincerity startled the Braves, and there was no more trouble after that from them. Later, he did the same for me in other ball parks."[3]

Regardless of which version of the Reese story you believe, the fact remains that despite all the positive parts of 1947, Robinson faced a whole new level of nastiness his rookie year.

And that's why I was on an Amtrak train headed to the so-called City of Brotherly Love.

PHILADELPHIA

The hate actually started on Brooklyn's turf of Ebbets Field early in that 1947 season, but it was indeed spewing from the Philadelphia Phillies' manager, Ben Chapman. In addition to shouting a question at Robinson about why he was not picking cotton, Chapman screamed from the dugout, "Hey, boy, I need a shine. Come over here and shine my shoes."

The Tennessee-born Chapman also encouraged his players to insult Robinson while they were on his home turf. Jackie heard another person from the Phillies shout, "Hey, black Nigger—why don't you go back where you came from?"[4]

As the Dodgers got ready for their first road trip to Philadelphia weeks later, the Phillies' general manager had the gall to urge Rickey to defuse the situation by keeping Robinson back in Brooklyn.

Rickey, of course, refused, but when the team arrived in the city, more trouble was brewing. The Dodgers had routinely stayed at the Ben Franklin Hotel, but this time the clerk, in a move reminiscent of the Charles "Tommy" Thomas incident, refused to let the "Negro" stay there.

It was shameful for the city, and Philadelphia is not just any city. It's the birthplace of our democracy and is now a racially diverse city that is 35.4 percent non-Hispanic white and 44.0 percent African American.[5] Helen Gym became the first Asian American ever to serve on the Philadelphia City Council, and after watching the movie 42 and seeing her hometown getting ripped, she had enough.

It did not matter to Gym that all the key participants had long since died, and the Ben Franklin Hotel—like Ebbets Field—was converted to an apartment building. She sponsored a spring 2016 resolution, timed to the sixty-ninth anniversary of Robinson's debut, to officially offer him a posthumous apology.

The resolution passed unanimously, and the apology was accepted by Rachel Robinson. The move was an attempt to make up for the way Jackie was treated throughout the city during his rookie year.

There was the phone call that Phillies general manager Herb Pennock placed to Rickey in May 1947, begging him to leave Robinson home for their four-game series. "[You] just can't bring the Nigger here with the rest of your team, Branch," Pennock said. "We're just not ready for that sort of thing yet. We won't be able to take the field against your Brooklyn team if that boy Robinson is in uniform."

Rickey was reasonably calm in his response, given the absurdity of Pennock's words. He said he was fine with the Phillies deciding to forfeit each of the four games, and the rules stipulated 9–0 victories for the Dodgers. "Very well, Herbert. And if we must claim the game, nine to nothing, we will do just that, I assure you," Rickey said.[6]

The Dodgers were coming with Robinson; clearly Rickey was not about to back down—even when officials at the Ben Franklin Hotel, which had welcomed the Dodgers for years, took hate to a new level. "And don't bring your team back here while you have any Niggers with you," shouted one hotel clerk, according to the Dodgers' traveling secretary, Harold Parrot.[7]

Even with the despicable attacks Chapman had already unleashed in Brooklyn, Robinson somehow took it in stride. "The Phils were rough on me when Ben Chapman managed them," Robinson recalled. "I remember he once was quoted as saying, he 'beat up Niggers in his spare time.'"[8]

But at least one Phillies player, Lee Handley, reached first base and apologized to Robinson. "Handley told me that the insults were coming from players who wanted to keep in right with Chapman but that there were other Phillies, like himself, who were ashamed of Chapman," noted Robinson.[9]

Ford Frick, president of the National League, warned Chapman to cut it out. The manager further insulted Robinson by claiming he was just trying to toughen the player up and make a better major leaguer out of him. Then he claimed he had also hurled anti-Italian slurs at New York Yankees great Joe DiMaggio. As if multiple wrongs made a right, Chapman also insisted he had previously shouted anti-Jewish insults at Hank Greenberg of the Detroit Tigers, as if it were all in fun.

Interestingly, Robinson had noted separately in a piece for *Look* magazine that Greenberg went out of his way to make him feel comfortable when they met on the field. "He told me that he, too, had run into discrimination as a rookie because he was Jewish, but he assured me that everything would turn out all right for me," Robinson recalled.[10]

Still, Frick and Phillies officials wanted to defuse the nasty situation. So a peace offering was hastily arranged where Robinson and Chapman could pose for a photo shaking hands before the Dodgers' first game in Philadelphia.

But Chapman couldn't even do that. Instead, the two men held on to a bat for the photo, so that Chapman did not have to directly touch an African American. "That was all right with me," Robinson fired back. "I didn't want to shake hands with him either."

Having to stand beside Chapman at all frustrated Robinson intensely. It was yet another example of him having to take it, which would lead some African American critics to later claim he was too accommodating.

"I hated to pose for that picture," Robinson wrote in 1955. "Today, I wouldn't do it, but I swallowed my pride and agreed."[11]

Yet a greater good came out of the terrible episode, because it was not only some of the Phillies players who were outraged by Chapman's behavior. The attacks actually drove Robinson closer to his white teammates who had been openly skeptical of playing with an African American. Eddie Stanky, a Dodgers infielder who was on that list of skeptics, confronted several players on the Phillies for slamming Robinson. And he basically called them cowards for going after someone who they knew could not respond because of Rickey's edict.

"The Dodgers told me, too, that they were just as disgusted," noted Robinson. "I always felt that day marked the welding of the club."[12]

In his unpublished manuscript, Robinson wrote about the impact these incidents had on him. "How could I be anti-white," he wrote, "after knowing a Branch Rickey, a Pee Wee Reese, a Carl Erskine" had stood up for him over the years?[13]

Erskine, who did not join the team until Robinson's second season, said this is another example of why the general manager deserves credit for instructing Jackie early on to turn the other cheek.

"Mr. Rickey was so wise that he planned that whole thing to bring it where he could put it in Jackie's mind and spirit that this was bigger than anything he had ever done," Erskine told me.

Still, Erskine added that for all of Rickey's planning, it was Robinson who had the will and determination not to fight back, even during the vile attacks from Chapman. "He not only listened—you know anybody can listen," Erskine said of Robinson. "What's hard in life is to *do* it. And I don't know how he did it."[14]

Chapman and others also misjudged the support network Robinson had—from celebrities like Frank Sinatra to average fans all across the country, many of whom told Jackie they were praying for him.

A NETWORK OF SUPPORT

Throughout the season, telegrams and letters poured in to Robinson from people all across America—white and black—telling him there was a prayer army out there rooting him on.

"I've kept close to my radio, and prayers," Mrs. Bernice Franklin of Tyronza, Arkansas, wrote Robinson on August 20, 1947, according to one of the many letters now kept in files at the Library of Congress.[15]

Wrote Harold MacDowell of Newark, New Jersey: "I pray that you will be granted the fullest measure of courage and good judgment—and I'm not normally a praying man."[16]

Then there was a moving letter from a Catholic priest in Harlem, New York. "This parish is one of eight Catholic parishes in Harlem," wrote the Reverend John F. Curran. "We are eager to impress upon our youngsters the fact that if you have what it takes ultimately you will be recognized. You know all too well the difficulties besetting the way of life of the Negro; and we are all so extremely proud of you and your accomplishments in the face of almost insurmountable odds."

Curran added a beautiful biblical reference: "The responsibility resting on the shoulders of him who would dare to be a Daniel would be tremendous."

Then the priest noted that beyond his talents on the field, Robinson clearly had gifts from God to endure the pressure of being the first African American major leaguer. "He would have to be little short of superman," wrote Curran. "He would have to be able to take what would be dumped . . . on him, come thru [sic] it unscathed, unmarked, smiling, the better man for it, and by sheer force of personal integrity and gentlemanly demeanor make those who had come to mock stay to praise."

"Thank God," Curran added, "you have what it took and takes."

The priest wrote that young people "with faces aglow in the rising sun of a new day" could now thank Robinson for showing them anyone in America can succeed, regardless of race. "You have made our youth realize that only the best can survive; and that best can even be embellished by cleanness in life at home and at work," wrote Curran.

"God spare you many years to your wife and family," he told Robinson. "May you continue further to inspire our youth to bigger, better and greater things in all fields of endeavor," Curran concluded, signing the letter "sincerely in Christ."[17]

Other fans urged Robinson not to lose his temper amid the taunts. On May 9, 1947, Eugene Carey—a deputy sheriff from Detroit who apparently knew Rickey—sent some encouragement to Robinson about the jeering that he faced.

"I read about the bench riding you are getting from opposing players," wrote Carey. "But Jackie, I know you can take it. You are made of that kind of 'stuff.' They are calling you vulgar names and using abusive language, thinking that it might cause you to loose [sic] your temper and 'blow your top.' This would affect your playing and hitting."[18]

Even Frank Sinatra was keeping close tabs on Robinson's history-making first season. Sinatra revealed this nugget to Brooklyn pitcher Ralph Branca, who had a pretty good voice and fancied himself a crooner. Branca would sometimes sing at nightclubs in between his starts on the mound, and as an Italian American, his role model, of course, was Sinatra.

Shortly after Robinson had made his debut, Branca and a friend went to see Sinatra at the Paramount in New York City, and they got past the guards to go backstage because of Branca's status as a Dodger.

"Big Ralph," declared Sinatra, then in the early days of his career, with a shake of the hand. "How could they do that to Durocher?"

In yet another sign that Leo Durocher had loved the nightlife a little too much—a fact that culminated in his suspension for the entire season of 1947 for hanging out with known gamblers—Sinatra asked the pitcher to give Durocher a "big wet kiss on the cheek" from the man who would become known as Old Blue Eyes.

"It wasn't fair, Frank," Branca said. "It wasn't right."

Suddenly Sinatra shifted the conversation to Robinson and quickly showed his reverence for the player, even though the language of the time was less than respectful.

"And this colored boy, what do you think of him?" asked Sinatra.

"I like him," said Branca. "Jackie's great."

"I like him, too, Ralph," said Sinatra, turning his attention to the World Series. "I like him enough to predict that he'll bring you the big prize this year."

"From your mouth to God's ear, Frank."

"Well," Sinatra concluded, "good luck to you, kid."[19]

Branca wound up helping Robinson in a major way when they traveled later that season to St. Louis.

TROUBLE IN ST. LOUIS

There were reports that Cardinals players had threatened to strike if they had to play against Robinson, though the rebellion may have really been a bluff. Ford Frick, president of the National League, stomped it out anyway by declaring any players who dared to strike would be banned from baseball for life.

Another man of character, Eddie Dyer, the Cardinals' manager, tried to give Robinson a warm welcome to the St. Louis ballpark.

En route to the field from the clubhouse, opposing players had to walk through the Cardinals' dugout. Robinson saw the players staring him down. "Then Dyer stopped me and told me, in front of his team, that he was glad to see me and that he wished me luck," noted Robinson. "It may not sound like much now, but at that time, it meant a lot to me."[20]

Later in the season, the Dodgers returned to St. Louis for a critical series of games with the Cardinals. The Dodgers had a tight, four-and-a-half-game lead over the Cards heading into the September series.

Robinson's nerves were fraying after nearly an entire season of taunts and abuse. The Cards' catcher, Joe Garagiola, was running out a hit in a September 11 game and stepped on Robinson's foot as he crossed first base.

Few believed the gregarious Garagiola was trying to maim him. But Robinson was on edge, and when he came to bat later in the game, he got a close look at Garagiola behind home plate. The umpire asked Robinson if he had cut his leg, and Jackie started ripping Garagiola.

"No, I didn't," Robinson said, nodding toward the catcher. "But it wasn't his fault I didn't."

Garagiola took the bait and ripped off his catcher's mask. Suddenly the two men were nose to nose, the crowd cheering on a possible fistfight.

They were separated without any punches exchanged, other than the knockout delivered by Robinson with his bat later in the game. He got the best revenge by smacking a two-run home run that gave the Dodgers a 4–3 victory and a little more cushion in the pennant race.[21]

A couple of games later, when Robinson was still on edge, he received one of the most important boosts of his career from Branca.

A Cardinals player hit a foul ball down the first-base line, and Robinson scrambled to catch it, racing at full speed. In his haste, Robinson did not realize that in foul territory there was a warm-up pitcher's mound between him and the Dodgers' dugout.

Robinson caught the ball but then immediately tripped hard. He was about to go flying into the dugout at full blast, headed for an all-but-certain injury.

Except Branca was waiting in the dugout to catch his friend.

"I jumped out of the dugout and made a perfect right shoulder tackle on him," recalled Branca. "I caught him and kept him from falling." That is the clinical, bare-bones version. Yet as Branca spun out more details, he revealed just how much affection the teammates had for one another.

"He wound up in my arms," noted Branca. "In describing the scene, someone said that Jackie and I looked like a married couple."[22]

Robinson noticed something more important: it sent a signal to the fans that the white Dodgers would not let the African American player get hurt.

"The others [in the dugout] crowded around and helped me back on my feet," Robinson wrote in a magazine article. "As I say, it was a little thing, but it surprised the spectators. I heard them talking about it during the next few innings. It seemed to break the ice between me and the Cardinal fans."[23]

And in a 1953 article he wrote for *Reader's Digest*, Robinson suggested this small gesture from Branca really broke the ice among the Dodgers as well. "That occurrence of my rookie days, out in the St. Louis ball park, proved to me once and for all that I was among men who did not give a hoot about the color of my skin," wrote Robinson. "What was important to them was that I was part of the team."

Robinson used this story to make the case that while there had been dramatic progress in race relations, there was still a long way to go. He would continue to recount it in the substantive civil rights speeches he delivered throughout the 1960s after his playing days were over, giving many of the talks in churches all around America.

"My own principal yardstick for men is this: Are they content to let themselves and their world rest on past advances—or do they use each new gain as a springboard toward the next one?" wrote Robinson.[24]

After that game, in the clubhouse, the tone of conversation showed just how strong Robinson's friendship with Branca had grown.

"Hey," Branca said, thinking back on his comrade's days on the gridiron with UCLA. "I bet there aren't many guys who can say they made a clean tackle on Jackie Robinson."

"Few in football," said Robinson. "And you're the first in baseball."

As Robinson took off his uniform, he noticed an annoying "strawberry," basically a skin abrasion, on his thigh from the tackle.

"I wouldn't call that a strawberry," Branca parried. "For you, I'd call it a blackberry."

A racial reference like that, even a joking one, could have started fisticuffs just a few months earlier in that kitchen in Panama, where Durocher had unloaded on the petition signers. In a sign of growing mutual respect and comfort between Jackie and at least some of his teammates, he shrugged this one off.

"You're the only guy who could get away with saying something like that," said Robinson. "Anyone else I'd have to run over."

"Only to be tackled," Branca smiled. "I did it once, Jackie, and I'll do it again."[25]

It was the kind of jocularity that teammates had not shared with Jackie before. And truth be told, Robinson himself had been keeping his distance too.

Robinson admitted in his unpublished memoir that dating back to the early years, "one thing that made it tough for me at the beginning was that I had a chip on my shoulder when I first came into the game."

He kept to himself, waiting for his teammates to make the first move out of a fear that he would make trouble for everyone if he tried to befriend them.

"It didn't take me long to realize that I was doing wrong," Robinson wrote. "If we were to be successful, I had to, in some way, get along with the fellows on the ball club, to get them to know and understand me. I couldn't expect them to take the giant step all by themselves, to create a friendship with me. I had to walk some of the way too."[26]

A NEW TEAM DYNAMIC

One legitimate reason for Robinson keeping a low profile is that he knew if he made one wrong move on the road, it could be used to undermine him and the entire Great Experiment as well.

"While traveling with the club, I was afraid to accept invitations to parties in strange towns or even to eat in a restaurant where I wasn't known," he wrote. "I worried about getting into a situation that would result in bad publicity. I was on guard night and day."[27]

Another reason for the distance was that he did not drink or smoke anyway, so he had fewer chances to socialize with his teammates. But he was also leery of forcing white players to hang out with him.

"I didn't want to rush things," Robinson wrote in a 1955 first-person account in *Look* magazine. "I figured that the others were having a harder time getting used to me than I was adjusting myself to them. At UCLA, I had been on teams with white boys, but no Dodger had ever shared a locker room with a Negro. It was an uneasy, touch-and-go situation."[28]

He added later, "I sort of had a chip in the beginning. I was looking for things. Maybe in the early years I kept to myself more than I should have because of that chip. I think maybe I'd be more—what's the word? Outgoing. Yeah. I know that. I'd try and make friends quicker."[29]

Of course, some players on the Dodgers were far less accommodating than Branca, and they also tested Robinson's promise to Rickey.

A bunch of Dodgers were in the middle of a card game on a train when everyone was startled by a comment from Hugh Casey, a relief pitcher born in Georgia. "Back home, when we used to need some good luck, we'd just reach out and rub an old Nigger woman's head," cracked Casey.

Tense silence filled the room as everyone peered at Robinson to see his reaction, as he seethed.

"'Mr. Rickey,' I was saying to myself, 'I'm sorry, Mr. Rickey,'" Robinson wrote in his unpublished manuscript. "'But here goes the real Jackie Robinson. No red blooded Negro lets a white man insult him like this.'"

In a sign of just how much respect and reverence that Robinson had for Rickey, he thought to himself some more about how many "I told you so's" he would get if he punched Casey.

"I wasn't then and am not now, the kind of Negro who will Uncle Tom for Uncle Tomming's sake," Robinson wrote later. "But, here, there was so much more important at stake than Casey's approval."[30]

It was a look indeed at the struggle for Robinson, who in the 1960s would face the "Uncle Tom" label from a new generation of African American leaders who were seen as being more radical, like Malcolm X and Muhammad Ali.

In 1947, though, Robinson was still more concerned about the support of white teammates. And he got that backing—even from Casey—after that nasty spat with Enos "Country" Slaughter.

SPIKED BY SLAUGHTER

Slaughter's vicious attack on Robinson, mentioned earlier, actually backfired. Once Slaughter's spikes ripped into Robinson's ankle, white players on the Dodgers rushed to his defense. "Hugh Casey, a Southerner who never had much to do with me, came off the bench and charged Slaughter," noted Robinson.

Branca went a step further. The pitcher offered to "stick one in Slaughter's ear" the next time they faced one another.

The white players were now so fired up that, remarkably, it was Robinson who was urging caution. "I calmed them down because I didn't want to be the cause of a riot, but that, too, made me feel that I belonged," recalled Robinson.

Robinson added, "It took every bit of my discipline to bridle my tempers! But when my teammates rushed to my support in white hot anger, it gave me the warmest feeling I've ever felt. At that moment I belonged."[31]

During his early seasons with the Dodgers, Robinson gritted his teeth and followed Rickey's demand. The truth is, he grew tired of staying calm, as he played the part of a model minority—or what he called a "freak role" on and off the field. Robinson was longing for the day when he could finally fight back, saying that would turn out to be his true Emancipation Day.

"Throughout all that seemingly endless period of being called names, facing snubs, insults, threats and sneak physical attacks, I was living for the day when I could step out of that freak role—the first Negro in the major leagues," remembered Robinson.

He added, "I was waiting and praying for the time when I could react naturally, explosively, if necessary, whenever I felt someone was treating me unfairly . . . The day I could sound off at a player on the opposing team who was riding me or my teammates . . . that would be the day of my emancipation."[32]

Here again, Rickey had been prescient during that first face-to-face meeting in 1945. "You can't fight except with base hits and stealing of the bases and the way that you catch the ball and the way you get along with the other players on the team," Rickey told Robinson. "You've got to act in such a way that you'll win the respect of your fellow players. You've got to win that so completely that they'll want to come to battle for you when you can't do it for yourself."

Robinson added: "The day that happened, the day my own teammates decided to take up the fight—that would be the day the crusade for integration in baseball would be won. That was the way Mr. Rickey had put it."[33]

Amid all of the hecklers and attackers, Robinson was named Rookie of the Year for 1947. He hit a strong .297 in that first season and led the major leagues with 29 stolen bases.

Another reason some of Robinson's teammates embraced him was that he helped get them to the World Series, and that meant bonus cash. For Jackie, his series share was $4,081.19, while he made just $5,000 the entire regular season.[34]

Robinson played valiantly in the World Series, but the Dodgers came up short against the hated Yankees. Still, he was all smiles in the clubhouse afterward, shaking hands and declaring to his teammates, "Thanks for all you've done for me."

He tried to shoot down a story that he was planning to quit after just three seasons. "I hope I've got six years of big league ball ahead," he declared.

Robinson would play far longer than that, but for now he had to worry about 1948, and there was more danger ahead.

CHAPTER 15

UNEASY ALLIANCE WITH CAMPY

As my research for this book accelerated, I was stunned by one particularly emotional letter that Jackie Robinson had received. It was from a longtime friend, and yet it signaled a rupture in their relationship. Apparently it meant enough to Jackie that he had decided to keep it in his personal papers until his death.

The writer of the letter, Joe Reichler of the Associated Press, was clearly personally wounded. He was defending himself after a blistering note had come in from Robinson in 1958 shortly after the player's retirement, in which he charged the writer made him look like a "patsy" in a magazine piece.

Reichler wrote to Robinson that he was shocked by the former player unleashing "unfair charges and accusations" at the reporter. It was clear that Robinson's tone startled Reichler.

"I'm not going to let a few hot-tempered words change my feeling toward you," wrote Reichler in the letter I discovered in Robinson's papers at the Library of Congress. "I think Ricky (my wife) is more disturbed about it than I am. She's fond of you, too."[1]

Robinson felt slighted by Reichler writing something favorable about his former teammate, Roy Campanella, the slugging catcher who joined the Dodgers in 1948, during Jackie's second season. That second year for Robinson was crucial in establishing that his strong rookie season had not been a fluke. He was also joined in 1948 by someone who became a key ally, that minor league pitcher he had met down in Texas, Carl Erskine, who would go on to throw two no-hitters in his career. Another key addition was the soft-spoken marine Gil Hodges, who played as a backup catcher in 1947. Then Hodges worked his way over to first base in the middle of 1948, after Robinson had moved to second base, which would be his home for most of his career.

"Campy" was another early African American star in baseball, so he was expected to be an important ally for Robinson. And, to be sure, they worked together plenty of times to advance the cause.

Roger Kahn noted in his book *The Boys of Summer* that as more African American players joined the Dodgers, as pitcher Don Newcombe did in 1949, Robinson would urge them to mingle as much as possible.

"Spread out," Robinson would say. "Don't sit together at one table. Mix it up. Eat with the white guys. You all sit at one table, you look like a spot." So on the dining car of their train, Robinson would eat with Erskine, while Campy would be at another table with pitcher Clem Labine.[2]

Why then was there so much resentment as time wore on? I wanted to find out more about what was really eating at Robinson.

With just a little bit of digging, I found that Reichler had passed away, but one of his surviving children actually lived near me in Washington, DC.

So in December 2015, I found myself walking near the White House with Paul Reichler to grab a table at Kellari, a Greek restaurant in Washington on K Street, the monied corridor where most of the lawyers and lobbyists work.

We were pretty easy to spot: Paul was the guy crossing the street in the middle of downtown Washington with a couple of big, framed photos of Jackie Robinson. Reichler was carrying a third framed picture of himself, at the age of no more than four or five, getting into his batting stance with a big league bat that was taller than he was. He was wearing a Brooklyn Dodgers jersey that covered him from shoulders to toes.

"I probably met Jackie in the clubhouse at Ebbets Field," he recalled. "My father would have brought me there in the 1950s. I remember being in the clubhouse with Jackie and shaking his hand."[3]

As a kid, he also got up close to other key Dodgers, including Campanella both before and after the 1958 car accident that ended his playing career and left him paralyzed for the rest of his life.

"Campy came to my bar mitzvah in 1960 in his wheelchair," recalled Reichler, adding about a New York Yankees great: "Whitey Ford danced the hora at my bar mitzvah."

Such were the perks for a kid whose dad was a respected sportswriter based in New York, when the city had three prominent baseball teams. "His religion was baseball," said Reichler. "Baseball was the king of sports then. He lived it and breathed it."

Reichler said his dad grew up on the Lower East Side of Manhattan, and he was most interested in cutting school to play baseball with his friends or sneak into the Polo Grounds for free to watch the New York Giants from the bleachers.

The elder Reichler experienced anti-Semitism early in his journalism career. Before landing at the AP, he was first offered a job at the old United Press International, but the offer was pulled back after a boss found out he was Jewish.

"I think that helped him identify more with Jackie," said his son. "He probably didn't come into contact with a lot of black people before he became the baseball writer at the AP, but they really clicked. He really admired Jackie for his bravery."

In fact, also included with Robinson's personal papers was an original copy of an AP dispatch by Joe Reichler, who interviewed Jackie right after Rickey declared he was being brought up to the Dodgers.

"I am on the spot and I know it, but I'm prepared for it," Robinson declared to Reichler. "I am certain I can win them over in Brooklyn as I did in Montreal."

Robinson added, "It feels wonderful to be a major leaguer, even if I haven't actually played in the big leagues yet. I hope I can justify everybody's faith in me."

Yet in the AP dispatch, Robinson admitted that even this piece of good news paled in comparison to what had happened in Branch Rickey's office in August 1945. "I thought I was dreaming," said Robinson. "Sometimes, I still think it is one long, sweet dream."[4]

The younger Reichler had never seen the original dispatch his father had written about Robinson in April 1947, and he was moved when I e-mailed him photos of the document.

"I heard my dad talking today," he e-mailed me about hearing his father's voice through the article. "What a gift!"

He also had never seen the rough letters exchanged with Robinson. But he noted his father had collaborated with Campanella on his autobiography, *It's Good to Be Alive*, around 1958, and Robinson must have objected to some of the characterizations in a magazine article excerpting the book.

"I also recall that Jackie did not respect Campy because Campy always tried to be liked by everyone and refused to complain or even acknowledge race discrimination," Reichler told me. "This made Jackie appear even more like an 'angry' black man, because he refused to let discrimination go unnoticed."

Though not always framed in such antagonistic terms, Reichler was not the only person to observe major differences between the two stars. In notes prepared for sportswriter Dick Young to help him write his own 1952 biography of Campanella, Rickey offered a comparison of Jackie and Campy with the excessive verbosity for which the Mahatma was famous.

Rickey was quick to assure Young that "there are no odious comparisons that can properly be made" between the players. But "if I may make a casual comparison between the two men, I might suggest as follows: Robinson would be strong and firm in argument of statement; Campanella might be convinced more quickly. Robinson would challenge, but Campanella would placate."

Yet, Rickey inferred in the notes included with his papers at the Library of Congress, Campanella was no "Uncle Tom"—contrary to the criticism he has faced. The two men just had very different strategies, attitudes, and temperaments.

"To a pitcher in incipient distress Campanella would urge, encourage with a 'rally 'round the flag' word and gesture," wrote Rickey. "Robinson might inquire with subtlety and might even be about to use, if he thought advisable, sarcasm or even satire. . . . [Robinson] presented with only one side of an argument might become a quick convert, but capable of change if the other side were later presented. The other would be inclined to think through a thing, less susceptible to early plausibles, or specious influence."[5]

Robinson always felt the tension of how hard he should be agitating for civil rights, continuing throughout his playing career and beyond.

Erskine, who, like Campanella, joined Robinson on the Dodgers in 1948, noted the other factor at play. For all of his abilities to listen to Rickey and not lash out in the early days, Robinson was still a human being; he bruised when he read a story he felt was negative.

"As unbelievable as it sounds, Jackie read *every* article of every newspaper—New York at this time had like twelve newspapers," Erskine told me. "And they all had editions throughout the day . . . Jackie was always quoted and misquoted so much that he never missed reading an article about himself."[6]

To be sure, Robinson and Campy got along as friends and shared an interest in making their race proud. But they would also sometimes operate more as rivals, with disputes over how hard they should both be pushing for civil rights off the field.

Author William C. Kashatus noted in his book *Jackie and Campy* that Robinson was not keen on Campanella's tight relationship with white sportswriters and fans, while Campy was jealous that African American sportswriters seemed to deify the one who came first.[7]

One of those writers, Sam Lacy of the *Baltimore Afro-American*, told author Arnold Rampersad, "Campanella resented Jackie who was a symbol for blacks because of his dark complexion."[8]

Campanella had a much different upbringing in Philadelphia than Robinson's tough childhood in Pasadena, and the catcher had a lighter complexion because he was the product of an Italian father and African American mother.

"Jackie was an assertive spirit when it came to politics and race; Campy had far less interest in such matters," pitcher Ralph Branca noted in his memoir. "The contrast between Jackie and Campy was fascinating—hot-tempered

Robinson and mild-mannered Roy. There were moments when Jackie considered Campy too passive, and times when Campy deemed Jackie too militant."

There may also have been some amount of tension between the two men, as Campanella seemed to steal some of Jackie's thunder. "As a three-time MVP, [Campanella] was the backbone of the iconic Dodger teams of the fifties," added Branca.[9]

Plus there was lingering strain over whether Rickey should have picked Campanella to make history instead of Robinson.

"There was always this question of whether Campanella could have been the first black player instead of Jackie," Erskine told me. "Campy had this passive, sweet, innocent, likable personality. Jackie was a little quick-triggered. So the question was, would Campy have been a better choice?"

Rickey clearly believed Robinson offered a better mix, and that choice panned out almost perfectly. "He said, 'I need a fireball for this role,'" noted Erskine. "'But he's got to know how to control it.'"[10]

CONFLICT OVER CAMPY

All this hung over the uneasy alliance between Robinson and Campanella from 1948, their first season together, through this exchange of letters with Reichler in 1958. In fact, Reichler suggested in his response to Robinson that Jackie was sore about the question of whether Campy should have been first.

Reichler was pleading with Robinson, stressing that Jackie had only been mentioned twice in the story. The first reference came when Campanella had allegedly told Robinson, "Don't spoil it, it's nice up here" in the big leagues, when Jackie wanted to make a bigger issue of discrimination.

"Another time . . . he said, 'I'm no crusader, I'm a ballplayer,' when it was your belief that he should speak up more for his race," Reichler wrote of the second reference to Robinson. "Is that making a patsy out of you? Is that saying, or implying that you were wrong, that you were a troublemaker, that you were bad for the game, that he, and not you, should have been the first Negro in baseball?"

Reichler added, "Certainly, I quoted him as saying how much he regretted not being the first, but that is more or less a credit to you—that you *were* the first."[11]

The timing of this exchange was particularly remarkable. Reichler's response was typed out on February 17, 1958, and he noted he was trying to react quickly to Robinson. That means Robinson sent his angry missive in early February, just days after Campanella's fiery January 28, 1958, crash.

During the baseball off-season, Campanella ran a liquor store in Harlem. That night he closed the store and then started racing home to Glen Cove, a beautiful hamlet on Long Island.

His rented Chevrolet hit a patch of ice around 1:30 a.m. He smashed into a telephone pole, the car overturned, and suddenly his neck snapped. Campanella was left paralyzed from the shoulders down, confined to a wheelchair until his death in 1993. Thanks to countless hours in physical therapy, he was able to use his arms and hands again.

Reichler received Robinson's angry missive in St. Petersburg, Florida, where he was covering the annual ritual of spring training. The writer was bed-ridden because of a virus. But sickness wouldn't stop him from having it out with Jackie in the 1958 letter.

"They're so unfair," Reichler wrote of Robinson's charges. "You couldn't possibly have come to this conclusion about me and about our relationship after all these years. If I didn't know you any better I'd swear you were kidding."

Reichler was mediating a dispute that was years in the making, a clear split between Robinson and Campanella over how hard to push.

"This business of 'don't spoil it,' etc., is typical of Roy," wrote Reichler. "So is the other phrase: 'I'm not a crusader . . .' Roy always has looked out for Roy first, he's never done anything that would tend to get him involved, or disliked, or in a position where he had to take sides. I've always known that. I've said to you more than once that he works at being a politician. And as you see, I'm not afraid to put it in writing here and now."

Reichler clearly did not like being put in the position of having to choose between the two African American stars.

"But that doesn't mean I can't like Roy," he wrote. "I always did. And I never hid that fact from you. Same way as I've always liked you—and still do, very much. Funny thing, many times and in many places, I've been asked to compare you two. I've always said that Roy you can like quicker but Jackie you like longer."

It was a full-on rant for Reichler now, and he let Robinson have it by guilt-tripping him with some kindness.

"I've always pointed out Robinson's sincerity, his honesty, his integrity, his frankness, his sense of loyalty," wrote Reichler. "At the same time, I've mentioned his stubbornness, his sometimes overzealousness and his *suspicion*."

Reichler went on to note he had just done a magazine piece with Warren Spahn, star pitcher for the then-Milwaukee Braves.

"He said the best news the Braves had during the entire winter of 1956 was your announcement that you were quitting," Reichler wrote about Robinson's retirement from the Dodgers, which would make it easier for Milwaukee to compete for the National League's spot in the World Series. "He went on to say how the Milwaukee pitchers dreaded facing you—how you somehow managed to beat them in the big games . . . how even if you didn't get the big hit, you inspired your teammates, etc., etc."

"Does this sound," Reichler asked, "like I'm your enemy?"

This was anguish for Reichler, who wrote that he never intended for the letter to go on so long but he had to get a lot off of his chest.

"You seem to have forgotten the many things you have told me off the record, which were never printed," Reichler added.[12]

Reflecting on it now, Reichler's son tells me, "Campy wanted to be liked by everybody. He would not object or complain if he saw racial slights. I think it made Jackie feel like, 'I'm carrying this cross all by myself. I'm fighting for you, but you won't share in the fight.'"

ROBINSON KEEPS FIGHTING

Robinson had plenty of fights to wage in 1948. Some were principled, like a dispute over his salary. Others were trivial, like a festering battle with manager Leo Durocher over Jackie's weight.

At the end of the 1947 season, Robinson had told *Look* magazine he was hoping to save enough money to set up a nice future for his son, Jackie Jr. "In 1948, I expect to earn much more than $5,000 from the Dodgers," he said. "I've got to make it quick, because I'm 28, older than most people think."[13]

Indeed, discrimination had meant Robinson got his start much later than white stars like Joe DiMaggio and Ted Williams. It meant he lost out big time in racking up statistics—home runs and runs batted in—that he should have collected in his prime.

While players of all races were paid poorly in those days, Robinson did get a raise in February 1948, $5,000 a year to $12,500.

Robinson was able to supplement his salary handsomely after his breakout rookie year with a speaking tour through the South, as well as a "vaudeville" tour where he answered preset baseball questions.

There was a huge downside, however, to his tours. Rickey, who prohibited players from giving speeches and attending banquets during the season, was particularly wary of fans showering Jackie with praise, inadvertently distracting him from the task at hand. So during the season that kept Jackie's focus on baseball and family because he got home most nights to Rachel and their one-year-old, Jackie Jr.

Once Robinson hit the speaking circuit after the season, he could not stop eating. He showed up for spring training, which started in the Dominican Republic, a full twenty-five pounds overweight.

Durocher was back from his one-year suspension, and he was primed to take out his built-up anger on the rest of the National League by having a monster 1948 season. He was furious with his star player for not being in top shape.

The fiery Durocher quickly saw Robinson's mistake as a chance to fire up his team by taking aim at his prized sophomore, declaring that the player looked like "the fat lady at the circus."

"You aren't pregnant with twins, are you?" jabbed Durocher.[14]

Robinson acknowledged later that he knew Durocher was a "magnificent tongue-lasher" who used his fiery personality to motivate players, and in this case he was justified in his alarm about the player's weight.

Yet Robinson, who had a legendary temper of his own, was furious that Durocher decided to air those concerns within earshot of the media, sparking a round of embarrassing stories.

"I had been on a personal-appearance tour in the South that winter, and I had been entertained in too many homes with too much food, especially hot breads," noted Robinson. "Leo was tough on me. He would hit grounders, fast ones that I had to chase and bend down for, and he would keep me hustling for ten minutes. Then he'd let me rest and start it again."[15]

Durocher had stood up for Robinson in Panama one year earlier, but now they were feuding. Jackie was able to bury the hatchet for a moment when it came out that Durocher would be moving to the Giants. In a July 1948 column, he called the manager a "human dynamo [who] expects the best that a player has at all times and when he figures a player isn't doing his best he tells you about it in no uncertain terms." But the two men would continue to clash, and they almost came to blows a few times.[16]

Robinson was furious when he came to bat in the Polo Grounds in 1951 and heard Durocher shout out that his former player now had a swollen head. "I turned to him and asked if he was still using Laraine Day's perfume," Robinson recalled in reference to Durocher's movie-star wife. "He blew up. From then on, for the rest of the season, no [holds] were barred. I could not repeat the things we said to each other."[17]

They eventually patched things up at the 1952 All-Star Game. But Durocher may have had another motive in cooling things down. The manager admitted to one of Robinson's friends that he knew making Jackie mad only fired him to play even better, so the Giants skipper realized he should stop giving the Dodgers star more motivation to beat him.

For all of his accomplishments on the field, though, Robinson always maintained that he was more proud of his willingness to take on bigger social battles, even if it caused friction with Campanella and others.

"Sure, everything would be a lot safer for me if I took it easy on the hot subjects," Robinson told *Sport* magazine in 1960, a few years after he had retired. "I'd probably get a little further. If I steered clear of controversy when I was a ballplayer, life would have been a lot more pleasant, too. I would have been better liked than I was. Being better liked, I would have got more awards. You know that. You know that a lot of people said after a couple of years that I was too aggressive, that I should have taken it easier in fighting and jockeying and yelling at umpires."

Robinson went on to invoke Campanella and Reichler, as well as an acerbic New York sports columnist, Dick Young.

"There is even a story that Dick Young and Joe Reichler insist is true," said Robinson. "They say they heard Roy Campanella tell me, 'Don't louse things up for us, Jackie.' I say that never happened, because I don't remember Roy ever saying that to me. But you see what I mean about people liking me more if I had stayed out of controversies when I was playing ball."

Robinson added, "But say I had and say I had won more awards. You know, if I had a plaque up on the wall and I thought I had won it because I was less aggressive about my rights—I wouldn't want to look at the plaque. I wouldn't have any pride in it and I wouldn't have any pride in myself, either."[18]

UN-AMERICAN ACTIVITIES

LIFE magazine ran a full-page editorial on August 1, 1949, defending Robinson in a major controversy—one of the first of his many forays into American politics. Robinson took heat from some fellow African Americans for testifying—he said reluctantly so—the previous month before the House Un-American Activities Committee, which had been formed to wipe out pro-Communist subversion in America.[19]

The tension came from Robinson discrediting his fellow civil rights activist Paul Robeson, who was heavily scrutinized by the US government because of his Communist and Soviet sympathies.

The actor and singer eventually had his passport revoked after a series of incidents, including a speech about the Cold War that Robeson made in Paris. There he reportedly claimed, "It is unthinkable that American Negroes would go to war on behalf of those who have oppressed us against a country [the Soviet Union] which in one generation has raised our people to the full dignity of mankind."[20]

These and other comments led to more than eighty of Robeson's scheduled concerts being cancelled in 1949 and 1950.

Robinson admitted later he was deeply conflicted about blasting Robeson, and he expressed regret. "I didn't want to fall prey to the white man's game and allow myself to be pitted against another black man," he wrote.[21]

But Robinson believed Robeson should not have held himself up as a spokesman for all African Americans, and he feared the activist's ties to Communism would set back the cause of the American civil rights movement.

After accepting the invitation to testify, Robinson received a mountain of outraged telegrams from fellow African Americans. Yet he plowed ahead, declaring during his testimony that Robeson's claim that his race would not fight the Soviets "sounds very silly to me."

"I understand that there are some few Negroes who are members of the Communist party, and in event of war with Russia they would probably act just as any other Communists would," testified Robinson. "Most Negroes—and Italians and Irish and Jews and Swedes and Slavs and other Americans—would act just as all these groups did in the last war. They'd do their best to help their country stay out of war; if unsuccessful, they'd do their best to help their country win the war—against Russia or any other enemy that threatened us."

Robinson wove in his own experience, including his faith in God and his time in baseball.

"I know that life in these United States can be mighty tough for people who are a little different from the majority—in their skin color or the way they worship their God, or the way they spell their names," said Robinson. "I'm not fooled because I've had a chance open to very few Negro Americans. It's true that I've been the laboratory specimen in a great change in organized baseball. I'm proud that I've made good on my assignment to the point where other colored players will find it easier to enter the game and go to the top."

There were more religious overtones as Robinson referenced Robeson's background as a singer to declare that people of different races and faiths had too much invested in America to "throw it away because of a siren song sung in bass."

"I am a religious man," said Robinson. "Therefore I cherish America where I am free to worship as I please, a privilege which some countries do not give. And I suspect that 999 out of almost any 1,000 colored Americans you meet will tell you the same thing. But that doesn't mean that we're going to stop fighting race discrimination in this country until we've got it licked. It means that we're going to fight it all the harder because our stake in the future is so big."[22]

At the end of the speech, someone in the audience on Capitol Hill cried out, "Amen!"[23]

In its August 1, 1949, edition, *Quick* magazine (in a story titled "Jackie Robinson: He Fights and Steals") hailed Robinson's testimony by tying it to the fact that he was now leading the National League in runs and runs batted in, while topping the American and National leagues in hits, stolen bases, and batting average.

"Jackie last week scored a few more points," declared the magazine. "In a speech that made him a national champion of democracy, Jackie said that singer Paul Robeson's claims that Negroes would not fight Russia were 'silly' and 'untrue.'"[24]

Meanwhile, *LIFE* magazine editorialized that the ballplayer had met Robeson's "libel with a very simple point: US Negroes are Americans." This advocacy on Robinson's behalf led to a headline that seemed to almost plead with Americans to accept African Americans as—well—Americans. "Negroes Are Americans," said the magazine's headline. "Jackie Robinson Proves It in Words and on the Ball Field."

The magazine added of Robinson, "He is also an intensely respectable man who takes proper pride in his handsome family (opposite) and in his success as the first Negro admitted to major-league baseball."[25] *LIFE* was referencing a beautiful portrait on the opposite page picturing Jackie and Rachel with their two-year-old son, Jackie Jr.

Yet this important story did not merit more than two pages or that week's cover story. Instead, the cover photo belonged to a smiling Joe

DiMaggio, the legendary outfielder for the New York Yankees. America needed six full pages of details about how "baseball's biggest hero" was back and better than ever after a heel injury nearly ended his career.[26]

It was a reminder that baseball was still a white man's game—being played in a white man's world. But Robinson had yet another major challenge to deal with. He was about to see a dramatic change in the relationship with his key protector and ally, Branch Rickey.

CHAPTER 16

LOSING RICKEY

Carl Erskine carefully thought over my question about how often he attended church during his days with the Dodgers.

Since most games were in the afternoon in those days, Erskine liked to get up early and start walking the streets of Brooklyn when the Dodgers were home. It gave him a workout—and a chance to look for a church of any denomination.

"I would just go into a Presbyterian church, whatever I could find, and sit in the sanctuary for five or ten minutes," Erskine said. "That was my worship for the day. That's a great exercise. I used to say at Sunday school years later, 'You've got to go to a church when it's *not* open. You find some really great moments in there at that time.'"[1]

Erskine was raised a Baptist in Anderson, Indiana, and his mother ingrained in him early the habit of attending church every Sunday.

Even if Erskine was not excited about that as a boy, he recalled with a chuckle, as a teenager he met a girl at that church. He started attending more eagerly to get more frequent contact with Betty, who became his wife. In 2017, they celebrate their seventieth wedding anniversary.

Branch Rickey was another motivating factor in Erskine staying serious about his faith. The former pitcher notes that after the general manager surprised him in their first meeting by asking if he went to church, Rickey expounded on that.

"I ask that of *every* young player that I sign," Rickey told Erskine. "Anyone who will discipline their life and sit in a place of worship on a regular basis, and think on the teachings of Christ, will develop something you can not get in the same measure anywhere else. A quiet self-confidence."

Erskine let that sink in. A quiet self-confidence.

Rickey was trying to mold young players and teach them that focusing on their faith would help them deal with the intensity of big league baseball and life in general.

"And it will stand you in great stead no matter what pressures life gives you," Rickey told Erskine about that confidence. "It's true for truck drivers, housewives, ditch diggers, and major league ballplayers."

Erskine often thought back on that first one-on-one with Rickey when he was pitching in front of huge crowds down the road. "I stood in Yankee Stadium my first time and I looked around—seventy thousand people," he recalled. "I said, 'That's more people than live in Anderson, Indiana.' It would shake your boots."

Well, that kid shaking in his boots grew into a pitcher who once set a record by striking out fourteen New York Yankees in a World Series game. That included the great Mickey Mantle four times, all in Game 3 of the 1953 World Series.

The point is, Rickey had a deep influence on many players beyond just Robinson. But it was probably Jackie who took it the hardest when the general manager and part owner of the Dodgers left the team in 1950.

Part of their close bond came from that longstanding commonality—the fact that Robinson also believed there were similarities between sports and religion. "My concept of religion is of people having faith in God, in themselves and in each other and putting that faith into action," Robinson wrote in his unpublished manuscript. "If you can find a better example of those four things than a team of sportsmen working as a unit, I'd like to know what it is."[2]

On that very point, 1950 was a breakout year for Robinson; he felt that many of his teammates beyond the usual suspects like Erskine and Pee Wee Reese were finally embracing him. But it was bittersweet because it came just as Rickey was being shoved out the door.

The man who pushed Rickey out was Walter O'Malley. The move became the first step in O'Malley taking over the Dodgers—and ultimately becoming reviled by the fans for ripping the team out of Brooklyn. In 1950, the team was divided into four 25 percent shares between O'Malley, Rickey, businessman John Smith, and Dearie and James Mulvey, whose daughter Ann would soon marry pitcher Ralph Branca.

O'Malley, the team's vice president and chief counsel, decided he wanted to consolidate power. Following Smith's death in July 1950, O'Malley got Smith's widow to let him control her share, and then set his sights on pushing Rickey aside.

O'Malley initially tried to lowball Rickey with a $300,000 offer, which is what he had paid to buy into the Dodgers a few years earlier.

Just in the nick of time, however, Pittsburgh Pirates owner John Galbreath hatched a plan to please both Rickey and himself. A good friend of Rickey, Galbreath wanted him for the Pirates. So he reached out to real estate mogul William Zeckendorf Sr. and got him to offer Rickey roughly $1 million for his share of the Dodgers, forcing O'Malley to up his offer. A previous agreement required partners to match any outside offers if the partner wished to purchase another's share.

Irritated as he was to have to shell out a heftier price, O'Malley begrudgingly matched Zeckendorf's offer, paying Rickey about $1 million for his 25 percent piece of the Dodgers. Rickey was instantly scooped up by the Pirates to be their general manager, pleasing both Rickey and Galbreath. (Zeckendorf got $50,000 for being the middleman, and the Pirates received the wisdom of Rickey, who ended up drafting the great Roberto Clemente for the team.)

Far less happy was Robinson, who knew Rickey was his partner in making history. Robinson was prescient in being nervous about his own status with O'Malley, concerns that he confided to Branca during spring training in 1950.

"He's my guy," Robinson said of Rickey. "He's one of the greatest men I've ever known. I don't know this O'Malley."

"I've heard he's okay," said Branca, comparing O'Malley favorably to "El Cheapo" in contract negotiations.

"He was fair with me," Robinson said of Rickey.

"I understand that, Jackie, and no one's gonna forget how he brought you up," said Branca. "Ultimately, though, you made your own mark. You're the guy—not Branch Rickey—who got the hits, made the catches, and ran the bases."

"I don't know, Ralph," said Jackie. "I feel kind of vulnerable without knowing Rickey's in my corner."

Branca saw a silver lining, though, noting Rickey had demanded that Robinson hold his tongue and not fight back for the first few years.

"Well, those three years are gone and so is Rickey," said Branca. "You can say what you want and be who you are. You can tell the umps where they can go—especially the ones who haven't been giving you the calls."[3]

Jackie had predicted this would be his true Emancipation Day. And suddenly, late in the 1950 season, with Rickey gone, something else liberating happened. His teammates were welcoming him even more.

WISECRACKS DURING BATTING PRACTICE

One afternoon in September at Ebbets Field, several Dodgers were standing around the netting behind home plate designed to protect fans from flying baseballs during batting practice before the game. "Waiting like a lot of hungry dogs, I thought, to tear this batting-practice pitcher apart," Robinson noted about the ravenous Dodgers ready to take their licks at the plate.

Robinson was feeling tentative because he had been out of the lineup for ten days with an injured left hand. Just to be safe, his thumb and pointer finger were padded with sponge rubber as he stepped up to the plate.

The first pitch came in. Robinson hit it weakly straight up in the air, which would be an easy pop out in a game.

"A home run!" jabbed outfielder Carl Furillo with a laugh. "That is, if we're playing this game in an elevator shaft!" (Furillo was known for his rifle-shot arm in right field, which author Roger Kahn wrote was so strong he could throw a lamb chop past a wolf.)[4]

Robinson mumbled something in return, and then took a cut at the second pitch. He hit a puny line drive that just barely made it to the outfield grass.

"What power that Number 42 has!" shortstop Reese yelled over to first baseman Gil Hodges.

Reese then turned to Robinson, and added in a mocking tone: "I do believe you're hitting the ball better now, Jackie, than before you were hurt."

Robinson normally could get his back up right quick, but this time he took it all in with calm confidence. He was making a remarkable discovery there in the batting cage.

"When they kid you, they like you," Robinson noted months later. "To them, as they said those things, I was just another ballplayer. Not black nor white, but just a right-handed hitter who could run pretty good and fitted in on this club at second base."

Robinson's hand was sore from the swinging, and his ears were burning from the wisecracks. But he actually felt good about the teasing. It meant he mattered to his teammates.

"What nice guys, I thought," Robinson recalled. "Lucky you, Robinson, to get into a bunch like this."

Just four years earlier, during Robinson's first spring training in 1946, he had noticed many of his teammates usually didn't openly try to taunt him or bring him down. Instead they just stayed mum, indifferent to his cause, feeling it was best to let Robinson sink or swim on his own.

"The same ballplayers would have stood around that cage stony-faced, saying nothing," he noted.[5]

In the final month of that 1950 season, Robinson also learned that he could no longer jump to conclusions when fans shouted at him, as he recounted in a first-person story for *Look* magazine.

Robinson was in the dugout grabbing a bat when he heard a fan shout, "Jackie, hit a home run and I'll give you a watermelon!"

A gruff Robinson told the man he was none too pleased at what seemed like a racial slur, except there was more to the story. Harold Parrott, the Dodgers' traveling secretary, brought the man to the clubhouse after the game.

The man was in tears as he declared, "I've always rooted for you, Jackie, and now you treat me like this!"

Robinson was confused, because he was the one who felt insulted. But the man explained that he was a fruit peddler who dragged his horse and cart around Brooklyn. He had previously brought watermelons to Robinson's teammate Gil Hodges for his family and was sincere about offering some to Robinson.

Robinson felt terrible about his mistake. He wrote that maybe it was a silly reminder of a serious fact about how easy it is to misunderstand one another, when in fact he felt race relations were starting to get better: "The road ahead is brighter and, as I've told you, there are many encouraging signs along the way. But none of us should let down now. We should fight all the harder—because our stake in the future is so big."[6]

Another humorous moment came during the 1951 season after Robinson received a particularly troublesome letter threatening his life. He was tense, but his teammates knew just how to diffuse the tension. "The next day the players got together in the dugout and said they'd all put on black face and wear my number '42' so the would-be killer wouldn't know who to shoot at," Robinson recalled. "That made me feel real good."[7]

Clearly, there had been a conversion in some of his teammates, who learned to welcome Robinson as just one of the guys. But Jackie had also made adjustments. He decided to be more forgiving.

During the 1950 season, someone on the Dodgers circulated a petition. This one was about a mundane team matter. While Robinson did not specify the topic of the petition, he suggested it was far more innocuous than that controversial one in Panama.

When the new petition was mentioned in the clubhouse in 1950, one of the outfielders who had signed the original petition (Robinson did not reveal which player) decided to make a point. "Wait a minute," the player said with a big wink and a smile. "I now read all petitions carefully. I don't want to make another mistake!"

Robinson knew what the player meant, and he appreciated his teammate going out of his way to acknowledge the previous error. "He had made a mistake, back in 1947," noted Robinson. "But it was a quick mistake. Give him time, and his decency came out. It was showing now, through that wink."[8]

Robinson was also hitting his stride on the field in 1950, with a strong .328 batting average leading him to his second consecutive All-Star Game. Yet tension would soon rise between Robinson and O'Malley.

JACKIE GOES HOLLYWOOD

O'Malley did little to mask his feeling that Jackie had a tendency to put himself above the team. "Robinson is always conscious of publicity and is always seeking publicity," O'Malley said at one time in their tense relationship. "Maybe it's a speech he's about to make or a sale at his store, but when Robinson gets his name in the headlines, you can be sure there's a reason."[9]

Robinson gave as good as he got. Before the 1952 World Series, Jackie went out of his way to tell reporters he wanted to bring home a championship for two people, and the owner was not one of them. "Rae and Mr. Rickey," he said, using his nickname for his wife, and, of course, referencing his original mentor.

Rickey had been replaced by O'Malley as the supreme leader of the Dodgers and was long gone, now running Pittsburgh's team. "But I wanted to let Mr. Rickey know where he stood in my book," Robinson said, poking O'Malley again.

Robinson added, in case O'Malley didn't catch the previous slams, that of all the people he had met in baseball, he considered Rickey "the finest, in a class by himself."

If Robinson had laid it on pretty thick, it may have had something to do with some acting skills he had recently started developing.

Shortly before spring training in 1950, Robinson went Hollywood, heading home to California to play himself in the film *The Jackie Robinson Story.* He got a cover story in *LIFE* magazine. The story noted when

Robinson was a kid, a pro ballplayer saw him play and remarked, "He'd be worth a million in baseball if he were white."

While Robinson grew up to prove that the color of his skin ultimately did not matter, he was still far short of reaching a million bucks. At the age of thirty-one, after several seasons of excellence, he was making $35,000 a year with the Dodgers (though that did make him the highest-paid member of the team at that time), and was getting $30,000 plus 15 percent of the profits for the Hollywood movie.

While he started out nervous, after convincing Rachel to be with him during the shooting he was flawless in delivering his lines. He got flustered only once: he was filming a romantic scene in his UCLA football uniform with his movie wife, Ruby Dee, when Rae walked onto the set.

The film included a scene where a fan tosses a black cat onto the field and shouts, "Here's a brother of yours, Jackie. Why don't you take him along? He wants to get into baseball too." Refusing to take the bait, Jackie brought the kitty into the dugout and decided to pet it.[10]

Robinson also got to bring his young son, Jackie Jr., just three years old, to Pepper Street in Pasadena to see his own boyhood home. The only hitch was the bellyache or two Jackie Jr. got after the film crew gave him a stash of candy, gum, and Coca-Cola.

Despite taking the time to shoot the film, it did not slow Robinson down at the plate. He was on fire his first week back with the Dodgers, hitting at a sizzling pace of .455.

Though there was a downside to going Hollywood. When he took a called strike without swinging the bat, a fan was heard taunting him, "What are you waiting for, Jackie, the camera?"[11]

MISSING RICKEY

Despite his busy life, it was difficult for Robinson to lose close contact with Rickey. Later he would express his feelings in a beautiful letter to his former boss in 1950, after Rickey had left the team.

"Dear Mr. Rickey: I have been intending to write for about a month now and it seems that finding the right words come hard so I will attempt at this time to put them down," Robinson began in the letter that is now with Rickey's personal papers at the Library of Congress. He wrote in blue ink on stationery from the Hotel Jaragua, located in Ciudad Trujillo (now Santo Domingo) in the Dominican Republic, where Jackie and Rae were relaxing after the 1950 season.

"It is certainly tough on everyone in Brooklyn to have you leave the organization but to me its [sic] much worse, and I don't mind saying we (my family) hate to see you go but realize that baseball is like that and anything can happen," added Robinson.

"It has been the finest experience I have had being associated with you, and I want to thank you very much for all you have meant not only to me and my family but to the entire country and particularly the members of our race."

Then Robinson turned overly modest as he heaped most of the credit on Rickey.

"I am glad for your sake that I had a small part to do with the success of your efforts and must admit it was your constant guidance that enabled me to do it," wrote Robinson. "Regardless of what happens to me in the future it all can be placed on what you have done, and believe me, I appreciate it."

Robinson stressed he did not know all the details that led Rickey to sell his share, and added that while he wanted to play his whole career with the Dodgers, he was open to going to the Pirates.

"I hope to end my playing in Brooklyn as it means so very much, but if I have to go any place I hope it can be with you," wrote Robinson.[12]

Rickey apologized for taking a long while to respond, but sent a gracious letter of his own on New Year's Eve 1950.

"I have observed that you have learned long ago that most things, good or bad, just don't happen to people by accident," wrote Rickey. "Your thoughtfulness in the field of so-called unimportant things has doubtless led to much of your success."

Rickey added that he hoped Robinson would become baseball's first African American field manager down the road.

"I do not know of any player in the game today who could, in my judg-ment, manage a major league club better than yourself," wrote Rickey. "I recently made this statement in the presence of several writers in the course of various remarks, but I have looked in vain for the reporting of the statement."

Since Christmas had just passed, Rickey said he had been thinking fondly of Rachel Robinson and the rest of the family. "I choose to feel that my acquaintanceship with you has ripened into a very real friendship, growing out of our facing and trying to solve common problems and our continuous record of seeing eye to eye in practically all of these problems that faced us," wrote Rickey.[13]

It was not just Robinson and Rickey themselves who believed their partnership was special—and perhaps even divinely inspired.

Rickey's papers at the Library of Congress include a copy of a sermon delivered on September 17, 1950, by Dr. F. Gerald Ensley at the North Broadway Methodist Church in Columbus, Ohio. He used the story of Robinson and Rickey to preach about creativity in the face of seemingly impossible challenges.

The sermon was based on Jeremiah 12:5: "If you have run with men on foot, and they have tired you out, then how will you keep up with horses?"[14]

Ensley's interpretation of this line was that life "tends to get tougher as it goes along," though he insisted that his congregation should not be discouraged by that. Rather, encouragement comes from us getting both stronger and more creative with each successive challenge. "Isn't it this very toughening of life that makes it interesting, and enjoyable, and worth-while?" asked Ensley.

"So with these mountainous social problems of our time, they can be circumvented or tunneled through, if creative intelligence is brought to bear upon them," declared Ensley. "Mr. Rickey's overcoming of prejudice in baseball is an instance of it."[15]

It's an inspiring cap to the Robinson-Rickey partnership. Now Robinson would have to go on without his mentor, and there was one incredible mountainous problem waiting for the Dodgers in 1951.

CHAPTER 17

"THE GIANTS WIN THE PENNANT!"

More than an hour had passed at the Clayton private cigar club in Chicago, and Jerry Reinsdorf lit his second stogie of the night.

He was trying to explain his hatred of the old New York Giants and Bobby Thomson, the man who hit that infamous home run to block Reinsdorf's beloved Brooklyn Dodgers from reaching the World Series in 1951.

"Did I tell you about my doctor friend?" he said. "A friend of mine from Brooklyn becomes a doctor. He's in New Jersey—Alan Fine—and Bobby Thomson comes in as a patient. He says, 'I can't treat you. You ruined my life.'"

The story is only slightly exaggerated. Thomson did walk into the office of Dr. Fine, who said all that. But the doctor, a mensch from Brooklyn, treated Thomson anyway.

"When Thomson hit that home run, ohhhh . . . people were crying in the streets," Reinsdorf said. "I remember taking a rubber ball and just throwing it against the wall over and over and over. Against the wall of a building—I just kept throwing it and throwing and *throwing it*!"[1]

Imagine what it must have felt like for Jackie Robinson, who was playing second base when the home run was hit. He was so competitive that he once famously said, "Above anything else, I hate to lose."[2]

The intensity of Reinsdorf's feelings so many years later reminded me of something Carl Erskine had told me at that IHOP in Indiana.

"The rivalry was intense—it was built up over decades," Erskine said of the battles between the Dodgers and Giants of the National League, who both desperately tried to win the right to face the hated New York Yankees of the American League in the World Series year after year.

These clashes even divided households in New York throughout the 1940s and 1950s. "I never knew a family that wasn't split two ways," said Erskine. "And many times they were split three ways."[3]

In the big game on October 3, 1951, Erskine was right in the thick of it at the Polo Grounds, the Giants' home turf.

He was in the bullpen in the ninth inning, when the Dodgers were clinging to a lead and manager Chuck Dressen had to choose which pitcher would relieve a tiring Don Newcombe. It was either Erskine or Ralph Branca, the man who won plaudits for bravely standing up for Robinson early on.

Dressen stood at just five feet, five inches, and after games, he swapped war stories while drinking a glass of Scotch mixed with black cherry soda. He was proud to be a simple man from Decatur, Illinois, quick to mention he had never read a book in his life.[4]

Author Roger Kahn recalled telling Dressen one time that one player was an "intelligent" man.

"What? What's that? What's that word? Starts with a 'I.'"

"Intelligent," said Kahn.

"Yup," said Dressen. "That's it. All ballplayers is dumb."

"All?" asked Kahn.

"And outfielders is the dumbest," the manager responded.[5]

When Dressen called the bullpen on the dugout telephone on that day in 1951, he was told that Erskine was bouncing his curveball into the dirt, so he should probably go with Branca instead. Dressen went with Branca, even though he had given up a homer to Thomson a couple of days earlier. It was one of several fateful decisions Dressen made that day.

Branca was still alive and nearing ninety years old when I started writing this book. After sending word through Erskine that he would talk to me, Branca did not return several phone messages I left for him. I finally reached his wife, Ann, who confided in the summer of 2016 that he was quite ill and unable to do an interview. He died in November and was widely and justifiably hailed for the class and grace he demonstrated throughout his life.

Giving up the home run was a heavy burden for Branca to carry, so I pressed Erskine on whether he ever woke up in the middle of the night thinking his whole career would have been different if he had been called into the game instead of his teammate.

Oh, yes, he has woken up feeling that way many times, Erskine said, adding with a laugh, "When people say, 'Carl, you pitched twelve seasons in the big leagues, what was your best pitch?' I say, 'The curveball I threw into the dirt at the Polo Grounds.'"

Branca received some vindication in January 2001, when *Wall Street Journal* reporter Joshua Prager reported that the famous headline may have really been, "The Giants steal the pennant!"[6] Prager ended up writing a terrific book, *The Echoing Green*, which laid out how the Giants had secretly set up an elaborate system at their ballpark in order to steal signs from the opposing team. That made it possible that Thomson knew a fastball was coming from Branca, and thus it would be easier to hit the home run.

Erskine praised Prager's book. "It was fascinating," he said.[7]

So when I met up with Reinsdorf, I asked if he had read it. After all, he has read everything on the Brooklyn Dodgers, and he is so meticulous about getting the facts about his beloved team correct that he offered to help copyedit the book you are reading. (Reinsdorf sent a letter to author Thomas Oliphant in 2005, pointing out eleven factual errors in his book *Praying for Gil Hodges*, though the owner cushioned the blow by writing he found the book "thoroughly enjoyable" and simply has a "compulsion" to fix mistakes because of incorrect stories written about his business over the years.)

So what did Reinsdorf think about the Prager book?

"I wouldn't read a book about the Giants," he said.

"Wait," I said. "At least half the book is about the Dodgers."

"I wouldn't read a book about the Giants," Reinsdorf repeated. "I still hate 'em."[8]

In contrast, love was on Branca's mind before the start of the 1951 season. He had mustered the courage to pop the question to Ann Mulvey, daughter of James and Dearie Mulvey, part owners of the Dodgers.

"Before I give you my answer, let's see what kind of season you have," Ann Mulvey told Branca.[9]

Branca's heart sank for a second, but she was just kidding. Still, he was old school and wanted to ask her father for permission. Mulvey ultimately gave his permission and said he and his wife would pay for the wedding.

"We're thinking late October," said Branca.

The couple would settle on October 20, 1951, at St. Francis Church in Brooklyn. That would be shortly after the World Series the Dodgers hoped to win. Mulvey wondered whether there might be another Subway Series with the Yankees. Yes, said Branca, adding boldly that it would result in the Dodgers' first World Championship in history.

"With a happy ending like this, I can't wait to get out to the mound," said Branca. "I don't anticipate any problems."[10]

Ouch.

But in fairness, there was a lot of optimism among Dodgers fans at that time, even after several consecutive years of heartbreak. In 1946, the Dodgers were tied with the Cardinals at the end of the regular season but lost a playoff series, sending the Cardinals to the World Series instead. Then in 1947, Robinson's first season was spoiled somewhat when the Yankees beat the Dodgers in a close seven-game World Series. Fast-forward to 1949, and the Yankees crushed the Dodgers in the Series this time, four games to one.

At the end of the 1950 season, all the Dodgers had to do was beat the Phillies on the last day of the regular season to force a playoff to decide who would go to the World Series. They lost.

So as the Dodgers prepared for the 1951 season, Branca was justified in telling his future father-in-law that they were finally primed to take their first world championship. And this time on the last day of the regular season, they did not lose the pivotal game.

Jackie Robinson would make sure of it.

PRESSURE COOKER

It was a roller-coaster year for the Dodgers. They were running on all cylinders early that season, building a huge thirteen-and-a-half game lead over the Giants for the National League pennant.

In the summer, the Dodgers started to struggle. The Giants beat them up in an August series at their home park, the Polo Grounds, thanks in part to strong play from a Giants rookie named Willie Mays.

Mays, of course, was one of several African American stars lighting up the National League, thanks to the road paved by none other than Robinson.

After the regular-season losses to the Giants, the Dodgers' first-place lead was shrinking a little, but Brooklyn was still in command. Yet Dressen—the pint-sized Dodgers manager—was starting to panic.

"Lose another series like this and we're dead meat!" he yelled at his team. "Dead meat! Do you hear me?"[11]

The team needed a calm, steady hand, but there was Dressen pushing the panic button. It was one in a series of dubious moves he made right up until the end of the season.

After the tongue-lashing he unleashed on his team, Dressen also seemed to lose trust in many of his pitchers. So he started using Branca and Newcombe over and over, eventually wearing them down.

In the fall, the Dodgers collapsed while the Giants won a stunning thirty-seven of forty-four games to close out the season and seize first place. Prager would reveal many years later that the Giants' cheating system was set up in the summer, just as they started tearing up the league.

But the Dodgers could still muster a tie for first place anyway, and the right to play the Giants in a best-of-three playoff series to decide the pennant. They first had to beat the Phillies in the final game of the regular season, on Sunday, September 30, with Branca headed to the mound for the Dodgers.

Branca woke up and went to Catholic Mass that Sunday, but he could not quite bring himself to pray for the Dodgers to prevail over the Giants. He recalled in his memoir that in church he simply thanked God for the gift of life and for giving good health to his family, and he left it at that.

After church, though, Branca started thinking about how bad he needed to beat the Phillies so the Dodgers could get to the World Series. He started rethinking his policy of not directly asking God to favor one team.

"Maybe I'd make this one exception," noted Branca. "But I didn't. I still didn't see God wearing a Dodger cap."[12]

In the pivotal game against the Phillies later on Sunday, Branca was pulled from the game in the fourth inning with the Dodgers already down four runs.

The Dodgers did rally to bail Branca out, tying the game and sending it into extra innings. Newcombe was called on to pitch a remarkable five and two-thirds innings of relief. Dressen continued his reliance on Newcombe and Branca to the point of exhaustion.

In the twelfth inning, the Dodgers were on the verge of losing it all, until Robinson thrust the team on his shoulders the way that Hall of Famers simply do.

The bases were loaded for the Phillies, so any kind of a hit could win the game if a single run scored. The batter smashed a low line drive heading toward the ground for a hit near second base, and it appeared the game was going to be over.

Yet Robinson made almost an impossible catch, lunging a long distance, snagging the ball a few inches before it hit the ground. "In doing so, he jammed his elbow into his stomach with such force that he lost consciousness," noted Branca.[13]

Sitting in the stands, Rachel Robinson broke into tears.

"She was sure I was dead," recalled Jackie, adding he also thought he was maimed as he regained consciousness and awoke face down in the dirt.[14]

It was Pee Wee Reese, the shortstop, who came to the rescue. He trotted over and started joking, pulling Robinson together. But Robinson felt too groggy and wanted to pull himself from the game.

It's a good thing Reese intervened, because Robinson came to bat two innings later. "The crack of the bat made that sound, that beautiful, satisfying, sensational sound that said cowhide had kissed wood, and the ball took off, the ball sailed, the ball soared into space—up, up into the left-field seats," added Branca.[15]

Robinson blasted his home run off Phillies pitcher Robin Roberts. More importantly, it won the game and sent the Dodgers into that three-game playoff versus the Giants with what appeared to be a head of steam.

Game 1 was on October 1, 1951, at Brooklyn's home park, and the Dodgers sent Branca to the mound. He had won two games against the Giants in the regular season, but Branca took a tough loss this time, 3–1.

And in a little bit of foreshadowing, Branca gave up a home run to Thomson, who even before then had swatted thirty home runs that season. It was potentially a key piece of information for Dressen to chew on as the series played out.

Game 2 was also at Ebbets Field on October 2, 1951. The Dodgers evened the series by cruising to a 10–0 victory, a shutout by pitcher Clem Labine. The win came thanks to four home runs by Brooklyn, including Robinson's nineteenth of the season, one of three hits he had on the day.

For Game 3, the series shifted to the Giants' park, the Polo Grounds, yet Branca was feeling good. The sometime-crooner remembers singing in the shower, "Oh, What a Beautiful Morning" from *Oklahoma!* even though he was nervous about the deciding game. "I was singing at the top of my lungs," noted Branca. "It was a beautiful morning. It was gonna be a beautiful day. My hopes were high. My spirit was strong."[16]

And the game on the road started beautifully for Brooklyn. Robinson rapped a single in the top of the first inning, driving in Reese for the first run of this pivotal game. That narrow lead held for a long time, as Newcombe and Sal Maglie of the Giants settled in for a pitcher's duel, until Thomson struck again by knocking in the tying run in the seventh inning with a hit.

Then in the top of the eighth, the Dodgers scored three runs to give them a commanding 4–1 lead.

Reinsdorf, who had been to that exhibition game at Ebbets Field at the start of Robinson's historic first season, was then fifteen years old and watching this game on his family's first television set. "My mother calls—she was at the grocery store—I guess she was late," said Reinsdorf. "She was calling to say she was on her way home. And I said, 'Well, by the time you get home, the Dodgers will be champions.'"

And to this day, the owner of the White Sox and the Bulls still believes he jinxed his team.

"I hold myself personally responsible," Reinsdorf said with a sigh.[17]

Newcombe was ready to pitch the bottom of the ninth inning to try to close out the victory for the Dodgers. He was getting tired, however, after being overused by Dressen in the final months of the season.

By comparison, modern-day pitchers are coddled. They might toss six or seven innings every five days, which is child's play compared to what Newcombe was pulling off.

Just four days before this playoff started, Newcombe had pitched a complete game of nine innings against the Phillies on the next-to-last day of the regular season. Then the very next day, in the big final regular-season game that Robinson won with the homer in extra innings, Newcombe pitched those five and two-thirds innings to keep the Dodgers in the game.

So Newcombe could be forgiven if the reports were true that he tried to pull himself from this game before the ninth inning. After all, in the span of five days, he had now pitched almost twenty-three innings.

The pitcher later insisted he never tried to beg out, and even if he considered it, Newcombe could not go through with leaving the game. He walked back out to the mound for the ninth inning after a stirring motivational pep talk from his friend Robinson, who urged him to pitch until his arm fell off.

Just in case, Dressen had three pitchers taking turns warming up in the bullpen: Branca, Erskine, and Labine. Since Labine had pitched that shutout the previous day, he was unlikely to come in and was just insurance.

The leadoff batter for the Giants was their captain, Alvin Dark, who got a single. He was one of the best shortstops in Major League Baseball history, and became a successful manager of the Giants in the early 1960s. (There was, however, a severe stumble in 1964 when a story claimed Dark questioned the mental capacity of African American and Hispanic players. He said he was misquoted, and Robinson defended the manager's character.)

Despite Dark's many achievements on the field, it was hard to beat starting one of the most dramatic comebacks ever as a career highlight. With the Dodgers holding a three-run lead, Dark was not going to risk a stolen base that might lead to an easy out and snuff out the rally. So Dressen should have dropped the Dodgers' infielders back to their normal positions in order to prepare for a potential double-play grounder.

Yet first baseman Gil Hodges held the runner on first base, staying close to the bag in order to prevent a stolen base. That left a big gap in the spot he would normally cover between first base and second base.

Sure enough, the next hitter shot a ball right through that hole, past a diving Hodges. In the bullpen, the three pitchers were stunned.

"The whole right side [of the infield] was open," Branca heard one of the other pitchers mutter. "Should have been a double play."[18]

That would have been two of the three outs the Dodgers needed to end the game and get their ticket punched to the World Series. Instead, it was a base hit, and the Giants now had men on first and third with nobody out.

Then came the first out. If the infielders had been positioned better and had gotten their double play, the game would now be over.

In reality, the Giants still had life—and the next batter slapped a double. The Dodgers' lead was cut to 4–2, with just one out and two men on base.

A laboring Newcombe was finally yanked, and Dressen had to choose a new pitcher from the bullpen. That man who played a critical role in Robinson's rise, longtime scout Clyde Sukeforth, was front and center again.

Sukeforth, the man who first tapped Robinson on the shoulder in Chicago, was now the bullpen coach. He noticed Erskine was bouncing those curve balls short of home plate as he warmed up at the Polo Grounds, so Sukeforth suggested the team turn to Branca.

Branca took the long walk in from the bullpen. On his way to the mound, he passed Robinson, who said simply, "Let's get 'em, Ralph."[19]

The first batter Branca had to face was Thomson. "*T-H-O-M-S-O-N*," Red Barber always stressed to his listeners, emphasizing the lack of a *P* in there.

Thomson represented the winning run at home plate. So if he hit a home run, it was game over.

Putting Branca in was another Dressen move that has long been second-guessed; Thomson had hit several home runs off Branca over the course of the year, including that one in Game 1 of the playoff series. But Dressen could fall back on the fact that Thomson's batting average was far worse against Branca than it was against Erskine (.265 compared to .545).

Leo Durocher, the former Dodgers manager, was now leading the Giants. He had a simple order for Thomson. If you're ever going to hit a home run, he barked, hit it now.

Dressen had a chance to take the bat out of Thomson's hands by giving him an intentional walk. Standing on the on-deck circle was Mays. He had gone hitless in three at-bats against Branca in Game 1, including two strikeouts, so it may have made more sense to pitch to a rookie in a pressure situation.

Then again, baseball managers traditionally do not intentionally walk the potential winning run in any game. Plus Mays was pretty good in his first season, 20 home runs in 121 games, and eventually grew into one of the best hitters the game has ever seen. So he could have risen to the occasion and knocked in the winning runs if given the chance. We will simply never know.

Per Prager, Branca's fiancée, Ann, was in the stands, silently praying that her future husband would get Thomson out. "Hail Mary, full of grace, the Lord is with thee," she said. "Blessed art thou amongst women and blessed is the fruit of thy womb Jesus. Holy Mary, Mother of God, pray for us sinners, now and at the hour of our death. Amen."[20]

The first pitch was a fastball down the middle, but Thomson let it go by for a called strike. Branca could hear Giants in the dugout screaming at Thomson for not jumping on such a juicy pitch.

"What the hell is wrong with you?" the never-shy Durocher screamed at Thomson.

Erskine thought the pitch choice was odd because the scouting report was that Thomson was a power hitter who loved low fastballs. Out in the bullpen, Erskine jumped in the air, knowing the best strategy was to try and throw a fastball high and inside because it was harder for Thomson to handle. "Not down there, Ralph!" Erskine yelled out, even though Branca could not hear him.

He figured the same directions were immediately shouted out to Branca from other Dodgers in the dugout, closer to the pitching mound. And in later years, Erskine wondered if Branca took a little speed off of his normal fastball—"less mustard" in the parlance of pitchers—in order to pinpoint the location higher and more inside for the second pitch.

Branca did then try to sneak a second fastball up and in past Thomson, hoping to set up a curveball low and away as the third pitch for a possible strikeout. Thomson never gave him the chance.[21]

He ominously clubbed the ball down the left-field line, though Branca was hoping it would fall just short of the wall.

"Sink, sink, sink!" Branca yelled in vain.[22]

The ball cleared the wall by mere inches, a game-winning three-run home run that quickly became known as "The Shot Heard 'Round the World."

This was one of the first baseball games ever televised nationally, but it was the call by Giants broadcaster Russ Hodges—a radio man—that would be remembered for the ages because of his elated shouting.

"There's a long drive . . . it's gonna be, I believe," Hodges began, his voice growing more excited by the second until he reached a full shriek with the refrain.

"The Giants win the pennant!" Hodges declared over and over. "The Giants win the pennant!! The Giants win the pennant!!! The Giants win the pennant!!!!"[23]

The historic call from Russ Hodges, no relation to Gil Hodges, would have been lost to history. But a man named Lawrence Goldberg, before leaving his Brooklyn home to get to work at the Automobile Club of New York in Manhattan, asked his mother to use his old-school reel-to-reel recorder to tape the game. Hodges himself long pushed a yarn that Goldberg was a Dodgers fan who wanted a tape of a Brooklyn triumph to play back and stick to his friends who were Giants fans. In fact, Goldberg was a Giants fan who simply believed something "climactic" was going to happen.[24]

It was one of the greatest games in baseball history, and there are probably millions of people who at some point have claimed they were there to witness it. Yet the reality is the game was played on a Wednesday and the Polo Grounds was half full: 34,320 tickets sold out of 56,000 seats.

Nonetheless, it was pandemonium among the fans who were there. They rushed the field. Video showed Branca turning and picking up the rosin bag, which typically sits behind the mound so pitchers can get a dry grip of the ball, and then slamming it to the ground.

"I wanted to believe that I was dreaming," recalled Branca. "I didn't want to believe that it was really happening. I wanted the pitch back."[25]

It was gone forever. Many of the Dodgers players rushed to avoid the crush of Giants fans and quickly get to the visitors' clubhouse to change their clothes.

When baseball players in the modern era want to head home after the game, they can easily walk through one of the two dugouts to enter the adjoining clubhouses. At the archaic Polo Grounds, players had to head all the way out to center field, head through a door, and navigate a set of stairs to make it to the clubhouse.

Branca now reversed that long walk of more than four hundred feet that he had made from the bullpen to the mound a few moments earlier. As Branca and the rest of his teammates made the painful trudge out to center field, there was one notable exception. Ever the man with an attention for detail who played the game the right way, Robinson stayed on the field.

Jackie immediately surmised that amid the confusion Thomson could make a mistake. He might fail to step on second or third base as he raced for home plate, which could nullify the home run.

"There's a photo of Jackie with his hands on his hips, just watching, making sure Thomson touched every base," said Reinsdorf, noting the savvy of Robinson, who still had the presence of mind to give his team a chance to win under the most difficult of circumstances.

Reinsdorf, of course, had told his mother on the phone that the Dodgers were going to be champions before she made it home from the grocery store. "And so I've always blamed myself for that loss," said Reinsdorf. "You never—you just can't count any game until it's over. But I remember that—ugh—never again. You gotta get twenty-seven outs. Until you get twenty-seven outs, the game is not over."[26]

Reinsdorf's agony was nothing compared to what Branca felt. He was ridiculed as a "goat," the man who blew the big game. Within seconds of the fateful pitch, Dodgers broadcaster Vin Scully saw just how devastating it was going to be for Branca and his loved ones.

When Scully first joined the Dodgers broadcast team, Barber was something of a second father to him, the senior guy suggesting later that Vin was the son he never had. "So he was determined that I would succeed," Scully told me. "And I am extremely grateful for that attitude towards me. And he was a disciplinarian towards me. And one of the things he insisted upon was that I not get close to the players. So they were all acquaintances."

Barber's point was that if you became buddy-buddy with one of the guys, and then that player makes an error during a game, the broadcaster could be tempted to downplay the miscue by his friend.

Scully had mostly taken that advice, but could not resist becoming friends with Branca, whose fiancée, Ann, was at the Polo Grounds praying the Hail Mary. They had gotten close because Scully had even had a few dates with Ann's roommate.

"We double-dated maybe three times," Scully said, stressing in that folksy way about him that they were "very ordinary" dates, mind you.

"Ann was going to Marymount. She had a roommate," recalled Scully. "And so Ralph and Ann, and then I would date the roommate, two or three times, not more than that. But that is why I would say I broke the code, where I got closer to a player" than Barber had instructed.

And so on October 3, 1951, as Scully sat in the broadcast booth, he knew Ann was not far away in the seats reserved for friends and family of the players. Barber was on to something, because when the ball was smacked, Scully was not just a passive observer.

"Instinctively with the home run I looked down to see how Ann was," Scully told me. "And as I remember it she bent down, opened her purse, took out a handkerchief, closed the purse, opened up the handkerchief, and then buried her face in the handkerchief."[27]

As Scully was quoted in Branca's memoirs, "Those few seconds said everything."[28]

Then it somehow got even sadder. Scully made his own way to the clubhouse. The broadcaster walked up a small flight of stairs that led to the door in center field. He recalled that there were four wooden steps that would take you up to the lockers, and the training room where players would get rehab for their injuries.

"And when I walked in, Ralph was spread eagled on the four steps," Scully told me. "And I actually had to kind of step over one arm."[29]

It was deathly quiet in the clubhouse, so Scully thought it was awkward to stay there alongside Branca. He kept walking to the trainer's room. He happened upon Robinson and Reese, who this time were nursing broken hearts.

"And I just—I didn't even say hello," Scully said. "I just sat down in a chair, and the silence was broken by Pee Wee. And he said to Jackie, 'You know the one thing I'll never understand?'"

Robinson did not offer an answer or venture a guess. He just stared at Reese.

"And Pee Wee said, 'How this game has not driven me crazy,'" remembered Scully.

Reese's first full season with the Dodgers had been in 1941, and the team lost the World Series. They lost the World Series again in 1947 and 1949. And now it was, in Scully's retelling, a crushing blow in 1951 that stopped them from even making it to the World Series.

"They lost all the time," Scully said, adding that Reese was the captain who tried to keep everyone calm. "They would get into the World Series and lose. Perhaps that's what he meant. Or maybe he just meant the ups and downs, the maddening ups and downs, throughout his entire career."

As he reflected later on the whole scene, Scully saw religious connections for Branca. He noted that despite the later revelations about the Giants stealing signs, Branca never whined.

"There was no sign of bitterness," Scully said. "And what made it very difficult for him was the fact that in New York, where the great moment occurred, everybody wanted to have lunches and dinners to honor Bobby. And of course part of the story had to be Ralph had to go [to the events] as well. And that had to be extremely difficult with one man exalting over the moment at the expense of the other. But I thought Ralph handled that wonderfully well."

Scully added, "I thought he carried his cross with a great deal of grace and dignity."[30]

That is a reference to the very image a Catholic priest used when he saw Branca shortly after the game ended.

Branca was doubting himself as he met up with Ann. She was waiting with Father Pat Rowley, dean of campus ministries at Fordham.

"At the moment when they needed their best pitcher, you got the call," said the priest. "That alone is a sign of the respect you have."

"*Had*," Branca responded.

"You're being too hard on yourself, son," said the priest.

"But why me, Father?" asked Branca. "I love this game so much. Why did it have to be me?"

"Simple," he said. "God chose you because He knew you'd be strong enough to bear this cross. This will not weaken your faith in God, it will build the strength of your spirit."[31]

A moving moment to be sure, though you will have to forgive Erskine for remembering something else more trivial, but also heartbreaking, about that day.

When he arrived early in the Dodgers' clubhouse, Erskine noticed that staffers were scrambling to move some of the props for a victory celebration to the Giant clubhouse. "All the champagne cases and the cameras were set up on the Dodgers' side because we went into the ninth inning with a 4–1 lead," said Erskine. "They're shoveling it quick across to the other side. And then the doors closed and our side was like a tomb while outside, you could hear, was bedlam."[32]

In the eyes of Scully, it was the worst circumstance. "The Dodgers' clubhouse was dead silent," the broadcaster said. "But the Giants' clubhouse was just across the hall, and on the field in the front of the clubhouse looking up, there were thousands of Giants fans celebrating. And the Giants players were celebrating."

Scully saw Eddie Stanky, the former Brooklyn infielder who was on the Giants, out on the steps of the Giants' clubhouse doing an imitation of Barber to further stick it to the Dodgers. "So all this, you know, hallelujah stuff, was going on ten feet away and we were listening to all that noise," Scully said.[33]

One more thing crossed Erskine's mind that day in 1951—a simple twist of fate that still eats at him today. It's the story he was mulling over at the IHOP in Indiana but was still not quite ready to tell.

That will come later in the narrative. First, Erskine wanted to talk about the day he learned the full measure of Robinson's competitive fire.

CHAPTER 18

"HOW DO YOU LIKE
THAT GARBAGE?!"

To try to explain Jackie Robinson's killer instinct—both on the baseball diamond and when it came to pushing for civil rights—Carl Erskine decided to dig out the story that seemed to bring him the most delight of all.

It was May 12, 1956, and the Dodgers were set to play their rival, the New York Giants, or "the invading Giants" as Red Barber used to declare when they visited Ebbets Field. (Barber refused to call the 1953 World Series after a dispute with the broadcast's sponsor, Gillette, and grew miffed that Dodgers owner Walter O'Malley did not support him in the battle. So by 1956, Barber had gone to work with the hated New York Yankees.)

The point is that even though it was just a regular-season game in 1956, the hype around this storied rivalry was ridiculously high. "Always a hot time in Brooklyn when the Giants come over," Barber would say in his broadcasts.

In those days there was usually only one nationally televised regular-season game per week, broadcast on Saturday as the Game of the Week and watched by millions.

"Pitching in Ebbets Field against the Giants on a Saturday afternoon, I don't think the World Series could top that," said Erskine, who was slated to be on the mound that day.[1]

But Erskine, Robinson, and Roy Campanella were all on the decline, as the pitcher was painfully reminded when he arrived at the Ebbets Field clubhouse that Saturday to find a blistering newspaper article left open on a trunk.

Erskine remembered the article quoting Tom Sheehan, the chief scout for the Giants, who suggested the Dodgers were over the hill.

"It was sub-headlined, 'Jackie's too old, too slow. Campanella's done. And Erskine can't win with the garbage he's been throwing,'" recalled Erskine.

This was seriously messing with Erskine's head. He'd already had a cortisone shot the night before to deal with a sore pitching arm. And now he had to face Dodgers manager Walter Alston, who had replaced Chuck Dressen after the 1953 season.

While Clyde Sukeforth had resigned as bullpen coach after the debacle of 1951, Dressen stayed on board. He led the Dodgers to the World Series in 1952 and 1953, but they lost to the Yankees again both times. So when he insisted on what the Dodgers management saw as a cushy three-year contract, he was replaced by Alston.

Like Robinson as a player, Alston got his seasoning as a manager with the Montreal Royals in the minor leagues. As broadcaster Vin Scully liked to say, Alston was "the quiet man from Darrtown, Ohio," who was grateful to have made it big and had no problem at all signing a short-term deal. In fact, he would famously sign twenty-three one-year contracts.

Now, however, Alston was on his third one-year contract on this day in 1956, when both Erskine's arm and head were bothering him. The manager walked out of his office for the customary gesture of handing the starting pitcher a warm-up ball to signify it was his game to win or lose today. A pained Erskine was secretly thinking of handing the ball back because he needed another day of rest.

But ballplayers didn't do that. Certainly not the Boys of Summer, anyway.

"I couldn't do it—I couldn't ask out of a starting assignment," Erskine told me. "So I took the ball. Now I'm cooked. I've gotta go pitch with all this anxiety."

Erskine's wife, Betty, was home in Anderson, Indiana, with their two young sons, ironing a tablecloth in front of the television.

The pitcher was just praying he could have an easy few innings at the start to steady himself.

It seems those prayers were answered. Erskine did not give up a single hit in the first four innings. His wife, who was not usually superstitious, decided this time to keep ironing the tablecloth, because she worried that changing her routine might disrupt a possible no-hitter.

Trouble came in the fifth inning. But Robinson, who had gotten so many personal assists from Erskine over the years, was there to save the pitcher. Willie Mays came up in the fifth, and he was no longer a rookie. After swatting fifty-one home runs in 1955, Mays followed that up in 1956 with thirty-six home runs and forty stolen bases, the first National League player to reach the "30-30 Club."

Erskine threw Mays a low inside fastball, and Mays smashed the ball to Robinson's left at third base. Robinson was aging; the Giants scout had suggested he was all but done. In fact, he had been moved from second base to third to make way for a younger African American star, Junior Gilliam.

It appeared that Mays's bullet would get through for a hit, but Robinson still had some quickness. He grabbed the ball before it could reach the outfield, but then he had to turn and throw out the speedy Mays at first base.

"Only Jackie could have made that play," noted Erskine. "He had the agility and instincts, knowing how to fire the ball to first after the pivot to beat out Mays."

No other Giant came close to getting a hit. As the game wore on, Betty Erskine was still ironing the same tablecloth. She had run out of cloth to touch up long ago, but she finally turned it over to iron the underside of it too.

It worked. Erskine got the second no-hitter of his career.

"And she ironed that tablecloth for nine innings," said Erskine. "And so I say, 'Well she didn't scorch a spot, I didn't allow a hit. That's teamwork.'"

Back at Ebbets Field, the first one on the mound to celebrate the Dodgers' teamwork was Robinson, followed by Campanella.

"Jackie had saved the no-hitter," said Erskine. "Campy had caught the no-hitter. And I had thrown the no-hitter. The three guys that Tom Sheehan said can't get it done anymore. So here is the classic, true story—as God is my witness."

Robinson had spotted Sheehan seated near the Giants' dugout. So he raced toward the dugout. Jackie had a surprise for him.

"Jackie had the newspaper clipping in the hip pocket of his uniform," marveled Erskine. "He had to have taken it off that trunk—he had to! He had that article in his hip pocket. And he waved it at Sheehan and the Giants' bench and said, 'How do you like *that* garbage?!'"

Erskine did not dub Robinson "Mr. Intensity" for nothing.[2] And that intensity did not come cheap.

OUT OF THE SANDBOX

We know that Jackie was forged in the fires of a rough childhood. He used those hard memories as motivation again and again, especially in the 1950s, when he seemed to be living in the stratosphere compared to where he had come from.

"My own childhood is one reason I try to win all the time," Robinson wrote in a 1955 article in *Look* magazine. "When I was one year old, my mother was left alone on a farm in Georgia with five small children. I've never seen my father."

Robinson again mentioned Mallie taking the family on "dirty Jim Crow coaches" on the train to Pasadena. "We never had much to eat, except for day-old bread that we dunked in sugar and milk," added Robinson. "Even now, Rachel has to remind me to eat green vegetables—I do as an example for our family—but I never developed a taste for them because I never ate them as a youngster. We had meat on Sundays only when my mother was able to get extra work."

Then there was the issue of childcare and Jackie having to sit in a sandbox while his sister attended classes at school. It was not the best of scenarios, but his mother was determined to stay off welfare. "If I quit working to stay home to take care of him, I'll have to go on relief," she told the school. "It'll be cheaper for the city if you just let him play in that sandbox."[3]

Robinson did not tell these stories with the goal of seeking pity. He was making the point that throughout the 1950s, he was still facing discrimination, long after he had been celebrated for breaking the color barrier.

He recounted in that *Look* magazine article, "Now I Know Why They Boo Me!," that he was catching flack for building a large house in a part of North Stamford, Connecticut, where no other African Americans were living.

Robinson noted whites and African Americans alike were slamming him, but "maybe those people who are criticizing me for building a new house in Connecticut don't know about the years I spent in a sandbox waiting for my sister."

In a sign of the pressure he still faced from his own community, one African American newspaper editor had sent Jackie a letter noting that there were major problems with juvenile delinquency near Jamaica, Queens, where the Robinsons used to live. "Not all of us are fortunate enough to be able to escape from Jamaica to the white society of Connecticut," he wrote acidly.

Robinson didn't take that attack lying down. He had the simple right to want his expanding family—there was now son David and daughter Sharon in addition to Jackie Jr.—to grow up in the country rather than the congested city.

And then he revealed Rachel first had dreams of settling in Westchester County, New York, but they were blocked because of their race.

They found a fabulous property in Westchester. While they were expected to haggle, they offered the owner the asking price. There was no reply for a long time. Then the owner came back to say the price had gone up $5,000, and Robinson called his bluff. "There was another period of confused silence," wrote Robinson. "At last, we were told that the land had been sold to someone else. Everywhere we went it was like that."[4]

He was an American hero, and he was still facing the same old discrimination and pressures from all sides. When he tried to move to a white neighborhood, white people balked and African Americans called him a sellout. Not much had really changed.

And when *New York Daily News* ran what was supposed to be an upbeat photo of Jackie Jr.'s third birthday, Robinson still got grief: white and African American critics noted the photo showed only one African American guest.

On the field there was trouble too. At the beginning, in 1947, Rickey had warned him, "They may throw at you."

"It isn't new to me," replied Robinson.

Yet here he was, near the end of his career, and pitchers were still throwing balls at him. He was hit sixty-six times over the course of his career.[5]

And now that Rickey's restrictions on fighting back had long since been lifted, Robinson's temper was getting the better of him in arguments with umpires. As the former general manager predicted, Robinson was being hammered with the charge that he was an "angry Negro," or some far more offensive term.

A prime example came in Chicago during the 1954 season, when Robinson also exploded at Alston—his own manager—not just the umpires. Duke Snider hit a long fly ball that appeared to be a home run after hitting a fan in the bleachers, but the ball bounced back onto the field. These were the days before instant replay, of course, so the umpires blew the call and ruled that the ball had hit the wall and was a double instead of a home run.

"I leaped out of the dugout," recounted Robinson, noting the team was down three runs and needed a boost. "The Dodger bench jumped up too, and I thought they were with me. Then I ran out to the field to argue."

Usually the manager would take the lead in racing out to the field to stick up for the team, but in this case Robinson was first to hammer the umpires, and he was stunned when Alston did not follow. "After a minute of argument, I saw I was alone," he noted. "No one had followed me out to protest. And the boos had begun."

Alston thought the call was accurate and saw no need to argue it. "Out there alone, with the fans riding me more every second, I felt foolish," wrote Robinson. "I wanted to find a hole and crawl into it."[6]

Robinson wrote that he heard boos "ringing in [his] ears," and he took out his frustration on Alston, yelling: "You don't protect your players! You sit there like a bump on a log!"

Alston replied quietly, "I thought the call was right."[7]

The most flack Robinson received in 1954 came during several games against the Braves in Milwaukee. It started when he had a "hot exchange" with some Braves players and one of their broadcasters called Jackie an "agitator," a characterization that did not sit well with him. During another game the Braves' Johnny Logan was batting with a 2–2 count. Always a close student of the game, Robinson noticed that when Logan fouled off the next pitch, the Milwaukee scoreboard showed him at ball three, even though the count should have stayed 2–2. When the next pitch was a ball, Logan walked.

When Robinson later came up to bat, he got into it with umpire Lee Ballanfant.

"Can I get a walk on three balls the way Logan did?" asked Jackie.

"Get in there and hit or get out of the game," snapped the umpire, who promptly threw Robinson out of the game.

Robinson flicked his bat in disgust toward the dugout. He claimed the bat slipped because it was a wet night. "It landed on the roof of the dugout, bounced into the stands and hit three spectators," he wrote. "So my reputation as a sorehead and a poor sport was clinched in Milwaukee, where the fans are the noisiest."

Fortunately, Ballanfant backed up Robinson and told National League officials that he had not thrown the bat on purpose. An usher who was hit with the bat said it was so light that he thought someone simply touched his head, so talk of a lawsuit went away.[8]

Robinson noted that plenty of white players and managers got into scrapes with little criticism. "Leo Durocher and Eddie Stanky kick up fusses all the time," he wrote. "But if I do it, I'm stepping out of line. Many people think that a Negro, because he is a Negro, must always be humble—even in the heat of sports competition. But, in my case, maybe it goes deeper than that."[9]

In another sign of tension with Campanella, Robinson even cited a journalist[10] who wrote about the fact that when Campy or other African Americans protested calls, they rarely got flack.

"They have resented me especially ever since I came up to the Dodgers, not just because I am a Negro but because I was *the* Negro who broke the color line in baseball," Robinson wrote.[11]

1955

Boos always hurt, but Robinson took it harder as his skills began to erode; the critics pounced on him without mercy.

"If I've been resented since the beginning in 1947, why did the fans get on me more than usual last year?" he wrote in 1955 about the jeers. "Well, during the last season, when it appeared that I was slipping, the people who didn't boo when I was on top felt free to let go, and did."[12]

Somehow there was still some dispute about whether Robinson was one of the game's all-time greats. *Saga* magazine even did an entire spread two years earlier on whether they thought Robinson would make the Hall of Fame after he retired.

The magazine noted, "It may not be long before the brilliant Brooklyn Dodger infielder hangs up his glove, and when he does, there is bound to be a noisy argument over the question of his qualifications for membership in the Hall of Fame at Cooperstown, New York. Jackie has been a controversial figure throughout most of his meteoric career, and for every fan who wants him in the Hall there is going to be one who wants to see him kept out."[13]

It seems absurd to think there was even a sliver of doubt about whether or not Robinson was a Hall of Fame player.

Yet, after he retired, Robinson himself had debates with sportswriter Joe Reichler about whether he would make the Hall of Fame. He did not want to go in as a token.

Paul Reichler told me, "I remember my dad saying that Jackie did not want to be in the Hall of Fame just because he was the first 'Negro' player."

He continued, "I remember them talking about this and my dad telling him, 'You were a great player. You were both.'"[14]

Being kept out of the major leagues until he was twenty-eight years old clearly meant some of his prime years were wasted. Yet he still racked up some remarkable statistics. From 1949, when he won both the Most Valuable Player award and the National League batting championship with an average of .342, Robinson went on a remarkable run. From 1950 to 1952, he batted .328, .338, and .308 respectively.

Sport magazine took stock of Robinson in October 1955, ten years after Branch Rickey signed him to that first minor league contract.

Author Roger Kahn spoke with Robinson's former manager Chuck Dressen, who summed up Robinson's career succinctly: "They told me when I went to Brooklyn that Robinson would be tough to handle. I don't know. There never was an easier guy for me to manage and there never was nothing I asked that he didn't do. Hit-and-run. Bunt. Anything. He was the greatest player I ever managed."[15]

CHAMPIONS AT LAST

In 1955, Robinson also finally saw the Dodgers win their first World Series championship, though it was bittersweet. He had the worst season of his career, batting just .256, and was kept out of the critical Game 7 of the World Series against the New York Yankees, a move that would have been unthinkable in previous years.

Early in the season, Robinson was struggling with a weak .244 batting average. Ever the leader who put his team first, Jackie himself approached Alston about whether he should be rested for a while.

In a *LIFE* magazine feature on the team in May, Robinson was described as a "sagging veteran," who was benched briefly. Five starters on the team were in their thirties, and the nagging question was, could they keep winning over the long haul?[16]

LIFE checked back in with the team over the summer for an August 1, 1955, story billed this way: "The disabled Dodgers: with most of their regulars out with injuries they suffer but do not sink."[17]

The story featured Campanella sans clothes, though key parts of his anatomy were obscured by a whirlpool tub as he soaked a bad knee and sore hand. Erskine was depicted shirtless as he received treatment for an ailing pitching arm. Robinson was shown being carried off the field by buddy Gil Hodges and manager Alston after his knee buckled, relegating him to part-time duty as speculation grew about the looming end of his career.

The magazine noted the team somehow still had a fourteen-and-a-half game lead for first place. The fans celebrated by giving shortstop Pee Wee Reese a touching tribute for his thirty-sixth birthday. It included a pile of presents that led Reese to shed tears, as well as a moment where the lights were lowered at the evening game so the thirty-three thousand spectators could illuminate the stadium with matches, lighters, and candles.

As the sun was setting on these Boys of Summer, they finally won the 1955 World Series by, in the words of Robinson, "beating our jinx club, the Yankees."[18]

"Yet in all honesty, I can't say this was the best Brooklyn team I ever played with," Robinson wrote in the *Dell Baseball Annual* magazine previewing the 1956 season. "I can't even pick them 1–2–3. Excluding pitching, I'd pick this club no better than fourth. The 1947, 1949 and 1953 teams were better. However, the one thing the '55 club had that the others couldn't match in any way was desire."[19]

Robinson was alluding to the painful reality that the Dodgers had several outstanding teams that fell short, losing seven World Series before 1955. And it also could not have been easy for Robinson to realize that when the team launched a comeback to win, it was Campanella—not Jackie—who carried the team.

The Dodgers lost the first two games of the series. In the critical Game 3 that was a must-win for Brooklyn, Campy clubbed a two-out, two-run home run in the first inning. The Dodgers won that game, and then were victorious in Game 4 as well, in part because of another Campy homer.

Game 7 at Yankee Stadium featured Dodgers outfielder Sandy Amoros making a dramatic catch of a drive from Yankee great Yogi Berra to save the game. That preserved a 2–0 shutout by Dodgers pitcher Johnny Podres, who won two games in the series and was named the Most Valuable Player.

Sadly, though, it marked the only time in the career of Robinson that he was not used in a World Series game that Brooklyn played. He was already suffering from diabetes and he had a strained Achilles tendon, but he was still a gamer who wanted to play no matter what. It had to sting that Alston left him out of the lineup.

This was apparent in the *Dell* article Robinson wrote after the Series, when he took a shot at Alston. Robinson suggested others had pushed Alston into key decisions, and he wrote that maybe winning a world championship would give him more "confidence" as a manager in 1956.

"I think he will assert himself more, make more of his own decisions and go to bat more for his players," Robinson wrote. "I think everyone knows of the problems Walt and I have had. We haven't always seen eye to eye but I've always given my best, regardless of my feelings. I have only one thought—to win."[20]

For all of the generosity he showed in his life, Robinson could hold a grudge. He was still poking at Alston years later, when he was asked by *LIFE* magazine to scout the 1963 World Series and he seemed to mock the manager's leadership: "When I played for him in Brooklyn some of us called him 'Pebbles' because he used to sit on the dugout steps and flip them."[21]

In Game 7 of the 1955 World Series, Alston started second baseman Jim "Junior" Gilliam in left field, while the beloved future coach and manager Don Zimmer (the pudgy guy known as "Popeye" who was thrown to the ground by Boston Red Sox pitcher Pedro Martinez in an epic Red Sox brawl with the New York Yankees decades later) got the nod at second base. Somehow the long-forgotten Don Hoak started ahead of Robinson at third base.

While *Sports Illustrated* reported before the Series started that Robinson was now "aging, aching, tiring, still crabby," the magazine suggested he would be a major factor because of his competitiveness and experience: "But Robinson is still all ballplayer, all fire and victory."[22]

Leaving Robinson out of the lineup may have been a questionable move from Alston, but inserting Amoros into the game was sheer brilliance. George Shuba, who had decided to shake Robinson's hand in that famous photo, pinch hit for Zimmer in the top of the sixth inning. Then Gilliam moved from left field to second base to replace Zimmer, and the speedy Amoros took over left field.

This loomed large in the bottom of the sixth inning, when the Yankees had runners on first and second with nobody out. The Yankees trailed 2–0, but then Berra came to the plate with a chance to take back control of the World Series.

When Berra smacked a pitch toward left field, Dodgers fans could be excused for feeling queasy about Amoros not being at 100 percent. *Sports Illustrated* had declared before the Series that Amoros "opened season in left, hit well until sidelined by thigh injury, which still bothers him; Series status is doubtful."[23]

That thigh injury was about to be tested as Berra's shot headed for the deepest part of the left field corner. It appeared the ball was about to hit the ground and rattle around the stands, potentially scoring two runs for the Yankees. Instead Amoros raced to the ball, helped by the fact that he was a lefty thrower instead of a righty thrower like Gilliam.

This meant that if Gilliam had still been out there, the fielding glove would have been on his left hand and he would have had to reach far across his body to catch the ball in the left field corner. The lefty Amoros had the fielding glove on his right hand and just barely snagged the ball to record one out. Then he fired the ball to Reese, who tossed it to Gil Hodges to complete a double play when Yankee Gil McDougald could not get back to first base in time.

Even with Amoros grabbing the spotlight, Robinson still left his mark with Berra in two other important moments in that World Series.

In Game 1 at Yankee Stadium, Robinson stole home in a daring play that left Berra furious. He famously and vehemently protested that he had tagged Jackie out before he crossed the plate. (In 2016 a current major league umpire confided to me that he and some colleagues had unofficially put the play through their modern television replay system for kicks, and with the help of technology they determined that Robinson had just barely scored ahead of the tag.)

The other moment came after the Yankees lost Game 7. Berra took the rare step of walking over to the visitors' clubhouse specifically to congratulate Robinson for winning his first World Series—especially after accomplishing so much beyond just baseball. Though Berra never forgot the dispute at home plate.

It has been reported that before Berra's death in 2015, every time he walked past a photo at his New Jersey museum of Robinson stealing home in that game, he would declare, "You're out!" Berra and Rachel Robinson also shared a poignant inside joke each time they saw each other over the years. "Safe," Rachel would say, waiting for Berra to reply simply, "Out."[24]

NEVER SATISFIED

It was a relief for Robinson to have finally won the World Series after years of frustration. But an earlier conversation he had with Erskine showed this was a man who was never satisfied with just one big victory—on or off the field.

Robinson caught Erskine off-guard at the end of the 1953 season, when the Dodgers lost out on another World Series and the fans started chanting their usual refrain, "Wait till next year!"

This was standard fare around Ebbets Field, so Erskine wondered if coming up short, yet again, had finally gotten to his friend. Instead there was something deeper gnawing at Robinson.

"Jackie, what's wrong?" asked Erskine. "You really hate that phrase, but why?"

"Carl, it's the same every year," said Robinson. "Whether it's our team or civil rights, it's always the same. It's not the phrase so much as what it says about our country."

Here he was, seven years after his first major league game, and the desire for change was still burning deeply inside Robinson. "It's the end of 1953, Carl, and some of the hotels around the league still won't allow us to stay with you guys when we go there," he said. "It's always 'wait till next year.' Carl, we've got to be persistent, you know that. We've got to change things in '54."[25]

This was a man who was running out of time, both in a Brooklyn uniform and out of it.

CHAPTER 19

ROBINSON TRADED
TO THE . . . GIANTS?

Jerry Reinsdorf had wrapped up his second stogie, and we were the last two people in the Chicago cigar club. But he had to get to one more story that was still eating at him.

He was perturbed about the time in December 1956 when the Brooklyn Dodgers broke his heart again. This time it was a baffling move that did not happen on the field, and it actually felt like two consecutive punches to the gut.

"First of all, I remember thinking, 'You can't *trade* Jackie Robinson!'" Reinsdorf said now. "But to the *Giants*?!"[1]

It was a shoddy way to treat a hero. The Dodgers traded Robinson in what was basically a fire sale. They got a journeyman pitcher named Dick Littlefield and $35,000 in cash.

It was the final insult—at least to Robinson—from Dodgers owner Walter O'Malley. The rest of Brooklyn would have to wait for about a year, when O'Malley officially moved the team to Los Angeles, to be slapped with a searing insult of their own.

"Get rid of him," O'Malley brutally told general manager Buzzie Bavasi.[2]

Author Roger Kahn suggested that this may have been another chance for the owner to take a slap at the former general manager, Branch Rickey, Robinson's longtime patron. Kahn obtained what seemed like a disingenuous note O'Malley fired off to Jackie and Rachel about how there was a "decade of memories," and maybe someday their paths would cross again. It was signed, "Au revoir, Walter O'Malley."[3]

A "decade of memories?" It sounded as though one of the nation's greatest civil rights heroes was getting a trophy from the local bowling club for ten years of really great effort.

For Reinsdorf, who was then off at college majoring in accounting at George Washington University, this was nothing short of despicable. And it was not just the end of Robinson's time in Brooklyn. It truly was the passing of an era—of an innocent time when stars like Robinson took the subway and were accessible to the fans who loved them. Dodgers center fielder Duke Snider played stickball—hitting a rubber ball with a broomstick—in the streets of New York City with kids like Reinsdorf. "There were these young mothers, they were probably in their twenties, and Duke was really good looking," Reinsdorf said with a smile. "So the mothers used to come out and watch the stickball games."

One day, Snider was still at Ebbets Field and had not made it to the streets yet. One of the kids playing stickball hit a ball that landed in a baby carriage. The baby was fine, but the tot's mother grabbed the ball and said she would only give it back to the boys on one condition. "She said, 'I'll only give it back to Duke Snider,' and we couldn't play because we only had one ball," recalled Reinsdorf. "We had to wait until he came home after that day's game."[4]

There was a brotherhood between the players and the fans, who would see their favorites parking their own cars in the lot on Bedford Avenue or having a cheeseburger at the go-to diner, Toomey's, on Empire Boulevard.

Erskine remembers unpretentious, humble attitudes from players like Gil Hodges, who is generally considered one of the best defensive first basemen of all time. Like pitcher Ralph Branca, Hodges was serious about his Catholic faith and was known more for being a gentleman than anything else. "He was genuine, he was just who he was," Carl Erskine said of Hodges. "He was quiet, didn't say a lot, but was real smart."

In the early 1950s, manager Charlie Dressen thought Hodges was too introverted and needed to show more emotion. Whenever there was a close play at first base and it looked as though the umpire blew the call, Hodges was too nice to start a fight. "Dressen said, 'Hodges, lookit, if you argue one time with an umpire and get thrown out, I'll give you a hundred bucks,'" recalled Erskine. "He couldn't do it. It never happened."

Dodgers teammates marveled about the time Hodges was too gentle with home plate umpire Tom Gorman at a game in Chicago. Gorman called him out on a controversial third strike; the pitch was ridiculously far out of the strike zone. "Gil comes back to the dugout and never says a word," said Erskine. "Puts his bat in the rack, puts his helmet down, doesn't say a word."

The next time up, Hodges had two strikes on him, and there was a ball in the dirt. Gorman called strike three again, and Hodges walked back calmly, placed the bat down, and put the helmet away without emotion. "So the guys really got on Gil this time," recalled Erskine. "'Gil, he's taking the bat right out of your hands! Bread out of your kids' mouths! You gotta say something to Gorman, come on now!'"

Hodges thought it over a bit, as his teammates continued to ride him. Finally he said, "Okay, okay, when I go up next time to hit I won't even ask Tom how his wife and kids are."

Classic Hodges. Which is why Erskine added, "I'll say this. I got booed at Ebbets Field. Pee Wee [Reese] got booed in Ebbets Field. Hodges was *never* booed in Ebbets Field."[5]

RETIREMENT

A year after Robinson was traded, Erskine, Hodges, Reese, Snider, and the remaining Dodgers would pull up stakes from Brooklyn forever, moving to Los Angeles, thanks to O'Malley.

And Robinson was out of baseball altogether, because he abruptly announced in January 1957 that he had already decided to retire, basically nullifying the trade between the Dodgers and Giants anyway.

The Dodgers did not know that Robinson already had lined up a deal to become an executive with the Chock full o'Nuts coffee company. And Jackie also sold exclusive rights to his retirement story, "Why I'm Quitting Baseball," to *Look* magazine for a cool $50,000.

The arrangement allowed Robinson to control the message, spinning that he jumped before the Dodgers pushed him, even though there were other signs that he still really wanted to keep playing.

"A lot of people will say I'm quitting because I was traded to the Giants last month. That isn't true," Robinson wrote in the January 22, 1957, edition of *Look*. "I started thinking about retiring from baseball almost four years ago, and have been looking around for the kind of job I wanted ever since. When it turned up a few weeks ago, I took it."

He added it was incidental that he learned about the trade just moments after inking a deal with William Black, who ran Chock full o'Nuts, the coffee company that also had cafes in New York.[6]

Kahn later found out that after a Giants executive quietly called Robinson to offer him more money, the player was mulling whether to undo the retirement. Kahn wrote in a 1971 story for *Sport* magazine that Robinson was still thinking about playing for the Giants "until the first day of the 1957 season. That morning his right knee, crippled by a thousand slides, was so swollen he could not get out of bed."[7]

And in a newspaper clipping from February 1954 among Robinson's papers at the Library of Congress, there was no talk of retiring. Jackie told a group of Oklahomans he was planning to play baseball for many years to come. "He has no thoughts these days of retiring despite his 35 years," declared the story in the *Tulsa World* newspaper by reporter Jack Kelley.[8]

In the winter of 1954, Robinson, always giving back, was serving as national chairman of Brotherhood Week, a series of events held around the nation, organized by what was then called the National Conference of Christians and Jews, to promote tolerance. He stopped in Oklahoma on his way home to California for a series of more speeches during the off-season. Kelley described Robinson as "the husky baseball star," a nod to the fact that his weight problems, which had become such a flashpoint with Leo Durocher, were creeping up again.

Robinson was moved by the sincerity with which the students at Will Rogers High School "recited their American creed" and sang songs praising America during a stop in Tulsa. "I don't know what it was about the Will Rogers kids that got me, but I just felt like crying when I got up to speak," Robinson told Kelley.

And Robinson was under the impression that his playing days were far from over. "He's going to be a Dodger as long as he can," concluded the news article in Tulsa.[9]

Well, Robinson's dream of riding off into the sunset with the Dodgers did not pan out. O'Malley and general manager Buzzie Bavasi treated the icon like an also-ran, trying to sell him off to a rival for the equivalent of spare parts.

Robinson clearly got a lot of pleasure out of beating the Dodgers to the punch. In the *Look* magazine article, Robinson recounted Bavasi essentially ducking his calls and then asking Jackie to come meet him in person and refusing to tell him what it was about. When they decided to have the conversation by phone, Bavasi finally revealed he had been traded to the Giants.

"I remember I was smiling when I put down the receiver," Robinson wrote. "I'd heard rumors of such a deal—along with a lot of other rumors—but it still came as a surprise. The reason I was smiling is that his announcement dispelled any lingering doubts I might have had about quitting baseball when I did—a half hour before."[10]

For all of his joy, at least for public consumption, Robinson was savaged in the media for his move. Sportswriters were furious that Robinson had sold the story; the famed journalist Red Smith accused him of "treason" for embarrassing the Dodgers, blocking the plans of the Giants, and deceiving the reporters who covered him for so long. "If it is true Jackie Robinson has, for a price, deliberately crossed his friends and employers past and present, then it requires an eloquent advocate to make a convincing defense for him," wrote Smith. "From here it appears true and no defense at all is discernible."[11]

Robinson had a retort for that. "Red Smith doesn't have to send my kids through college. I do."[12]

Meanwhile, African Americans were thrilled by the fact that Robinson appeared to get the better of the Brooklyn bosses—and the press.

"White folks sure get mad when we Negroes out-smart 'em," one Brooklyn bartender told *Jet* magazine.

The magazine teased a provocative story on its January 24, 1957, cover: "Did Jackie Robinson Betray Baseball?" The resounding answer in the pages of *Jet* was "no way"; the article declared Robinson had shrewdly taken charge of his own life as the Dodgers brass tried to move him like a "second-hand automobile" to the Giants.

"When Jackie Robinson's final and most spectacular 'steal of home' placed his Florsheims under the polished desk of a plush office as vice president of a chain of New York coffee snack bars, sports writers and his former Brooklyn bosses cried 'foul!'" journalist Dan Burley began his story. "But Jackie, at last his own umpire, scored on a play that goes in the record books as a financial grand slam."

On top of the $50,000 he received from *Look* magazine, Robinson would be earning $30,000 a year from Chock full o'Nuts, which the magazine noted, "employs 750 Negroes among its 1,000 workers."[13]

"I haven't double-crossed anybody," Robinson told *Jet*. "From the way I see it, Bavasi was double-crossing me because he, knowing how strongly I felt about playing for some other club, didn't tell me a word about it until he had sold me to the Giants for $30,000—30 pieces of silver—and a pitcher."[14]

Jet followed this up with another provocative cover story the very next week, January 31, 1957, with a photo of the retiree and the headline: "Does Jackie Robinson Talk Too Much?"

"The classic pattern of the 'universally beloved' Negro athlete is cast along the lines of one who speaks only when spoken to, lets sportswriters put words in his mouth, never calls a white man by his first name without putting 'mister' before it, is always short of cash, doesn't know what to do with money and reads only the Bible and the funny papers," blared the magazine. "For some white folks just don't like Negroes who talk back."

The magazine noted that after complying with the demand to keep quiet his first few years, Robinson did everything from "sassing umpires to expressing his views on civil rights," and was now getting into hot water immediately after retiring.[15]

Robinson had done a simple Q&A forum with a church in Waukegan, Illinois, and he let slip that the Milwaukee Braves "blew" the 1956 pennant race because "two or three" of their players spent too much time in night clubs. He subsequently apologized for saying it but made clear it was true by adding, "If they call me a liar, or have me with my back against the wall, I'll name names."[16]

If Robinson felt a bit under siege from the attacks, he at least had many fans rallying to his side. Telegrams of support poured in from around the country, as shown in his personal papers at the Library of Congress.

"It was with much disappointment that I heard of you leaving the Brooklyn baseball club," said a blunt telegram from Charles Phillips of Miami Beach. "I consider the Dodgers not only ungrateful but also stupid."[17]

O'Malley and the Dodgers came under heavy fire in one telegram after another. Thomas Kirksey of Chicago wrote: "I doubt whether I would be far wrong if I said that America was no little stunned and saddened that one of the Dodgers' all-time greats had been 'under the hammer.'"[18]

At least one fan put Robinson's battle with O'Malley in starkly religious terms, casting Jackie as Jesus Christ and the executive as Judas. "Sometimes I compare you and Our Lord together," wrote one fan from Jamaica, Queens. "You had to endure great sufferings and abuse to play baseball in the majors and to show the way for your race whereas Christ had that Cross to carry to Calvary. You both carried your Crosses to prove to the world that all men are created equal."

The fan added, "Walter O'Malley and Buzzie Bavasi I guess could be compared in my opinion to Judas Iscariot who sold our Lord for 30 pieces of silver. They sold you for 30,000. I guess if you do decide to don a Giant uniform you will make them sorry. This is certainly my way of saying it is entirely up to you in your choice. Ask that other great Man who carried the Cross. He will show you the way and tell you what to do."[19]

An elderly couple urged Robinson to read Psalm 35 and Isaiah 41. "Fear not thou worm Jacob," wrote the couple, adding: "you did your best at all times, you have a lovely intelligent wife and family. The Lord [has] blessed you."[20]

Still others recalled big games, such as Robinson's heroics in the final game of the 1951 regular season when his diving catch saved the game and he knocked himself unconscious, putting the Dodgers into that anticlimactic playoff series with the Giants.

"You gave me my greatest thrill in 1951 in Philadelphia," one fan wrote. "That play you made in extra innings was terrific and that 'homer' in the 14th won the game."

Another added: "I was nine years old when you came to Brooklyn, and I could never repay you for the many happy moments you have brought me along with countless millions."[21]

And more important, many telegrams talked about how much of an inspiration he had been, such as the note from a sixteen-year-old Chinese American: "My family and I came to this country during this time of crisis because we knew that this is a country of true democracy. I think that this element has never been as well demonstrated as in the story of your life."[22]

Others showed humor, such as one fan—before learning about the retirement—who wrote, "Millions of fans like myself who are admirers of you and what you have done for America will now turn our loyalty to the Giants."[23]

There was an outpouring of demands that Robinson spurn their nemesis, the Giants, with one fan urging that he not "play for that other team, if you want to call it that. You have always hated the Giants, even you must admit that."[24]

A Brooklyn doctor, a Dodgers fan going back to 1930, tried to find middle ground in the event that Robinson did end up playing for the Giants: "It'll be a little like hoping you hit a home run every time up with Brooklyn winning the game."[25]

But another supporter declared, "Having been a Dodger fan for all my life and having been one of your keenest fans, my advice to you would be to retire."[26]

And that is exactly what Robinson did. The Giants tried to tempt him to come back and play in 1957, and he seemed to be talking tough in *Look* magazine about how he could still perform at a high level. In the end, though, with his health already starting to fail, Robinson wisely stayed retired.

"And I'm glad my last season with the Dodgers was a good one and that I had a good Series," he wrote of another World Series loss to the Yankees. "Maybe I have another good season or two in me—but at 38, you never know. I'm glad I ended strong."[27]

In fact, Robinson was a shell of his old self in 1956. He collected a measly ninety-eight hits, after getting twice as many in his prime. He was down to ten home runs and forty-three runs batted in. Perhaps most tellingly, the man who once terrorized opposing teams with his speed had only twelve stolen bases.

The aging Dodgers that year faced a stiff challenge in the National League from the Milwaukee Braves, led by a young African American star named Henry "Hank" Aaron. After Aaron drove home the winning run at Milwaukee's County Stadium in a July game against the Dodgers, forty thousand fans were chanting, "The Bums are dead!"

Sports Illustrated noted the veteran Dodgers had a long familiarity with winning and were motivated by the cold hard cash they could collect from World Series bonuses. But the magazine warned that the Dodgers had sunk to third place in the National League. And with injuries mounting, including a bum leg for Robinson, their run of five National League pennants in ten years—including finally beating the Yankees for the World Series in 1955—might be done.

The article suggested that while the Dodgers' dynasty was on the verge of collapse, Robinson and his teammates were making a comeback in the National League. That surge came in part because the players had the guts to take personal responsibility for their weak start, an uncommon move in modern-day sports. Guys like Erskine stepped up to defend manager Walter Alston, who had been the subject of anonymous sniping in the media, saying it was the players' performances that were the cause of the losses early in the season. Robinson noted he and his teammates were grownups who aired their grievances and then grew as a team.[28]

Robinson also showed his competitive flame had not been doused yet, as he openly goaded Milwaukee for being too green, declaring that their players were starting to choke, while the old-school Dodgers were rising to the occasion.[29]

In the end, Robinson was right. The old guys beat Aaron and the Braves to take the National League pennant in 1956.

The Dodgers lost to the Yankees yet again in the World Series that year, thanks in part to Don Larsen pitching the only perfect game in World Series history. And Robinson was correct in the *Look* magazine piece. He had a strong World Series, playing all seven games this time, and collecting six hits, including a home run and two runs batted in.

Perhaps more important, he left an impression on that kid on the Braves named Hank Aaron, who had gone to that drug store in Alabama back in 1948 just to get a glimpse at Robinson.

In April 1974, Aaron, as a member of the Atlanta Braves, would end up breaking Babe Ruth's record of 714 home runs in a career. The previous month, on March 20, Aaron had written a newspaper article in a publication called *Guideposts*.

In the story, Aaron credited Robinson for being his inspiration, specifically citing his faith in God as a key factor. "What fascinated me so much was that Jackie was an emotional, explosive kind of ballplayer," wrote Aaron. "Yet during that crucial first year in the big leagues, he didn't lose his temper in spite of a steady barrage of insults from fans and other players."

Aaron added, "How did he keep control? I learned later that he prayed a lot for help. And he also had a sense of destiny about what he was doing, so much so that he felt God's presence with him. He learned to put aside his pride and quick temper for the bigger thing he was doing."

Aaron claimed that he now knew he needed to rely on someone stronger and wiser and not just hope to do accomplish something so monumnetal alone.

"I don't do it on my own," wrote Aaron. "God is my strength. He gave me a good body and some talent and the freedom to develop it. He helps me when things go wrong. He forgives me when I fall on my face. He lights the way."

Aaron concluded, "The Lord willing, I'll set a new home run record. If I don't, that's okay too. I've had a wonderful time in baseball and have enough great memories to last two lifetimes. I have been blessed."[30]

Yes, in the end, Robinson's legacy on civil rights and faith has been passed to many people of all races. And now it was time for me to go see the woman who was by Jackie's side to see all of it unfold, the ever-classy Rachel Robinson.

CHAPTER 20

THEIR BELIEF IN GOD'S SPIRIT

I went to Lower Manhattan to visit Rachel Robinson at the offices of the Jackie Robinson Foundation, which has been mentoring young people for several decades, keeping his incredible legacy alive and well. A key part of what Rachel is trying to pass on to future generations is the fact that her husband's ability to accomplish so much came in large part from working together with Branch Rickey, someone with whom he had a lot of differences on the surface.

"I wish we saw more of that," she told me. "I wish we could create more partnerships like that. So we wouldn't have so much contention, and we would make a lot more progress."

For all of the men's differences, though, Mrs. Robinson knows better than anyone that faith was their key similarity.

"The Branch Rickey that I got to know after all of this happened was kind of a very thoughtful person, deeply religious," she told me. "So was Jack. So one of the things that brought them together as partners was their belief in God. And their belief in God's spirit pervading things."[1]

The truth is, none of it could have happened without Rachel either. Jackie credited Rachel—or "Rae" as he affectionately called her—for repeatedly calming him down in tense situations, particularly during those horrible bus rides in 1946 on their way to Florida after being bumped from their plane.

Rachel had allowed their honeymoon to be cut short so that Jackie could get to spring training, and he said later that without his wife, he would never have gotten through the challenges lined up in front of him. "She hadn't been wearing [her wedding ring] more than a few weeks before she got a dramatic example of the kind of problems she was going to have to share with me," said Robinson.

The player said he was torn between anger at the cruel things being done to the couple and the fact that he had to listen to Rickey and make sure his career did not get off on the wrong foot. "I could have lost my temper and ended up clobbered unconscious in some obscure Southern jail—or worse," suggested Robinson. "Maybe this would have happened if it hadn't been for Rae."

It particularly tortured him to watch his new wife treated so poorly as they traveled from California to Florida. "To be a Negro man in the South—or other parts of our country where such savage discrimination faces you—is bad enough," he said. "To have to watch the woman you love and respect treated in such an inhuman way—and to know that there is nothing you can do about it, nothing to protect and shield her, nothing to keep her from bleeding and suffering insults—well, it is almost impossible to find a way to express your feelings."[2]

Rachel ached over it as well, which she revealed in a book she wrote about her husband, *Jackie Robinson: An Intimate Portrait*.

She wrote that when they boarded the first bus before dawn, it was not very full, so they took some empty seats near the front, and Jackie fell asleep. But as white people eventually started boarding over time, the driver told Rachel the couple needed to move to the back of the bus. She was nervous that her husband, the man with the infamous temper, would lose it.

Instead, Jackie was passive about it, which actually upset Rachel even more.

"I woke Jack, concerned about his reaction, especially given his fight in the army over this very same order," wrote Rachel. "But, instead of challenging the driver, he docilely led me to the last seat in the rear. I followed in a mixed state of disbelief, relief, and pain. The relief did not last, and in the darkness I silently wept. My man had become the white South's 'boy,' in order to keep us safe."[3]

If Jackie did not fight back, he would be seen—even for a brief moment by his own loving wife—as too weak. If he lashed out at the bus driver, he would infuriate Rickey and possibly ruin the entire mission.

Once the couple did make it to Florida, they had to change cities within a few days because of the threat of violence. "We had to pack and move in a hurry because a white mob was threatening to run us out of town," Robinson wrote in a 1955 article for *Look* magazine.

Robinson confided he almost threw in the towel as exhibition games were canceled because of racist cities blocking him with local ordinances. "I was deeply embarrassed and upset by the trouble I was causing the Montreal club," he wrote. "I wanted to quit baseball before the season opened. But Rachel and Mr. Rickey talked me out of it."[4]

Reflecting on that exchange when he sat down to write his unpublished memoir, Robinson was blown away by how prescient Rickey's advice about the importance of his "girl" turned out to be. "How true were those words of Mr. Rickey's about a man needing a woman by his side," wrote Robinson. "From the very beginning of my baseball career there have been so many times when I needed Rae by my side. I can't even estimate how much would have been lost without her."[5]

As Ralph Branca noted years later, "Rickey felt everyone should marry and encouraged his players to do so, the sooner the better. The way Rickey saw it, marriage—especially for athletic young men—was essential for moral integrity."[6]

Broadcaster Vin Scully recalled being a "wide-eyed kid" who heard the exact same message when Red Barber sent him for an interview with the man that everyone called "Mr. Rickey" without fail.

"I thought he was going to ask me about the infield fly rule or some other part of baseball," Scully told me. "And instead he wanted to find out about me, and eventually after talking for quite some time, he said to me, 'Are you engaged?' and I said, 'No sir.'"

Scully continued. "He said, 'Are you going steady?' and I said, 'No sir.'

And then he took one hand, kind of pounded it on the desk and he said, 'Get a girl, go steady, get engaged, and get married.' And that was that. That was his advice. Because he always worried, especially about young single players on the road. And of course here I was, not a player, but I was single and I was going to be representing the team on the road. It wasn't a lecture, but it certainly drove home the point."[7]

And Robinson got the message loud and clear. He cited the great Duke Ellington in calling his wife the "perfect accompanist" on his history-making journey. "My wife and my mother have been the two most powerful influences for good in my life," he added.[8]

Rachel was, of course, there for him again when he made it to the big leagues. On one road trip that rookie season, he was on so many long-distance telephone calls, getting encouragement from his wife, that at one point he ran up a twenty-eight-dollar phone bill in two weeks—serious money in those days.

Those were times when Rachel needed to be gentle to encourage Jackie. But she also proved to be as tough as nails when it was needed.

Jackie's battles with Walter O'Malley reached a boiling point in 1952. The owner of the team lashed out at Robinson for missing exhibition games, even though the player had the legitimate excuse of being injured.

But O'Malley made the mistake of inviting Rachel to join their meeting. She grew furious as O'Malley suggested Jackie might be faking the injuries, and then he also had the gall to say Jackie should not be complaining about being assigned a separate hotel in spring training.

"That burned me up," Jackie wrote in his 1972 autobiography. "I told O'Malley that if he thought I intended to tolerate conditions I had been forced to stand for in the past, he was dead wrong."[9]

That was nothing compared to what happened when O'Malley went on to call Robinson a "prima donna" and "crybaby" because his leg had been bothering him. Rachel ripped into the owner, declaring she had seen Jackie endure a series of injuries over the years without ever telling the team, because he wanted to stay in the games.

"Nobody else spends more time worrying about Pee Wee Reese's sore foot or Gil Hodges' batting slump or Carl Erskine's ailing arm," she said. "Jack's heart and soul is with the baseball club, and it pains me deeply to have you say what you just said."

Then she delivered the knockout punch by doing what O'Malley hated most, comparing him unfavorably to Rickey.

"You know Mr. O'Malley, bringing Jack into organized baseball was not the greatest thing Mr. Rickey did for him," she said. "In my opinion, it was this: Having brought Jack in, he stuck by him to the very end. He understood Jack. He never listened to the ugly little rumors like those you have mentioned to us today. If there was something wrong, he would go to Jack and ask him about it. He would talk to Jack and they would get to the heart of it like men with a mutual respect for the abilities and feelings of each other."[10]

With a partner like that, it is clearly no surprise that one of the key sources of Jackie's strength in fighting for civil rights came from Rachel.

FAITH FOR FIGHTING

Rachel and Jackie also shared the crucial element of faith. Jackie directly tied that faith to the struggle for civil rights in a series of sermons and speeches he delivered in churches and other venues all across the country in the 1960s, when parts of the nation were literally engulfed in flames.

In July 1963, a month and a half before Dr. Martin Luther King Jr. would deliver his famous "I Have a Dream" speech, Robinson spoke of how the church could effect social change in an address at the Fourth General Synod of the United Church of Christ in Denver, Colorado.

"It is the ministers, the church people of America, who can, almost overnight, cure the ills of our system which make so many of us commit the sin of acknowledging the Fatherhood of God on Sunday and rejecting the brotherhood of man on Monday."[11]

This theme—that you cannot believe in the Fatherhood of God without acknowledging the brotherhood of men of all races—is one that Robinson would repeat in speech after speech throughout the 1960s. To Jackie, religion and racism could not go hand in hand.

In the same speech, Robinson hinted that all of the taunting and exclusion he faced over the years had wounded him. He told the story of an African American boy who moved to a neighborhood "where Negroes never lived."

There was a church across the street from the boy's new house. His curiosity piqued, on Sunday morning the boy decided he wanted to go to Sunday school at the church. The minute he walked through the church doors, however, he was blocked by an usher who told him that he could not come in because "this church was for white people."

Surprised and anguished, the boy went outside and started to cry.

Then God—personified as a pedestrian in Jackie's story—walked down the street and saw the boy crying.

"Little boy, why are you crying?" asked God.

When the boy explained that he had been forbidden from entering the church because of his skin color, God—in Jackie's words—"sat right down at that little boy's side and started to cry too."[12]

The image of God sitting on the street and crying with the boy is arresting in its simplicity. And it shows that for Jackie, racism was not only an affront to his legal rights as an American citizen or his right to fair play on the baseball diamond. Nor was it only an affront to his pride. He felt it was an assault to his entire conception of human dignity, a conception fueled at least in part by faith.

Robinson was also making the point that, as with schools, hotels, and water fountains, Jim Crow was alive and well in the church.

"For years, as it has been pointed out often in the past, it has been a national shame that 11:00 a.m. was the most segregated hour in America," Robinson said in 1963 and then reiterated during that 1967 sermon in New Rochelle, New York.

When he stood in the pulpit of that New Rochelle church, giving the sermon mentioned near the start of this book, there were no fewer than 159 race riots in America over the course of that year.

During what became known as the "long, hot summer," there were major riots in June 1967 in cities from the South (Atlanta and Tampa) to the Northeast (Boston and Buffalo) and the Midwest (Cincinnati).

Then, in July, there was an explosion of riots in several more American cities, the most tragic ones wreaking havoc on Newark, New Jersey, and Detroit, Michigan (the infamous Twelfth Street riots).

"The stones and the rocks and the Molotov cocktails were hurled in Detroit and in Newark and in Rochester," said Robinson. "And they were answered by the sharp retort of bullets, the merciless banging of police billies against head and limb."

He warned that as the summer passed, an even worse situation could be bubbling in America.

"For the sticks and stones of physical combat are vicious, but the stones of white backlash, the stones of 'hate the white man propaganda,' are more deadly weapons than any others that exist," Robinson added. "These are the weapons which can destroy our beloved country and bring death and destruction and slavery to all Americans. For it is as true as when Mr. Lincoln said it: 'A house divided against itself cannot stand.' And America, slowly but with grim certainty, is becoming a divided nation."

The long, hot summer sparked President Lyndon Johnson to form the Kerner Commission to investigate. America was facing another seminal moment in the civil rights movement, with complicated questions to consider again.

Yet Robinson did not need a commission to tell him what was wrong. He had wrestled with these questions before. In baseball parlance, this was "in his wheelhouse"—as in a pitch others might whiff at but he could knock out of the park.

The answer to the troubles, he knew, came from the Bible. And even in his declining health, the man delivering the sermon on this Sunday was still far ahead of his time.

"I think we need to think less in terms of 'helping' the Negro and more in terms of making sure he has the tools with which to give God a little help by helping himself," said Robinson, who had clearly learned this principle from his mother.

By the end, it must have sounded to the people in the church that Robinson, in his declining health in 1967, was actually back in his prime. "The final question: What more does the black man want?" Robinson asked from the pulpit. "The simple answer: Everything he should have to put him on a status of equal opportunity with his white brother. He should not seek more. He cannot settle for less."[13]

As Robinson delivered those words in 1967, there was no Internet or cable television, so the speech was not broadcast far and wide. I found this sermon in his personal papers at the Library of Congress, along with several other moving speeches in which he intertwined progress in civil rights with faith in God.

In May 1968, Robinson delivered a speech titled "The Church and the World" to the Eighty-First Annual Assembly of the Texas Association of Christian Churches in Austin. He was pinch-hitting for President Johnson, who could not make it.

"Many people believe me to be a Republican and I am sure there are any number of Republicans who would like to take the president's place," Robinson said. "But seriously, I am not here to talk politics but to seek to tell the truth as I see it."

Robinson warned that he planned to be frank, even though "some people like to pass out candy instead of candor." He was still willing to tell uncomfortable truths.

"Ladies and gentlemen, there are just too many people going around the world and about the country, in your town and in mine, in your church and in mine—too many people telling everyone who expresses an opinion, 'You're right,'" said Robinson. "I made up my mind a long time ago that I would rather be true to myself and to my beliefs and principles than to buy popularity at the cost of truth. When all is said and done, I'm the one who has to live with me."

Robinson repeated a line he often liked to use in these speeches, "I'm no goody-goody," to make clear he was not holding himself up as perfect before God.

"And I believe that the necessity for being true to oneself is one of the crying needs of Christian laymen in our disturbed world," he said. "We live too much, these days, by the rule of consensus. What one does is fine if everybody's doing it. The opinions one has must be popular opinions."

He added, "We must have a society of conscience, not consensus."

Words so prescient, in fact, that they could be plugged into a speech today.

"For when we, as Christians or heretics, fail to speak the truth, fail to live the truth—when we lie by the words we utter and deceive by the phrases we fail to speak—we pave the way for division and hatred and strife," he said.

He warned of racial strife and divisions over the Vietnam War tearing the country apart. And he suggested bluntly that faith in God was the solution.

"It is a terrible mess, this whole situation," he said. "And if it can be cleaned up ever, at all, it will only be the church and church people who will be able to do it. But it's not going to be done by just Sunday-go-to-meeting Christians, or just by Monday-morning halfback Christians, or by just let-John-do-it Christians, or 'I-don't-want-to-get-involved' Christians."

Robinson declared, "It will have to be done by dedicated Christians of understanding, creating goodwill for their fellow man."[14]

POLITICAL LEANINGS

In that sermon, Robinson was targeting President Johnson and his once-strong commitment to civil rights. "But not too long ago, when his own [Kerner] Commission on Civil Disorders issued a courageous, astoundingly honest report which placed much of the blame for our social ills on white racism—a report which warned that we were in great danger of going the disgraceful Jim Crow route of South Africa—the president acted as though the cat had got his tongue," said Robinson.

He warned that Johnson could let the commission become a "mockery and an empty gesture," and raised questions about the president failing to seize the mantle of leadership in the wake of the assassination of Dr. King.

"True, another civil rights bill was quickly passed," said Robinson. "But doesn't it seem to you that America is swiftly returning to business as usual?"[15]

While Robinson often leaned Republican, he was not an ideologue, and he challenged both sides. He endorsed Republican presidential nominee Richard Nixon in 1960, declaring he did not believe the Democratic nominee, John F. Kennedy, was really committed to civil rights.

Yet Nixon still angered Jackie. He just did not seem willing to try to understand the complexities of the black community, as when he passed over the chance to campaign in Harlem. And when a white judge in Georgia unjustly sentenced Dr. King to four months in prison where he'd have to do hard labor, Nixon refused to contact King to show his solidarity. Though Jackie implored Nixon to make the call, the Republican thought it would be perceived as too overtly political. In fact, had it not been for a last-minute conversation with his old mentor, Branch Rickey, Jackie might have dropped his endorsement of Nixon.

While Kennedy exceeded Robinson's original expectations on civil rights, a torch that Johnson took up after the president's assassination, Jackie stepped down from Chock full o'Nuts in 1964 to campaign full-time to help the presidential run of a moderate Republican, Governor Nelson Rockefeller of New York. According to historian Michael Beschloss, Robinson stressed, "we must work for a two-party system, as far as the Negro is concerned."[16]

When Republicans instead nominated for president a conservative who opposed the Civil Rights Act of 1964, Republican senator Barry Goldwater, Robinson became disillusioned. At the Republican convention in San Francisco, the former ballplayer nearly got into a fistfight with a male delegate from Alabama who was held back by his wife.

"Turn him loose, lady, turn him loose!" yelled Robinson.[17]

Robinson ended up backing Johnson in the 1964 election, though he challenged him hard in this 1968 "Church and the World" speech. And in the same address, Jackie slammed Nixon, who was running for president again that year, for allegedly not even pretending to want to help the poor.

"In one of my less wisely considered stages of political development, I once believed in Mr. Nixon as ardently and sincerely committed to racial justice," Robinson said acidly. "We all make mistakes and that was one of mine which was a beaut."

Robinson added, "The late Dr. King did not accept the doom of the poor. He believed with Mr. Lincoln that God must have loved the poor to have allowed there to be so many of them. Dr. King believed that God meant for all men, black and white, rich and poor, Protestant, Catholic and Jew, to be able to have a dream."[18]

This was nothing new for Robinson. Complacency was something he bashed leaders in both parties about. He loved to write letters as forceful as his speeches, and they crackled with anger and impatience.

Ten years earlier, he had fired off a missive on Chock full o'Nuts stationery on May 13, 1958, addressed to President Eisenhower.

"I was sitting in the audience at the Summit Meeting of Negro Leaders yesterday when you said we must have patience," Robinson began. "On hearing you say this, I felt like standing up and saying, 'Oh no! Not again.'"

Robinson continued, "I respectfully remind you sir, that we have been the most patient of all people. . . . As the chief executive of our nation, I respectfully suggest that you unwittingly crush the spirit of freedom in Negroes by constantly urging forbearance and give hope to those pro-segregation leaders like [Arkansas] Governor [Orval] Faubus who would take from us even those freedoms we now enjoy."[19]

As he neared death in March 1972, Robinson sent a tough letter to then-President Nixon, accusing him of "polarizing this country."

"I want so much to be part of and to love this country as I once did," Robinson wrote.[20]

Robinson also had the guts to take on fellow African Americans, which Erskine saw up close in between a doubleheader the Dodgers were playing one day.

"Now the maddest I ever saw Jackie was not at an umpire or another player," said Erskine. "It was at a black fan in Cincinnati."

It was a hot July afternoon early in Robinson's time with the Dodgers, and excursion trains had brought African American fans into Cincinnati from major Southern cities like Atlanta and Birmingham so they could see Robinson play. Some of these fans had a little too much to drink on the train or during the first game of the doubleheader.

"We were warming up for the second game, Jackie and I were standing near the edge of the dugout," said Erskine. "And a black fan came down the aisle. He's disheveled, he's roughed up, he's drunk."

In a slurred voice, the fan started yelling, "I wanna see my *boy*, Jackie!"

Boy was a trigger word, and Robinson at this point in the 1950s would not take that from a white fan—or an African American. "Jackie was incensed," said Erskine. "He was furious. And he yells at this guy about halfway down the aisle coming toward him, 'Get outa my sight, you slob! Go home and clean up! I'll bet your front yard looks just like you do.'"

The man stopped in his tracks and retreated into the stands.

"That's the maddest I ever saw Jackie," said Erskine. "Everything he stood for was being exposed in the wrong way, and he was over-the-top mad."[21]

THE CIVIL RIGHTS TRAIL

Robinson proudly continued to take up the cause after his playing days, marching in Birmingham in 1963 with Dr. King as well as other sports stars, like boxer Floyd Patterson. But it was Robinson who caught the eyes of many of the marchers, some of whom shouted, "Show us, Jackie!"

When they first reached Birmingham after a flight from New York, Robinson joined King and the others at the Sixth Avenue Baptist Church. Jackie had invited Bill Stephenson from a Canadian magazine, the *Star Weekly*, to accompany him.

Stephenson reported that Robinson was jokingly introduced as "an old, broken-down ballplayer who just happened along," as he headed to the pulpit with sweat filling his prematurely gray hair.

"I don't think you realize [what] you mean to us," Robinson told the church members. "With your quiet courage you've touched the conscience of the whole world. There's no doubt now that we'll succeed."

Talk about modesty. The man who had shown the way a couple of decades earlier was now giving credit to a church full of people in Birmingham.

Robinson told the hushed church that he was motivated to come to Birmingham after seeing a photograph in a newspaper of an associate of the notorious Bull Connor, the ruthless white commissioner of public safety in Birmingham, sticking a knee into the neck of a young African American girl.

"This is the picture the whole world will remember about Birmingham," said Robinson.

After the speech, a minister had to tell the crowd to stop asking Robinson and the others for autographs because they had to meet up with six hundred teenagers waiting at New Pilgrim Baptist Church. Many of the youngsters still had bandages from being beaten by police, but when the dignitaries arrived, they were singing, "This little light of mine, I'm gonna let it shine."

After a pastor suggested to the teenagers they had to love everyone, even Connor, Robinson got his turn. He seemed to be angered by the sight of young people who had been injured, and he openly wrestled with whether he could stick with nonviolence.

"He plunged into a fiery denunciation of Bull Connor, begging the children to forgive him for he couldn't find it in his heart to love men like that," reported Stephenson. "He turned his biting invective against President Kennedy for what he called his betrayal of the Negroes, then against all white America for 'letting men like George Wallace be their spokesmen at this critical hour.'"

Robinson abruptly sat down, looking embarrassed about perhaps being too harsh with his rhetoric. But he was still bubbling with anger after local African Americans told him countless stories of harassment by white police officers, like getting arrested for public drunkenness after a drink in a bar or getting a ticket for loitering while standing on church steps.

When Robinson reached the airport to head home, a white man looked around to make sure nobody could hear him before whispering, "I've seen you play ball a hundred times, Jackie. More power to you, fella!" Robinson stopped and seemed to weigh the hypocrisy before finally saying, "Thanks, fella. Be seeing you."[22]

RICKEY PASSES ON

Rickey was still Jackie's confidant during this period. In a letter sent only a few weeks after the voting rights march from Selma to Montgomery following the infamous "Bloody Sunday" in 1965, Rickey told Robinson that he "would have been there if I could have walked. I thought about hiring a couple of able-bodied pushers for a wheel chair, but the kind I use at airports would not stand up for a sixty-mile hike."

Robinson knew Rickey was suffering from heart problems, and there were only so many more letters they would be able to exchange.

"Things have been very rewarding to me," Robinson wrote back. "But had it not been for you, nothing would be possible . . . Even though I don't write to you much, you are always on my mind."

Robinson then invoked Rachel to let the former Dodgers general manager know how much they were still thinking about him. "We feel so very close to you and I am sure you know our love and admiration is sincere and dedicated," wrote Jackie. "Please take care of yourself. P.S. Rae sends her love along with the children."[23]

It was too late. In November 1965, Rickey was quite ill but insisted he wanted to make the trip to deliver the speech accepting his induction into the Missouri Sports Hall of Fame.

"Now I'm going to tell you a story from the Bible about spiritual courage," Rickey said at the podium.

Suddenly he stopped. "I don't believe I'm going to be able to speak any longer," Rickey said, before collapsing in front of the shocked audience.[24]

Rickey had survived several heart attacks. But this time he slipped into a coma, staying there for twenty-six days until he died on December 9, 1965.

Ten years earlier, Robinson had modestly written, "It isn't even right to say I broke a color line. Mr. Rickey did. I played ball. Mr. Rickey made it possible for me to play."[25] Upon Rickey's death, Robinson added, "the passing of Mr. Rickey is like losing a father."[26]

And even in death, Rickey brought different races together. At Rickey's funeral in St. Louis, Robinson found himself in the back of the church near a former teammate, Bobby Bragan. He was a white player who had served as one of the ringleaders circulating that petition back in 1947 trying to block Robinson from joining the team.

The onetime adversaries looked at each other, and Bragan signaled for them to go to the front of the church, where they sat together in one of the pews closest to the altar.

Rickey essentially wrote himself a pretty darn good epitaph in his memoir, *The American Diamond*: "The game of baseball has given me a life of joy. I would not have exchanged it for any other."[27]

His grandson, Branch Rickey III, ended up going to the old baseball man's office to clean it out days later. One particular part of that experience was burned into his memory. The younger Rickey told me in an interview he started taking a pile of plaques off the walls: awards for starting the modern minor league system and citations for all his work with the group he helped to found, the Fellowship of Christian Athletes.

Yet there was not a single plaque on the wall congratulating Rickey for what would be his real legacy, helping to break the color barrier.

"He thought it was inappropriate to accept an award for something which was common decency—that any person with a soul should have an understanding of why it needs to be done," Branch Rickey III told me.

"It was his position," he said, "that you should not take credit for it."[28]

CHAPTER 21

"MY SON DESERVED BETTER"

Jerry Reinsdorf has few regrets at age eighty-one. He has a wonderful family and a comfortable bit of wealth, and he won a World Series with the Chicago White Sox, plus six NBA championships with the Chicago Bulls.

But he had one chance to meet Jackie Robinson. And he blew it. "Oh," he sighed. "I would have loved to have met Jackie."

Reinsdorf and his friend were sitting at Ebbets Field before a Dodgers game, when a guy came by and said, "Would you kids like to be on the *Jackie Robinson Show*?" Robinson did have a radio show. But Reinsdorf and his friend were convinced they were being tricked because they had arrived early to grab front-row seats in the general admission section, first come, first served.

"We thought we were pretty savvy—he just wants to get our seats," Reinsdorf told me. "So we refused—we wouldn't give up our front-row seats. Half an hour later, two other kids came by and said, 'We were just on Jackie Robinson's show!'"

This is why Reinsdorf had agreed to get together with me in Chicago for the second straight night. He wanted me to meet Ed Goren, the former vice chairman of Fox Sports, another Brooklyn native who actually did get to know Robinson.

This being Chicago, we met, of course, at Gibson's Bar and Steakhouse on North Rush Street.

And this being Reinsdorf, there would be a couple of more cigars after-ward, mixed with banter about the Dodgers.

"They were lovable losers," Goren said.

As for the melting pot of races and ethnic groups in Brooklyn back in those days, Goren said there was a sense that nobody was better than any-one else.

"We all got along because we were in the same boat," Reinsdorf chimed in from the other side of the booth.

"There was a comedian who said he was up for secretary of state," he said. "Somebody said, 'What do you know about foreign affairs?'" He said, 'I have ten relatives in Brooklyn!'"

Goren's father, Herb Goren, was a sportswriter for the old *New York Sun*, and the son was hooked on the Dodgers at an early age. Ed was not yet three years old when his father brought him to Havana for the team's spring training and he got to meet Robinson for the first time.

For spring training starting in 1948, it was on to Vero Beach, Florida, which became known as historic Dodgertown. Branch Rickey had leased an abandoned naval air station, enabling him to house white and African American players at the same training facility rather than dealing with pri-vate hotels still operating under Jim Crow.

"I swam with Jackie Jr. in Vero Beach," Ed Goren said with a smile, though he quickly added not all of his stories about Robinson's first son are that sweet.

After Herb Goren left sports writing, he went into public relations as a press agent for the New York Rangers hockey team. In the early 1970s he brought the elder Robinson to a series of games over the course of a couple of years. Ed Goren was now a young man, and he got to tag along. He has the distinct memory of Robinson almost being on a roller coaster of emo-tions. At one game, the younger Goren listened as Jackie spoke proudly about how Jackie Jr. was serving his country in Vietnam.

The next time they met at a hockey game, Robinson had a much differ-ent demeanor, after his son had returned home from war.

"Jackie is distraught," Goren remembered. "His son got hooked on drugs."

It was one of many challenges weighing on Robinson. His own health was declining rapidly, and he was worried about providing for his family.

Before his broadcast career on CNN, Larry King had a local show in Miami. He remembered having Robinson on as a guest about a year before his death on October 24, 1972. "He was half blind," King told me bluntly about how diabetes was ravaging Robinson's body.[1]

Jackie's daughter, Sharon Robinson, told me in an interview that she remembered going to a special event together at the famed Apollo Theater when she was a young girl. At some point they got separated, and her father could not find her for an agonizingly long time. His sight was that bad.

And for someone of his stature, Robinson had not earned nearly as much money as he deserved, so he was concerned about how much he was leaving behind for his family. Rickey had long been accused of being motivated by money and not sharing enough of it.

There was even a poem created to point out the gap between the crowds of fans that came out to see Jackie play and his actual compensation: "Jackie's nimble, Jackie's quick, Jackie makes the turnstiles click."[2]

While Rickey substantively proved that he clearly cared about more than just money, there is no question that Robinson helped provide major economic stimulus to the Dodgers, and he saw very little of the profit.

That may provide a little context for why Robinson said this about the game he loved: "Baseball, like some other sports, poses as a sacred institution dedicated to the public good, but it is actually a big, selfish business with a ruthlessness that many big businesses would never think of displaying."[3]

In January 1957, *Jet* listed some astounding numbers, showing that in the pre-Robinson era of 1930 to 1945, the Dodgers only topped attendance of one million fans in four seasons. Yet in what the magazine dubbed the "Decade of Jackie," the Dodgers brought in more than a million fans in every season from 1946 through 1956, including a high of 1.807 million in Robinson's rookie year of 1947.[4]

Nevertheless, Robinson never earned more than $42,000 a year for the Dodgers, while white stars for other teams—from Joe DiMaggio to Stan Musial—all earned around $100,000 per year at their peaks.

It was not just the antagonistic Walter O'Malley who short-changed Robinson in his later years. Rickey never really gave him what he was worth either.

"I knew I was underpaid, but so were a lot of other Dodgers," said Robinson. "We were all told that we were playing in a small ballpark and the team couldn't make much money. We never knew the actual break-even point for the team; ballplayers hardly ever do. I didn't argue because I figured that if you cooperate with people, they will cooperate with you later on."

In a sharp contrast from the modern era, retiring athletes like Robinson did not have multimillion-dollar endorsement contracts and cushy positions in the broadcast booth waiting for them when they hung up their spikes.

An October 25, 1956, letter to Robinson from C. R. Brookbank, executive director of the Canadian Council of Christians and Jews, tells the story dramatically. Brookbank had been clamoring for Robinson to spend some time in western Canada, noting "your following out here is terrific, and we will be delighted to have you come if you will do so."

According to the letter I found in Robinson's personal papers at the Library of Congress, he was being asked to spend an entire two weeks on a goodwill tour of speeches and glad-handing far from home in January 1957.

His time would be worth thousands of dollars, right? Guess again.

"I hope you will give some serious consideration to this now, Jack, and in consultation with the planning people out here I can now offer you $75.00 a day plus expenses," Brookbank wrote to Robinson. "How about it?"[5]

It was unclear whether Robinson said yes. Though we know with certainty that Robinson did not let any of this pay disparity impact his desire to continue fighting the good fight on civil rights.

In October 1959, he delivered a speech in Greenville, South Carolina, and headed to the airport for his flight back to New York, a standard trip on the rubber-chicken circuit. Except he decided to take a seat in the "Whites Only" waiting room at the airport.

This was the same man who, before he was a celebrity, refused to move to the back of the bus when he was serving in the army. Whether he was recognized or not in Greenville—he was heavier and grayer now—an African

American sitting in that spot in the South still caused a stir. A policeman was called over, and he was asked to move.

Robinson refused.

Perhaps it reminded him of spring training 1946, when, after scoring a run, he was accosted in the Montreal Royals' dugout by a Florida sheriff, handcuffs at the ready, for the high crime of playing baseball with white people in violation of local ordinances.

In Greenville, Robinson did not budge. He calmly—at least according to his account—told the police officers that the airport was built with federal funds and segregation was not allowed. "My taxes and other Negroes' taxes helped build this place," Robinson declared. "I have the right to sit anywhere I like."

Told to leave, Robinson nonetheless remained in the whites-only waiting area until his plane arrived. But he was not satisfied. He pressed for more action, and he turned his experience into a test case. "The National Association for the Advancement of Colored People took it to court," he said. "We think we can win and possibly put an end to white waiting rooms wherever the airport was put up by federal funds."

Finally he got to the real point.

"Small win, perhaps, but important," Jackie Robinson said. "They're all important."[6]

After all these years, he was still fighting the good fight. There was no closing his eyes to the struggle, even though he would be bestowed with an honor that finally gave him the license to kick back and relax.

HALL OF FAME

On July 23, 1962, Robinson became the first African American to be inducted into the Baseball Hall of Fame in Cooperstown, New York.

In a delicious irony, Robinson was elected in the same class of inductees that included former Cleveland Indians fireball pitcher Bob Feller.

Jet magazine could not resist pointing out Feller "admitted he greatly misgauged Jackie, when, in 1945, he remarked that he 'couldn't foresee any future for Robinson in big league baseball . . . If he were a white man, I doubt if they would even consider him as big league material.'"[7]

Robinson certainly did not miss the connection. "First let me say how much of a thrill it is to be coming into the Hall of Fame with Bob Feller," he began, before thanking the other inductees.

Humble as ever, Robinson ended his remarks by shifting the focus away from himself and vowing to continue dedicating his life to helping others. "I want to thank all of the people throughout this country who were just so wonderful during those trying days," said Robinson. "I appreciate it [to] no end. It's the greatest honor any person could have. And I only hope that I will be able to live up to this tremendously fine honor. It's something that I think those of us who are fortunate again must use in order to help others."[8]

In fact, Robinson had already opened many doors for so many people starting—but not ending, of course—with baseball players.

The following summer, timed to the one-year anniversary of Robinson's Hall of Fame induction, Associated Press sportswriter Joe Reichler wrote a story about one of the most important legacies Jackie would leave.

"Today 90 of the 500 players are Negroes, about 18 percent, compared to the 10 percent Negro population in the United States," Reichler wrote in July 1963. "Some of the game's greatest stars are Negroes. Willie Mays, Ernie Banks, Don Newcombe, Frank Robinson, Henry Aaron, Roy Campanella, Maury Wills and Robinson [all] earned Most Valuable Player awards. Mays, at $100,000, is one of the highest salaried players in the history of the game."

Reichler added that football now had a slew of African American stars like Jim Brown. And pro basketball had everyone from Oscar Robertson to Bill Russell and Wilt Chamberlain.

Then Reichler casually mentioned at the end of the piece that for the first time in 1962, local Florida businesses near the spring training camps stopped barring service to African American ballplayers. Hotels and restaurants had still been discriminating, sixteen years after Robinson's rough first visit to Daytona Beach.

What Reichler left out, modestly, is that the reporter had personally helped overturn the remnants of Jim Crow, a move that still makes his son, Paul, proud.

In the early 1960s, the elder Reichler spent a lot of time covering the St. Louis Cardinals' spring training around St. Petersburg, Florida. African American players like Bob Gibson, Curt Flood, and Bill White told Reichler they were still feeling the sting of Jim Crow, despite all of the vows of progress post-Robinson.

"Nobody had really written about it," Paul Reichler told me. "Reporters in those days were less critical."

Joe Reichler decided it was time to blow the whistle. He knew his Associated Press dispatches ran in hundreds of newspapers across the country. "He wrote this exposé on the treatment of the 'Negro' players. They couldn't stay in the same hotels, couldn't eat in the restaurants," said his son. "He just catalogued it. And because it was the AP, it was picked up everywhere."

A feel-good moment, right? But after the story ran, Reichler was slated to attend an annual chamber of commerce event for the teams and all the writers, who then—and now—bring major business to these Florida communities. At the event, the emcee would call out the names of all the baseball players attending, and then all the writers. But this time the local business owners were furious with Reichler for calling them out in print.

Paul Reichler was still just a kid, and he was sitting at a family table with his mother, in a different spot from his father. So he got a little scared by what happened when he heard the reaction to his father's name being called. "There's booing and screaming and everything from people in the audience," he recalled. "My mother, who was a very timid woman, was cowering. I was a kid. I didn't know what to think."

Then the ballplayers, African American and white, had their own say.

"And then gradually, one by one, the players stood up and started applauding," he recalled. "And it quieted the crowd. It was really chilling. But it's my best memory. That was really a special moment."[9] Joe Reichler had taken a stand, undoubtedly inspired by his friend Jackie Robinson.

When Jackie was finally inducted into the Hall of Fame and given a bigger portion of the recognition he was due, he sounded a bit wistful and even nervous.

"I feel quite inadequate here this afternoon, uh, this morning," Robinson corrected himself. "But I think a lot of this has been eliminated because today it seems everything is complete. First of all, I want you to know that this honor that was brought upon me here could not have happened without the great work and the advice and guidance that I've had from three of the most wonderful people that I know."

Robinson said the day would not be complete without those key people in the crowd, starting with his mentor. "I just hope you don't mind if I just pay a word of thanks and a tribute to my adviser and a wonderful friend, a man who I consider a father, Mr. Branch Rickey," he said.

Then he acknowledged Mallie Robinson: "And my mother, who taught me so much of the important things early in life, I appreciate to no end, my mother Mrs. Robinson."

Robinson then stressed that he would not be at Cooperstown without the person who was so critical to getting him through all of the struggles, his wife, Rachel.

"Ladies and gentlemen, my wife who has been such a wonderful inspiration to me and the person who has guided and advised me throughout our entire marriage," he said.[10]

It was supposed to be a nice retirement. Robinson wanted to manage a baseball team someday. They had that dream house in Connecticut that Rachel wanted.

It did not work out that way. Robinson, though, was not looking for pity. "Don't complain, work harder," he liked to say. He did just that.

JACKIE'S BRAVE NEW FIGHT

The September 10, 1970, issue of *Jet* magazine had Jackie on the cover, stooped over and far heavier than he was during his playing career. The headline declared, "Jackie Robinson Joins War Against Dope in Ghettos."

The story featured Jackie declaring drugs were a new "form of slavery" in America, while some African Americans complained he was a "Johnny-come-lately" to the cause.

The truth is Robinson was again ahead of his time, since illicit drugs have remained a scourge long past his own death. "We have them coming out of high school, coming back from Vietnam with no real future to look to and seemingly no one to turn to, then the problem is further complicated with our youngsters because they are black," Robinson said in the 1970 interview.

Jet detailed how painfully personal this was for Robinson, because his own son, Jackie Jr., had become a drug addict upon coming home after about a year of military service in Vietnam.

"Regardless of how a parent tries to bring up a son, you can never be around 24 hours a day to know who their associates are," an anguished Robinson told the magazine. "We didn't know whether to throw up our hands to say, 'Well, Jackie, you got yourself in this problem, get yourself out of it.' I really can hardly describe the numbing feeling that my wife and I had at that time."

Rather than shun their son, they got him help. He spent two years as a resident at a treatment center in Connecticut.

"Prestige didn't mean a thing," said Robinson. "I mean, who cares about prestige when you have a boy whose very life could hang in the balance. Our feeling was, 'The hell with the next-door neighbor or anybody else who was going to look at us and talk.' Our only concern was for Jackie and how we could help him."

At the time of the interview, Jackie Jr. was twenty-three and had two more months before he was expected to graduate from the treatment center. There had recently been a picnic for the parents of the residents.

"When it was time to leave and I was getting ready to leave I extended my hand to Jackie," Robinson recalled. "And for the first time in many years, he brushed that hand aside and embraced me. Nothing has pleased me more than that one particular incident."

That joy, though, soon turned to tragedy.

Jackie Jr. made it out of the treatment center after, in the words of his father, "he had fought his way back up out of the hell of drug addiction."[11]

Then Jackie Jr. took his recovery a step further, dedicating himself to working at the Connecticut treatment center to help others get off drugs. He had been clean himself for three years before he was killed in a tragic car accident at the age of twenty-four.

He was driving home from the treatment center in the early morning hours of June 17, 1971, in his brother David's sports car. He lost control of the car, which crashed into the guardrails, leaving Jackie Jr. pinned under the wreckage.

The elder Robinson admitted in his memoir that he felt guilty that his son never quite learned how to deal with the pressure of being the son of a hero. People peppered him with questions like, "You think you'll ever be as famous as your father?"[12]

Rachel Robinson added, "He'd been told time and again he couldn't be better than his dad. So he didn't have the fierce competitive spirit that his dad did."[13]

Young Jackie ran away from home as a teenager in response to a widening gulf with his father. When the elder Robinson searched the teen's room, he was surprised to find a photo of himself that his son had once carried in his wallet. "It meant that Jackie had cared a lot more for his old man than his old man had guessed," recalled Robinson. "I couldn't hold back the tears. I broke down and cried in the terrible way a man cries when he's someone who never cries. Through all the bad times Rachel had never seen me cry, and it made a bad experience that much more painful to her."[14]

Jackie Jr. returned home, and they made up. Then he volunteered for the army in 1964. After less than a year of training, he was sent into combat and was awarded a Purple Heart for combat wounds. "It wasn't all that much," the son insisted. "I just got shrapnel in the [rear]."[15]

As he recuperated in the military hospital, Jackie Jr. joined some of his African American comrades in questioning why they were fighting for democracy across the globe while being refused basic human rights in America.

Indeed, in some cases it wasn't hope in American-style democracy that inspired African American men to enlist. "Many of them found opportunities in the armed forces that were denied them in civilian life," said the elder Robinson, who had his own racial strife to deal with in the army more than twenty years earlier.[16]

Jackie Jr. was discharged from the army in June 1967, and when he came home, he was smoking marijuana but insisted it would not lead to harder drugs. (He would later admit that, during this time, he was also regularly popping pills and drinking cough syrup to get a high.)

His father's skepticism was substantiated when a call came in from the Associated Press. "Don't you know that your son was arrested about one o'clock last night on charges of possession and carrying a concealed weapon?" the reporter asked.[17]

While the police had previously warned the elder Robinson that his son might have a drug problem, Jackie and Rachel, stunned by the news, went to the jail and posted $5,000 bail. Then they helped him through treatment.

That's what made his death even more painful: Jackie Jr. was clean when it happened. Yet people assumed it was because of a relapse, so Robinson would stress that drugs had nothing to do with it.[18] The pain was eased a bit by the letters, telegrams, and phone calls that came in from people whose lives had been made better by Jackie Jr.'s efforts to use what he had learned to help others with addiction. The pallbearers at his funeral were residents of the treatment center that he had aided.

When Jackie and Rachel emerged from the church after the funeral, they spotted a bunch of little kids all wearing baseball uniforms, part of a Jackie Robinson fan club.

"For me they signified that none of the suffering had been in vain," recalled Robinson. "They were the bright hope of tomorrow. They were the age that Jackie had been when I dreamed that what I was doing in baseball might make things easier" for future generations.[19]

It needs to be noted that Jackie and Rachel's surviving children, David and Sharon, have made their own marks dedicating their lives to social justice and are active with the Jackie Robinson Foundation. David, the youngest, has lived in Tanzania since 1983, where he has focused on economic development in East Africa, running a coffee farm. Before leaving America, he founded a group that was focused on housing issues in Harlem,

New York. After serving as a nurse-midwife and an educator, Sharon became a consultant for educational programs for Major League Baseball. She is also the author of several books about her father and his legacy.[20]

Ed Goren, who had seen the elder Robinson at a series of hockey games during Jackie Jr.'s fall, noticed a series of shifts in the hero's moods. It started after Jackie Jr. had testified on Capitol Hill about his recovery. "Jackie was so proud" about the progress his son was making, recalled Goren.

Then, in early 1972, Robinson came to another game a short time after Jackie Jr. had died. Goren was standing outside Madison Square Garden.

Up the street came Robinson, prematurely gray and shuffling slowly. "That night Jackie was distraught again when I saw him," Goren recalled. He remembers Jackie telling him, "Ed, my son deserved better."

Robinson was not just upset about the death. He was second-guessing himself and why he had not spent more time with his son when Jackie Jr. was growing up.

"You have to understand he deserved a better father," Robinson told Goren. "I was fighting for a bigger cause. He deserved more of me. My son is the one who deserved better."

Robinson was also questioning why he had saddled his first son with Jackie Jr. as his moniker. "Why would I name my son after me?" Robinson told Goren. "It put too much pressure on him."[21]

Paul Reichler also saw Robinson up close in those years, and he confirmed the hero did feel guilty about what had happened to his son.

"How do you live up to the name?" Reichler told me. "I mean Jackie Robinson's son, and you have the name? It can be a real burden."

Reichler's father, Joe, had covered Robinson for the Associated Press. Fortunately, Joe and Jackie's friendship recovered from that nasty exchange of letters in the late 1950s that had stemmed from an article the elder Reichler wrote about Roy Campanella. "If anything the disagreements brought them closer together," said Paul Reichler. "Sometimes in a relationship when you have a fight, if you work it out, it gets stronger."

Such was the case for Robinson and Reichler, who left the AP in the mid-1960s and went to work for Major League Baseball in public relations and as a historian. His office was near where Robinson worked for Chock full o'Nuts in midtown Manhattan, so they would meet for lunch.

Reichler also sent his son up to Robinson's office to get some advice on college and life. Robinson was famous and busy, and he was getting old and tired, so he easily could have begged off, but of course he obliged; he was always mentoring and teaching.

But like Ed Goren, the younger Reichler noticed a much different Robinson when he saw him in the later years. "Jackie was never the same after his son died," Reichler told me. "There was a sadness about him. There was a heavier face. And a heavier walk."[22]

FADING STARS

The years and hard times were certainly catching up with Jackie. Then the rest of the Boys of Summer started fading. The first bit of heartbreaking news for the old fraternity of Dodgers came on April 2, 1972: it was about their former first baseman, Gil Hodges, who managed the New York Mets to their first World Series championship in 1969.

Pitcher Ralph Branca had jotted a note by his telephone to call Hodges in two days for his birthday. But suddenly the phone rang. Former Dodger Rube Walker, who was catching when Branca threw that pitch to Bobby Thomson, was now one of Hodges's coaches on the Mets. He was calling to reveal Hodges had had a massive heart attack in West Palm Beach. "Ralphie, you're not going to believe this, but Gil's gone. We were all with him on the golf course," said Walker, adding: "He was smiling, he was joking, and then he fell. Just like that."

Two days later, on what would have been Hodges's forty-eighth birthday, Branca was driving to his funeral at Our Lady Help of Christians Church in Brooklyn. He glanced out of his car window and realized Robinson was driving right next to him.

The first thing Branca noticed is that when he honked and waved, there was absolutely no reaction from Robinson. The second observation was that

Robinson's hair was now snow white, and he was wearing very thick eyeglasses. Branca figured out a moment later the reason Robinson did not turn when he honked was because he was struggling with his vision and needed to concentrate.

They parked alongside each other, and when Robinson got out he struggled to walk on an uneven sidewalk. "It's the diabetes, Ralph," said Robinson. "It's affecting my vision."[23]

As they got closer to the church, Robinson tripped. Branca rushed to catch him, and suddenly they both flashed back to the moment they had bonded over so many years ago. "Just like '47, Ralph," said Robinson. "When you tackled me before I crashed into the dugout."

It was a bittersweet moment there on the flagstone pavement in Brooklyn. Yes, when Branca caught Robinson in 1947, it told Jackie that he belonged. His teammates were finally embracing him and protecting him, and the stress of being the first African American baseball player was eased ever so slightly. But in reality the stress of being the first never really went away. What was happening on the sidewalk in Brooklyn was a sad reminder of Robinson's decline.

Perhaps the sharpness of that decline was in direct proportion to his intensity as a player. Roy Campanella remembered sitting in the dugout one time with Robinson about to come to bat, when Jackie said if nobody got on base ahead of him, he had a plan to get the Dodgers a run. "I'm bunting my way on," Robinson told Campy. "Then I'm gonna steal my way around the bases."

A puzzled Campy asked, "What makes you say that, Jackie?"

"I need the exercise," quipped Robinson.[24]

Robinson played at such a high level that he sometimes used his skill to simply toy with other teams. But years later, at the church, he could barely walk up a couple of steps.

"His reflexes were lightning-fast, and his timing at the plate was uncanny," noted Branca. "In a few short years, he had become old and sick."[25]

Robinson was moved by Hodges's death and Campanella's decline. He expressed shock about it all and said publicly that he was getting afraid for himself.

The fact that he was seeing his own mortality became even more clear when famed broadcaster Howard Cosell brought Gil Hodges Jr. inside a car parked outside the church where Hodges's funeral was held. There in the back seat was Jackie Robinson, crying like a baby, according to Carl Erskine.

Erskine also had a tough time at Hodges's funeral. The pitcher was an honorary pallbearer, since he and the former first baseman both hailed from Indiana and were close. Back at Ebbets Field, organist Gladys Gooding had a special song to play whenever Hodges walked up to bat or Erskine came in to pitch. "I always said that other than the National Anthem, back in the 1950s the song played more than any other was 'Back Home in Indiana,'" Erskine told me with a smile.

Gooding was invited back to perform at the Catholic church for Hodges's funeral. Erskine and the other pallbearers started wheeling the casket to the back of the church, and Gooding was playing the organ.

"And she played, 'Back Home in Indiana,'" recalled Erskine. "It got me. Really got me. As I stepped out the church door, Howard Cosell thrust a camera in my face and said, 'Carl, can you give me a reaction?' And I said, 'No, Howard. I can't speak.' I couldn't do it."[26]

Just seven months later, Erskine would be attending another funeral for a member of the Boys of Summer. This time it was Jackie Robinson.

CHAPTER 22

"CARL, I PRAY FOR YOU EVERY DAY"

Carl Erskine and I had just about worn out our welcome at IHOP, tying up a table for three whole hours while running up a small tab.

"Separate checks?" the waitress asked.

"No, I'll take care of it," I said.

"Oh, whatever," Erskine said cheerfully. "I can host you here in my hometown."

Even with a generous tip, the tab was only twenty-one bucks, so I insisted that this one was on me. After all, I had gotten a full notebook of material from Erskine, and there was still one more story he wanted to share.

"I'm taking a chance here," Erskine had said, as he struggled with whether or not to tell me.

Our time was running out, because Erskine had to go pick up his son Jimmy, his fourth child, who has Down syndrome. When Jimmy was born in 1960, everyone from doctors to friends were less sensitive about the birth defect.

Jimmy faced one prejudice after another as he grew up, and over time Carl saw some similarities between his son's struggles and those of Jackie Robinson. And that is why, for all of his achievements on the baseball diamond, Erskine sounded most proud of the fact that Jimmy had grown into a fifty-six-year-old man who had his own job, setting up tables at the Applebee's across from this IHOP.

"Jackie and Jimmy—living in different times in history and coming from uniquely different circumstances—have travelled a parallel journey far more alike than different," Erskine wrote in a self-published book titled *The Parallel.*

"The one parallel factor that made them both successful is that what they were striving for was right," he wrote. "In the end, what is right will always prevail."[1]

And maybe that philosophy of striving for what is right inspired the one last story he wanted to get off his chest. It had to do with the Dodgers' devastating loss in that 1951 playoff game, where the New York Giants won not quite fair and square.

Erskine told me that early in that 1951 season, months before the Shot Heard 'Round the World, he witnessed something that may have brought the Dodgers some bad karma. "It is one of the weirdest strokes of fate that I ever witnessed in my life," he said.

Remember, author Joshua Prager revealed in 2001 that the Giants had set up a system for spying on other teams. They hid a high-powered telescope trained on center field at the Polo Grounds. This allowed team officials, without anyone on the outside knowing it, to peek at the catcher and whether he was giving the pitcher a sign to throw a fastball, a curveball, or an off-speed pitch.

It gave some measure of exoneration to Ralph Branca, the Dodgers pitcher who talked with that Catholic priest about carrying a big cross after he threw the pitch that Giant Bobby Thomson smacked for a home run on October 3, 1951.

"We was robbed!" Branca wrote in his memoir.[2]

By the 1954 season, Branca had been dropped by the Dodgers and was now playing with the Detroit Tigers. He grew close with a teammate named Ted Gray, who had friends who played for the Giants in 1951.[3]

Branca's and Gray's lockers were next to each other, and they were hotel roommates on the road.

"I was sworn to secrecy," Gray finally revealed to Branca one night.

"I promised not to, but when I hear you talk about '51 and that pitch to Thomson, it breaks my heart that you don't know."

"Don't know what?" asked a puzzled Branca.

"He knew you were going to throw him a fastball," revealed Gray.

"You mean he guessed," said Branca.

"No, he knew," confessed Gray. "They were stealing the signs."[4]

As it was explained to Branca, the telescope had been used during World War II, and it was so precise it could see a fly on a chimney from a few hundred feet away.

In July 1951, when the Dodgers still had a strong but ever-shrinking first-place lead, Giants manager Leo Durocher moved forward on a plan to set up the telescope in his center-field office. Remember, Branca had to make that long walk out to center field to get to the clubhouse after Thomson's homer; Durocher's office was near that clubhouse—with a window facing directly at home plate.

A coach for the Giants would turn off the lights in Durocher's office during the game so nobody in the crowd could see him, then point the telescope directly at the opposing team's catcher. It was used against teams all across the National League, not just the Dodgers in that playoff series.

The cheating plan was so sophisticated that Giants management secretly put down wires underneath Durocher's office. That allowed the sign-stealing coach to use buzzers to send his own coded messages to the Giants bullpen and the dugout on the field about which pitch was coming.

Catchers universally put down one finger if they want the pitcher to throw a fastball and two fingers for a curveball, which is a slower pitch with more movement. When the buzzer said a fastball was coming, Giants in the dugout would shout to the hitter, "Sock it!" When a curve was coming they'd scream, "Be ready!"

Catchers sometimes change up the signs if they suspect somebody on the field stole one in a targeted strike, as opposed to an elaborate cheating system. The Giants had a backup if an opposing catcher switched the signs. Someone in the bullpen would hold a white towel if a fastball was coming and wave it for a curve.

Mark down Jerry Reinsdorf as someone who thinks the scandal of the stolen signs is actually overblown.

As the current owner of the Chicago White Sox, Reinsdorf noted that even today it is far easier for a runner on second base to peek at the catcher's signs and try to steal them. Then the runner can touch his helmet or wave a specific arm or give some other signal to tell the batter which pitch is coming.

Thomson had a runner on second base in the ninth inning of that game in 1951, Reinsdorf told me, and it would have been far quicker to get help from that teammate than relying on a telescope and buzzers to get him a sign within a few seconds.

"Besides, it's *your* fault if your signs are stolen," Reinsdorf said of the Dodgers' game in 1951. "Come on. I don't buy this."[5]

Nonetheless, the Giants somehow won thirty-seven of their last forty-four games in that 1951 season, an astounding run of victories that suggested the cheating helped. And if a hitter like Thomson got any kind of secret message telling him that a fastball was coming from Branca, it would have changed his entire approach, enabling him to start his bat sooner and making it more likely he could hit a home run.

Maybe Branca had not really been a goat after all—and he did not deserve all the abuse he received anyway, even if the home run was his fault. The attacks started in the moments right after Thomson smashed that home run. At the Branca home in Mount Vernon, New York, his mother got a call from a man who jabbed, "Why couldn't anyone teach your sorry son to pitch?" More than a few callers simply hung up after declaring, "Drop dead, Branca," to whomever answered.[6]

After learning about the cheating in 1954, the Catholic in Branca felt self-righteous. He told himself that teammates like Robinson and Pee Wee Reese never would have gone forward with such a cheating system if Dodgers management had suggested they use it. But here's the thing about Branca: he was a kind and decent man, and he did not want to rat out Thomson.

After he told Ann what he had learned, she asked whether he'd consider filing a complaint with the commissioner of baseball.

"I don't want to be a crybaby," said Branca. "I don't want to be seen as a sore loser."[7]

Who among us would not want to shout this grievance from the roof-tops and try to clear our names? Instead Branca kept it in for many more years, choosing to continue carrying that cross.

Regardless of his faith, Branca was simply a gentleman who did not want to try to destroy Thomson. In between the time he learned about the cheating in 1954 and Prager's reporting in 2001, reporters had asked Branca about such rumors, but he always refused to speculate.

In March 1962, Joe Reichler—that Associated Press reporter who was close friends with Robinson—broke a story quoting an anonymous source who suggested the Giants stole signs and used a buzzer system during the 1951 season. Shortly after the story ran, Branca appeared on a previously scheduled segment with broadcaster Howard Cosell. Cosell repeatedly pressed him for comment, but Branca would not weigh in.

In the 1980s, Branca and Thomson even began profiting off of their brush with fame as they appeared at sports memorabilia shows together to autograph photos of the Shot Heard 'Round the World. Branca would still sometimes wake up in the middle of the night fretting about the pitch, but he had grown to feel a kinship with Thomson. "I saw that he was a good guy with values not unlike mine," he wrote. "He loved his family, and his politics, like mine, were conservative. The chip on my shoulder fell off. I saw Bobby not as the perpetuator of the cheating scandal but as a foot soldier and not one of the generals who initiated the sign-stealing."

When Thomson died in 2010, Branca attended the funeral and said, "Even though I had lost a game, I had made a friend."[8]

Before Branca passed away in November 2016, he expressed some measure of peace with what happened on that October day in 1951. Branca spent some of his last moments in hospice care and was comforted by the war stories he shared with his son-in-law, Bobby Valentine, himself a for-mer major league baseball player and manager.

Valentine told New York-based sports talk radio host Christopher "Mad Dog" Russo that Branca confided to him that he was going to his grave believing the Giants players did steal signs throughout the season of 1951 to help them win. However, Branca said he did not think that Thomson had gotten the sign during that key at-bat, and that it was simply a bad pitch that was socked into the left-field seats.

"He said something like, 'Heck, anyone could have hit that pitch,'" Valentine told me.

The pitch also did bring Branca some fortune from all of those autograph shows with Thomson, and he noted in his final days that he did not mind the fame that came mixed with the heartache. "Well, I never would have sung on *The Ed Sullivan Show* if I didn't throw that pitch," Branca told Valentine.[9]

Valentine added to me he did not think his father-in-law had a grudge with Thomson. "He thought it was a shallow mind that would try to define him by that pitch," said Valentine. "Other people defined him that way. But I don't think Ralph did."

Pressed on Branca's faith, Valentine said, "He was a devout Catholic who went to church every Sunday, no matter where he was. He believed there were rules and tried to abide by them. He was a God-fearing man who knew he was a piece of the puzzle, but not the whole puzzle."[10]

Yet there are a couple more twists on the story. In 2011, Prager reported in the *New York Times* that after his own book, *The Echoing Green*, was published, including the detail that Branca's mother, Kati, had emigrated from Hungary, a reader contacted the author, wondering if Kati was Jewish. Kati had been a practicing Catholic, but Prager found records showing she actually was Jewish, and that two of her siblings were killed at concentration camps during the Holocaust. By traditional Jewish law, the pitcher was Jewish too.

Branca had always been a practicing Catholic himself, and he smiled as he told Prager, "Maybe that's why God's mad at me—that I didn't practice my mother's religion. He made me throw that home run pitch. He made me get injured the next year. Remember, Jesus was a Jew."[11]

That brings us to Carl Erskine's twist on the story. Why had he suggested the Dodgers earned some bad karma that 1951 season?

It all started with Chuck Dressen. He had served as a coach under Durocher when he was managing the Brooklyn team, and he never felt that he got enough credit as Leo's understudy. Now that Durocher was running the Giants, Dressen was obsessed with his Dodgers crushing his nemesis.

During the regular season, the Dodgers swept a series with the Giants at Ebbets Field to go up big in the standings, and the Brooklyn clubhouse was exultant.

"Charlie Dressen, he's up there—he's in hog heaven, believe me," said Erskine. "He has just now 'killed' Leo Durocher. And he is so happy he is going up and down the line, 'Nice going! Atta boy!'"

Dressen decided to up the ante because he knew there was a door between the Dodgers' clubhouse and the dressing room for the opposing team, and the door was never locked.

Durocher was getting dressed after the game on the other side of that door, so Dressen wanted to rub in the series of losses. He wanted his pitchers to gather as a group and serenade Durocher with a little ditty. The song would be a parody of the "Beer Barrel Polka," turning the lyrics into: "Roll out the barrel, the Giants is dead!"

It was just the type of song that could wake up a sleeping Giant, but Dressen wanted to tempt fate. And so did Branca.

All the Dodgers pitchers had lockers lined up in one section of the clubhouse: Branca, Rex Barney, Erskine, Joe Hatten, and Erv Palica. "Come on back to the door! Come on back to the door!" Erskine remembered Dressen shouting. "We're going to sing to the Giants!"

Then Dressen went down the line of his pitchers, exhorting each one of them to join him in running over to the door.

"I'm serious now, this is God's truth," said Erskine. "Palica wouldn't do it. Hatten wouldn't do it. I wouldn't do it. Barney wouldn't do it."

Erskine was standing right there. And Branca, who had his own beef with Durocher, decided to go sing with Dressen.

Branca had won twenty-one games for the Dodgers at the age of twenty-one in 1947, while Durocher was serving his one-year suspension during Jackie's first season. When Durocher returned to the Dodgers the following year, Branca felt the manager mishandled the pitcher. Now that Durocher was managing the Giants, Branca enjoyed taking a shot at him.

Branca also had that backstage meeting with Frank Sinatra and considered himself a bit of a crooner. So it seems natural that if anyone were to join Dressen in rubbing Durocher's nose in the losses, it would be him.

In fact, Erskine told Prager part of this story for his outstanding 2006 book, *The Echoing Green.* "Palica and I didn't have any appetite to do that," he told Prager about the singing. "But Ralph went with him. Dressen pulled him in."[12]

Prager reported that Robinson also joined Branca and Dressen in blaring out that the Giants were dead, though Erskine told me he did not remember Jackie joining the song.

The reason all of this was gnawing at Erskine is that he had long wondered whether rubbing Durocher's nose in the early season losses backfired on the Dodgers. The Dodgers had tempted fate and given Durocher more motivation to knock them out of first place in the National League.

"So they sang to Leo, who was the firebrand of the century," Erskine said. "He would do anything to beat you. Now play out the rest of the year."

The Dodgers had a huge edge over the Giants before Brooklyn began collapsing. Then, on October 3, Branca and Erskine were warming up with Clem Labine in the Dodgers' bullpen. But Labine had pitched the day before and was tired, while Erskine bounced those curveballs in the dirt. Branca got the call. The home run was hit.

Erskine was still in the bullpen, so along with Labine and bullpen coach Clyde Sukeforth he was one of the first Dodgers to reach the clubhouse.

One by one, the other dejected Dodgers arrived in the clubhouse, and in the agony of defeat each one showed off his dominant personality traits.

Gil Hodges, the soft-spoken warrior who was always a gentleman, was one of the first players who had been on the field to make it to the clubhouse. "I remember this vividly," said Erskine. "He just takes his glove—and typically—folds it quietly and puts it in the top shelf of his locker."

Then the hot-tempered Robinson showed up. "And he fires his glove in to the back of this metal locker," said Erskine. "It sounded like a cannon—*boom!*"

Then Dressen walked in. "He takes his shirt and rips it," said Erskine. "All the buttons [on his uniform] came off."[13]

Branca eventually made it to the clubhouse, shell-shocked, slumped. What could his teammates possibly say to console him? They all stayed away and left him alone—except for one.

Robinson walked over and threw his arm around Branca's shoulder. "Ralph, try not to take it personally," he said. "If it weren't for you, we would have never made it this far."[14]

This was a conversation that would stick with Branca for the rest of his life. When I asked Valentine about Branca's memories of Robinson late in life, he mentioned this very moment.

"Jackie came over to him after he threw the pitch," Valentine recalled. "Jackie said that he shouldn't hang his head."

Added Valentine, "He loved Jackie. He thought Jackie was an intelligent person with the will of a gladiator who was tested and never cracked."[15]

It was particularly amazing in 1951 that many of the white players, and the manager, were losing their cool after the epic meltdown. The African American player, who had been conditioned to turn the other cheek and was seasoned for brutally tough moments, was standing tall in the lowest of moments.

Branca thanked Robinson and then sat there alone.

"I wanted to die," Branca recalled.[16]

Erskine saw that celebratory champagne, chilling in the Dodgers' clubhouse when they had the ninth inning lead, get dragged over to the Giants' dressing room instead.

Then Erskine spotted Branca sprawled out on the steps, face down, and could not stop thinking that maybe the Dodgers had tempted fate with that darn song.

"I could not erase from my mind," Erskine told me, "Dressen coming down to a line of pitchers, 'Let's go sing to the Giants! The Giants are dead!' And one pitcher after another, 'No, no, no.' . . . I thought Ralph might have gone back there to sing."[17]

Erskine was too much of a gentleman to finish the thought. He did not want to make things any worse for Branca.

But left hanging in the air was the strong whiff of the idea that God had been watching, and the handful of Dodgers who had stuck it to Durocher early in the year left some of their teammates feeling as though they never should have stirred the pot like that.

After I told the story to Reinsdorf, he stirred a bit and nodded his head. It reminded him of his own silly decision to tell his mother over the telephone, in the ninth inning of that game, that the Dodgers were going to be champs.

Reinsdorf felt like maybe Branca had picked a fight with Durocher and the Giants while they were pretty harmless to the Dodgers early in the season. And if the pitcher wanted to rile them up, he should have found a way to put them away long before the playoff series.

"I had a friend who used to say, 'Never spit on a man unless you're going to drown him,'" said Reinsdorf.

Looking back, though, Reinsdorf saw no shame in the Dodgers losing in 1951 and so many other times. He notes that it's not as if they were in last place. They came in a strong second many times to great teams like the vaunted New York Yankees and should have counted their blessings.

"My mother used to say, 'God didn't intend for you to be happy every day,'" he said.[18]

INSPIRATION FROM CAMPY

And this was a point Erskine wanted to weigh in on as we sat at IHOP. He had long believed that Roy Campanella taught him a lesson about losing, and more importantly about faith.

"I would liken Campanella to Job," said Erskine. "He was in a wheelchair for thirty-five years. But he never cursed his maker when he lost everything. He never said, 'Why me?'" Erskine added, "He said to me, 'Oh, I lost a few things, but look at what I got left.'"

A year after Campanella's crash, even Brooklyn's longtime nemesis— the New York Yankees—rallied to his side. The Yankees agreed to crisscross the country to the Dodgers' new home in Los Angeles on May 7, 1959, for Roy Campanella Night. All proceeds from the exhibition game went to help pay off Campanella's hefty medical bills.

Dodgers fans responded: the exhibition game at the Los Angeles Memorial Coliseum was attended by 93,103 spectators, a record for the largest crowd in Major League Baseball history.

A few years later, Erskine took a friend to meet Campanella. After so much time in a wheelchair, Campy often suffered from complications, and on this particular day, he was in the hospital. "He was on his stomach to heal his bed sores," said Erskine. "We spent a half hour with him, and afterward my friend said to me, 'I thought we went to cheer *him* up.' Roy never hit bottom."

Another time, when Erskine was recovering from hip surgery, Campanella was now doting on him. "How ya doing, Oisk?" Campanella asked Erskine, slipping back into the Brooklyn chatter.

Erskine noted that even though Campanella was in the wheelchair, he was wearing a new suit, and his shoes were shined. Campanella asked Erskine about his son Jimmy, who was competing in the Special Olympics, and how the family was coping with everything.

"Carl, I pray for you every day," Campanella told Erskine.

As Erskine thought back on that as he sat at the IHOP, tears started filling his eyes all over again.

"I tell you what . . . ," Erskine said, before his voice trailed off and he never quite finished the sentence.

It was finally time for me to go catch a flight home, and Erskine had to go pick up Jimmy at work. But first he wanted to make one last point about Robinson and Campanella and the rest of the Boys of Summer.

Despite all the setbacks and challenges, the heartbreaking losses to the Giants and Yankees, Erskine thought it was worth every second.

"Those Dodger teams—people think losing is all bad," Erskine told me. "From the spiritual standpoint, losing is necessary. Otherwise you would have no thanksgiving or praise for success. The best comes out of people when they have some form of failure."[19]

CHAPTER 23

THE LAST HURRAH

The first thing I noticed about Jackie Robinson's grave was one of his most famous quotes etched into it: "A life is not important except in the impact it has on other lives."

As if to confirm the idea, baseballs and bats were lined up along the grave and on top of it. Many of the bats and balls said "RIP" and were autographed by average people who left them behind because they wanted to say that Jackie's life left an impression on their own lives.

"Thank you! You have paved the way for us. God bless you!" said the inscription on one baseball, which was signed simply, "Rosado family."

I was observing all of this in a quiet section of Cypress Hills Cemetery in Brooklyn. On the top of the gravestone there were pennies and other coins visitors had left behind. There was also a small American flag draped over the side. Someone had written out some of Robinson's own words on the white parts of the flag. "Life is not a spectator sport. If you're going to spend your whole life in the grandstand just watching what goes on, in my opinion, you're wasting your life," it read.

The person who left the flag behind added, "#42 Breaking Barriers. Thank you."

When Robinson was inducted into the Baseball Hall of Fame in 1962, it was clear that his achievements were about far more than just statistics.

"To see Robinson's career in numbers is to see Lincoln through federal budgets and to miss the Emancipation Proclamation," Roger Kahn wrote in *Sport* magazine on the twenty-fifth anniversary of his first game. "Double plays, stolen bases, indeed the bat, the ball, the glove, were only artifacts with which Jackie Robinson made his country and you and me and all of us a shade more free."[1]

At the Hall of Fame induction ceremony, Robinson was overjoyed about the recognition. "We have been up in cloud nine since the election," he declared. "I don't ever think I'll come down."[2]

Alas, in just ten years, Jackie would fall fast. Rachel recalled in her book that when they posed for a family photo at the 1972 World Series, he whispered, "the last hurrah."[3]

How fitting then that he prodded the powerful one more time. His old friend Joe Reichler was also there as Robinson was honored before Game 2 of that year's series between the Cincinnati Reds and the Oakland Athletics.

"I'd like to live to see a black manager, I'd like to live to see the day when there is a black man coaching at third base," Robinson said, his voice choked with emotion on October 15, 1972.[4] (Frank Robinson, no relation, became the first black manager two years later.)

One week after his remarks, Jackie and Rachel were home watching a football game on television together. "Jack suddenly got up and turned the TV off, saying he had detected a flash in his good eye," Rachel wrote. "Such bright flashes often signaled the rupture of a small blood vessel in the eye. A sickening thought raced between us."

They feared blindness was coming, so an appointment with Robinson's doctor was set up for the next day. In fact, it was far worse.

In the morning, Jackie was getting dressed while Rachel prepared breakfast. Suddenly Jackie came speeding toward the kitchen. She met him in his tracks. "He put his arms around me, said, 'I love you,' and just dropped to the floor," she remembered.[5]

The great man had passed on to meet the God he had sought for so long.

Of the many tributes, one of the most poignant was from Dixie Walker, the Dodger from the Deep South who had helped circulate that petition in 1947 threatening a walkout if Robinson got a chance to play in Brooklyn.

"I'm as sad as I could possibly be," said Walker. "Oh, I said and did some stupid things when Jack came up. But before the end, Jack and I were shaking hands."[6]

It had come full circle: some of the old Dodgers who never wanted Robinson to take the field now recognized how much of a mark he had left.

That mark was clear when more than two thousand people turned out to mourn Robinson at his memorial service at the historic Riverside Church in Harlem, where Roberta Flack sang an African American spiritual.

"I told Jesus, it would be all right to change my name," she sang. "He said your father wouldn't know me if he changed my name, but I told Jesus it would be all right to change my name."

Sharon Robinson later wrote that it was a one-mile caravan that took the hearse with Robinson's body through Harlem and on to Brooklyn for burial at Cypress Hills Cemetery.[7] It is no surprise then that several ballplayers were among the more than a dozen honorary pallbearers—including Roy Campanella, who was there in his wheelchair, and Willie Mays.

But to actually carry the casket from the church, Rachel Robinson selected five of her husband's former Dodgers teammates—Joe Black, Ralph Branca, Junior Gilliam, Don Newcombe, and Pee Wee Reese—and one other special person.

Rachel called Bill Russell, the African American basketball great, and asked him to serve as the only non-teammate handling this solemn duty.

"That's an overwhelming honor. Why me?" Russell asked her.

"You were one of Jack's favorite athletes," she responded.

Looking back at that conversation many years later, on a panel at the LBJ Presidential Library in Texas, Russell's familiar, gravelly voice quivered.

"Jackie had done a tremendous thing for us," said Russell. "That he was the first black to play baseball, but he was never a pushover. And he took us to a place that opened up this whole world for us. But I was not going to revisit that place . . . I wanted to take it to the next step."[8]

WHAT IF?

But what if that very first step had not been taken?

Branch Rickey had those second thoughts that led him to visit the minister in Brooklyn. Then the minister's widow, June Fifield, wrote her essay saying she wanted Robinson to know about Rickey's careful contemplation and how there was a hidden hand of God in the decision.

Did that message ever make it to Jackie? The only person who would know for sure was Rachel Robinson. She was still every bit as elegant as ever, though, sadly, as she closed in on ninety-five years old, she had lived more years without her beloved husband than she lived with him.

Mrs. Robinson's voice had grown softer, but it was still powerful when it came to the cause of civil rights. She was smiling warmly when I arrived in New York to visit the Jackie Robinson Foundation, where she carried on the legacy of her husband with grace. She still affectionately called him "Jack," never "Jackie," as one last intimate connection with him.

I told her that President Obama had told me to tell her he saw a straight line from her husband to the first African American president.

"I love that," she told me. "I'm very happy to see that he endorses that idea. So you link the progress we've made in the country from one period to another, you know? I think it's very important to acknowledge that."[9]

Then I told Mrs. Robinson about what I had learned about Rickey's forty-five-minute walk with God in 1945. June Fifield had written, "I hope Jackie will see his fellow man in a new light, knowing this story. May he ever remember Branch Rickey's soul searching in the presence of the God of us all, on his own 'days of decision.'"[10]

Rachel told me she had never heard that story, and she was certain her husband never did either because he would have shared it with her.

"It just reinforces what I knew of him," she told me about Rickey. "I believe he was very thoughtful about making this decision. And he knew he was going to be pretty well isolated in making it. So he needed all the strength he could summon up to take the step."

She noted she was already aware of the broader point of the story to her: Rickey was very thoughtful about the decision and went through every nuance of it.

"He agonized over all aspects of the idea," she said. "He was a pioneer in some ways. And so he had to do what pioneers do—they have to step out and do what they have to do and take the consequences. And he was prepared to do that."

As for reaching out to a minister, it seemed to be part of Rickey's careful game to get everything just right. She was a witness to those preparations, the executive making adjustments to the experiment on the fly, and informing the Robinsons about details of the impending storm.

"He was one who always extensively prepared for changes in the plan," she told me. "He would always alert us to things that were developing over time."

Meaning, of course, Rickey was informing both Rachel and Jackie about the challenges that were popping up, from the first meeting the two men had in August 1945 through that trying first big league season of 1947.

"I think the collaboration was extraordinary in the face of what they were trying to do," Rachel told me. "They knew they couldn't do it without each other. The interdependence between them was solid."

Jackie wrote in his unpublished memoir that he believed that South Bend incident with Charlie Thomas had led Rickey to make a promise with God.

"The promise was that if he succeeded in becoming a power in baseball, he would dedicate himself to breaking down the barriers which kept Negro players out of the major leagues," wrote Robinson. "Knowing these things about Mr. Rickey and seeing how he stuck to his guns during the desperate battle which came about after he took the first bold step to integrate baseball, I realized that his promise had not been made lightly."[11]

Knowing that Jackie saw how critical Rickey's faith was in sustaining his determination, I wondered how integral their own faith was for Jackie and Rachel in 1945 and beyond. I was surprised when she gently corrected me, and I feared I had said something wrong.

Instead her body language said very clearly that they did not wait to rely on their faith until Jackie was on the precipice of breaking the color barrier.

"I think our faith had been important through our lives," she said. "You know we came from religious families, who really believed that—we had beliefs that supported us in our activities. And in our judgments, and in plans we made."

She added, "And there's a leap of faith when you go and get into an experiment like this. And you need to know—not just be thoughtful about—but you have to think, 'Where is my support coming from? How am I going to manage the challenges?' And we knew there were going to be challenges."

When I reflected on her powerful words later, it got me to thinking about just how much faith had shaped Jackie and Branch for their entire lives.

When it came to Branch, learning about his indecision and hesitation did not make him any less of a hero in my eyes. It showed me he was not just the fast-talking wheeler-dealer who was always dead certain about signing Jackie.

In my view, he turned out to be more human, weighing concerns and doubts, and leaning on God to help him find the right path forward.

When it came to Jackie, after several years of research about him, in travels from Pasadena to Brooklyn and a lot of places between those coasts, there was one detail I learned that guided almost every word I wrote.

It was a ritual that had nothing to do with baseball, even though there were plenty of those that I found fascinating, such as the fact that like a lot of players, Jackie was superstitious. On the drive to Ebbets Field each day, he would fret about whether being stopped by certain red lights on his normal route to the ballpark would mean he was headed for a bad day on the field. When he was doing well at the plate, he would keep his uniform out of the washing machine for days on end, just to make sure the hot streak didn't get wiped out.[12]

But no, there was another detail that was a lot more powerful to me, since it provided insight into Jackie's core, and clearly was quite meaningful to him.

Rachel remembered that every single night during his rookie season in Brooklyn, Jackie would go through the simple ritual of kneeling beside their bed to pray, just as his mother Mallie taught him.

Yes, Jackie and Branch had a bond that was formed thanks to baseball and Brooklyn, the whiff of hot dogs and draft beer in the stands at Ebbets Field. Plus the sounds of the crack of the bat and the crash of the ball into the catcher's mitt on a pitch from a hurler named Branca or Erskine.

But another key ingredient brought these two men together—faith in God, though that faith was not absolute or perfect. For both of these men, their faith was tested in ways the public never fully knew. Yet, as Rachel saw up close, that bond remained solid.

And the image of Jackie getting down on his knees like a little boy got me thinking about another boy, who is quickly becoming a young man, and inspired me to finally make this book a reality.

One publisher after another had the same reaction after looking at the book proposal I had pieced together. Sure, they were inspired by the spiritual message, but they rejected the book on the same premise again and again. The public already learned about Robinson and Rickey in other books and the big Hollywood movie.

I was disappointed and truly had given up hope of ever getting it published until one afternoon in the fall of 2015. My then-fourteen-year-old son Patrick came bounding down the staircase from his bedroom.

I had instilled in him a love of baseball that I had been taught by my own father. And now that father-and-son bond, handed down through the generations as in so many American families, was about to remind me about the importance of faith.

"Dad, it's pretty amazing we have a baseball autographed by Jackie Robinson," Patrick said. Then he asked innocently, "How did you get it again?"

I was momentarily stunned, because I had given the ball to Patrick when he was younger and had not given it much thought since then.

The ball had been in my possession since I was his age, and I came by it in an unconventional way. My journalism career had started with a paper route delivering copies of *Newsday* on Long Island. I used to talk baseball with one of my customers, and one day he asked how much money I made per week on the route.

The man pulled a baseball out of his jacket pocket. The ball had belonged to his brother, who worked the front desk at a Brooklyn hotel. I was too young at the time to remember the precise name of the hotel, but I thought the man said it was the "Saint" something or other.

Unfortunately the man also did not know which year the ball was signed, but it was autographed by the entire Dodgers team at some point in the late 1940s or early 1950s.

And then he made an offer I could not refuse. "If you pay me five bucks a week for the next ten weeks, the ball is yours," he told me.

I scooped it up and held on to it for years, moving it from college dorm rooms to starter apartments and then the place my family has called home in the Washington, DC, area for more than a decade. And then, as Patrick and I collected newer signed baseballs from various ballparks across America, I had given my son the historic Dodgers ball so he could give it an honored spot on a shelf in his bedroom, and then I put it out of my mind.

For some reason, just as I was despairing about my failed book project, Patrick pulled it down from his shelf and handed it to me. It was hard not to see it as a sign.

Did I mention that Patrick's birthday is April 15, the anniversary of Jackie's first game?

I resolved to rewrite the book proposal, and within a couple of months I had a deal with HarperCollins. So when I went to meet Carl Erskine at that IHOP in Indiana, I had to bring along the baseball in its protective case.

Erskine took off those indoor sunglasses he wore to protect his eyes from the light. Then he started scanning the old ball. "Oh yeah, there it is," he said, spotting his own signature.

I told Erskine I had never learned which year the baseball was signed. So he inspected the other names on it, and based on which players had signed, Erskine finally figured out the mystery.

It turned out the ball was from, yes, that heartbreaking season of 1951.

But another fact that I learned during my research had a more profound impact on me. I was reading Duke Snider's autobiography and he mentioned that early in his career, he and other players lived at a temporary place in Brooklyn, the St. George Hotel.[13] That was the hotel where my son's baseball was signed.

I decided to use Google to type out "St. George Hotel" and "Brooklyn," where I found the address. It happened to be on Henry Street, a nice little coincidence.

More interesting was what Google Maps told me. The hotel where a lot of those players lived was just a short, three-minute stroll to Plymouth Church. The spot where Branch Rickey paced and paced, thinking and praying and ultimately gaining strength from God to take that first courageous step to sign Jackie Robinson.

ACKNOWLEDGMENTS

Whenever I had writer's block, I sought out Red Barber, the longtime broadcaster for the Brooklyn Dodgers, to give me a lift. Of course, "the Ol' Redhead" died twenty-five years before I began writing this book. Yet thanks to YouTube, I was able to find an audio gold mine of various Dodgers broadcasts from yesteryear. I was instantly transplanted back to Brooklyn in the 1940s and 1950s, the radio broadcasts giving me infusions of the charm and intimacy of Ebbets Field, and the words would start flowing again.

For some reason, my searches over many months kept taking me back, over and over, to one particular game called by Barber in Brooklyn at the start of the 1950 season against the Giants.

Barber was a master with words, making the routine sound poetic, painting beautiful pictures for his radio listeners. At one point, Roy Campanella struggled to grab a foul tip behind home plate, which the broadcaster described as the catcher trying to grab a "mad bumble bee." Rather than calling Bobby Thomson fast, he said simply, "This fellow can fly, long strides."

But the line from Barber that stopped me each time I listened to this particular broadcast was his description of Gil Hodges, a marine who served in combat during World War II. The strapping slugger had gotten seven hits in his first ten at-bats to start the 1950 season, and "has really been hotter than a two-dollar pistol," said Barber.

"Hodges is a magnificent athletic specimen," he added, his Southern drawl dragging out the syllables. "I don't know of anybody who has ever seen him who wants any part of him. He has the least trouble of any man on the face of the earth. And he's awfully good-natured. Everybody says he's just grand. But if you're that strong, you oughta be good-natured."

That stopped me in my tracks because it reminded me of my father, Edward Sr., and I wanted to acknowledge him first here. My dad has always been a sort of gentle giant, working so hard to provide for his family, setting an example for me with both his strength and his smile.

And my dad has always been fearless, especially in 1981, when he took me to my first World Series game. This was a rare World Series when the Dodgers (the Los Angeles version, anyway) actually beat the New York Yankees. I have to finally admit here that I am a Yankees fan, so I was sad at the end of that series. But that emotion paled in comparison to the fear I felt after we attended Game 2 together at Yankee Stadium.

There was so much hype around the game that all the parking lots around the stadium were full when we arrived, so my dad had to park our beat-up Datsun on a public street far from the ballpark in a tough Bronx neighborhood. After the game, when we arrived back at the car, four or five men were waiting for us. They must have watched us park hours earlier, seen my Yankees jacket and cap, and figured we would be coming back a few hours later.

I was only ten years old, and it all happened so fast that I did not process what was happening in real time. But when the men started walking away from the car and toward us menacingly, my dad knew we were in danger and did not flinch.

It was dark, and this was long before cell phones, so my dad clearly did not think we were going to get the police in time. He told me he would confront the men so that we could try to get into our car to make it home. He pointed to a bodega a couple hundred feet away that was still open at this late hour, and told me to wait at the doorway a minute. If he got hurt, I should go inside and demand the man behind the counter call the police. If the men left him alone, which seemed like a pipe dream, I should rush back to the car so we could escape.

It was unclear if the men had guns or other weapons. Because my dad worked in a supermarket, he had a cardboard cutter in his pocket. In the ultimate bluff, he pulled the cutter out and charged toward the group of men! Somehow they all ran. It was only one of many times he stood up for me, and I wouldn't have written this book without the many sacrifices he and my mother, Christine, have made for me.

After reading an early draft of this book, my mom was moved by the section I wrote about Hodges's 1972 funeral. She sent me a text saying the reason was that while there was no way for me to remember this, I had actually attended Hodges's wake the day before the funeral. Both of my parents respected Hodges and decided to bring me to the Brooklyn church to pay our respects. I was only about fifteen months old at the time, so my mom noted, "I was holding you in my arms." She still is.

My sister, Colleen, is the most loving person I know, and watching what she does for my nephew, Frank, and niece, Carla, always inspires me to be a better parent. Thank you, Ching, Emily, and Natalie too.

I dedicated this book at the beginning to my wife, Shirley, because she is so strong and loving, and to my children, Patrick and Mila, because I am more proud of them than anything else in this world.

This book became a reality because my friend Jeff Carneal believed in the power of this story so much that he stuck his neck out for me and called Brian Murray, the CEO of HarperCollins, on my behalf. I will be forever grateful to Jeff, as well as to the great Ken Burns, who was very gracious in helping me get my arms around the story early on, as was my friend David Fauvre.

I owe a remarkable debt of gratitude to my indefatigable researcher, Joshua Bucheister, who did simply outstanding and meticulous work day after day on the overall project. The Brooklyn piece of the narrative took off because of the hard work of Jennifer Williams, one of the best producers in television. Peggy Grande was invaluable with her knowledge of Pasadena, while Tim McCaughan and Rich Johnson got the ball rolling with research and rewrites. Thank you, Donna Shor and Kathy Kemper, who hosted that dinner at the Belgium ambassador's house that sparked this book.

Sending Josh Bucheister to me was just one of dozens of things my dear friend Juan Williams did selflessly to aid this project. I first broached the idea of the book at a dinner with Juan on October 13, 2011. I know that because I have an e-mail from the next morning where he wrote: "I was thinking about how many baseball players make the Sign of the Cross when they approach the plate or point to Heaven after a big hit. You are on to a really powerful theme."

The following April 15, Juan e-mailed me from a Washington Nationals game, "It is Jackie Robinson Day at the ball park. Wearing my Robinson jersey and every player has on number 42!" His enthusiasm continuously encouraged me when few others believed.

The same needs to be said for the remarkable Jerry Reinsdorf, who was my champion in the Midwest. From the moment we met over a cigar, he has been a true-blue friend, and not because he complimented me. To the contrary, the man had the guts to tell me, through various drafts of this book, when it was not measuring up to his high standards. I was even more impressed that he didn't just say, "Fix it," and wash his hands of it. Instead, he somehow found the time, in between running two sports franchises, to show me how to make the book better. When he read one of the final drafts and e-mailed simply, "It's really good," I finally exhaled and felt as though I had gotten somewhere. The man who connected me to Reinsdorf, Mark Sullivan, is the very definition of a gentleman.

My champions in the South were in Kentucky, starting with Kelly and Joe Craft, who never wavered when I needed them most. And this other guy in the Bluegrass State, John Calipari, offered endless encouragement through endless texts and calls about sports, mixed with the occasional talk of politics. Not to mention the pearls of wisdom over coffee at Dunkin' Donuts in Lexington or dinner in New York's Little Italy with Barry "Slice" Rohrssen and their simple preseason toast, "Good friends, good health—and how about a few wins."

I was set up to win because of the strength gleaned from these dear friends, but still I have to admit I was scared out of my mind when I got that sit-down with Brian Murray at HarperCollins, and he told me to give him the "two-minute version" of a book I had been noodling over for a few years. Then I realized most of my live shots are supposed to be ninety seconds or so long, and I mostly figured it out. Brian was a kind listener during my stammering pitch, and I was honored when he told me a few days later he wanted to publish it. He put me in touch with David Moberg, senior vice president at HarperCollins Christian Publishing, who exuded nothing but class. Matt Baugher was a terrific cheerleader for the book from the start; Joel Kneedler made the manuscript better every time he touched it, as did Meaghan Porter. Thanks as well to Lori Cloud in marketing and to Kimberly Golladay, Jesse Wisnewski, and Rhonda Lowry.

I am donating a portion of the proceeds of this book to the Jackie Robinson Foundation. I am sad that I never got to meet, let alone interview, Jackie. But I was inspired by the sheer dignity of Rachel Robinson when I met her. Thanks as well to others at the foundation: president and CEO Della Britton Baeza, director of communications Josh Balber, and board member Ziad Ojakli. In honor of Jackie's service in the US Army, I am also donating some of the proceeds to Folds of Honor, an impressive charity dedicated to helping with the educational needs of the children and spouses of military heroes killed or disabled in action. And, finally, a donation is being made to the Negro Leagues Museum in Kansas City, Missouri.

I am grateful for the support and friendship of so many at Fox News Channel that I could fill several pages, but special mention to Bill Shine, Jack Abernathy, Suzanne Scott, Jay Wallace, Dianne Brandi, Lauren Petterson, and our entire Washington bureau. Gratitude also to my attorney, Bob Barnett.

Your real friends shine brightest when you need them most: thank you, Fred Graefe; Msgr. Peter Vaghi; Bob and Emily Jones; Jack, Jocelyn, and Susanna Quinn; Judge Andrew Napolitano; Bob Massi; Maria Bartiromo; Ali Velshi; Tim Burger; David DiMartino; Erik Smith; Christopher Cuomo; Brian and Steph Gullbrants; Jim and Frann Gray; Donald and Dawn Levy; Richard and Karen Levine; Randy and Mindy Levine; Dr. Albert and Lauren Hazzouri; Lee and Erika Lipton; Vic and Victoria Damone; Pat Welsh; John Pucci; Dr. Joseph Johnson; Ken Korach; Ennis Jordan; Tom Jolly; and Jonathan Wackrow.

And a special shoutout to Debbie Saunders. Long dinners with Flip and his "win the day" mantra helped me finally get this book written. I know he is smiling down on the whole family, particularly my new "little brother" Ryan.

A NOTE ON
UNPUBLISHED SOURCES

42 Faith: The Rest of the Jackie Robinson Story uses unpublished material from the Jackie Robinson Papers and the Branch Rickey Papers, both of which are held at the Library of Congress.

In particular, *42 Faith* quotes heavily from an unpublished book manuscript by Jackie Robinson, titled *My Greatest Day*. Though undated, it was most likely composed between March and September 1961. *My Greatest Day* was supposed to be part of the Great Days series, edited by Walter Lord and published by what was then called Harper & Brothers.

Based on a March 1961 agreement between Robinson and Harper, a September 1961 letter from an editor at Harper to Robinson's literary agent, and a February 1963 addendum to the March 1961 agreement (all held in Box 10, Folder 21 of the Robinson Papers), one can assume that the book manuscript was dropped at some point. Then it was significantly revised, and parts of it were published as *Breakthrough to the Big League* in 1965 by Harper & Row (formerly Harper & Brothers), also edited by Walter Lord.

The sequence of each book is distinct. Some content appears verbatim in both *My Greatest Day* and *Breakthrough to the Big League*; some content appears in both books but with different words, phrasing, and context; and some content is unique to each book. When I quote from *My Greatest Day*, I indicate in endnotes whether the content also appears in *Breakthrough to the Big League*.

Apart from the body text, which is ninety-six pages long, *My Greatest Day* includes a "Forward" [sic] and a "Religion Chapter," each of which has its own set of page numbers.

In addition to *My Greatest Day*, *42 Faith* references speeches, sermons, letters, fan mail, and newspaper clippings from both the Jackie Robinson Papers and the Branch Rickey Papers. When the date of a speech is unavailable, I have done my best to infer it from the content. Most of the speeches referenced have no page numbers.

These and many other materials are available for public perusal in the Manuscript Reading Room, a truly wonderful place, at the Library of Congress in Washington, DC.

I am eternally grateful that Sharon Robinson told me the family wanted me to use as much material as possible from her father's personal papers because her mother donated them to the library so that the public can see his legacy. What a terrific gift.

NOTES

INTRODUCTION

1. Press release, October 9, 1940, 93:4, Franklin D. Roosevelt Library, Hyde Park, New York, quoted in Neil A. Wynn, *The African American Experience During World War II*, The African American History Series (Lanham, MD: Rowman & Littlefield Publishers, Inc., 2011), 50.
2. Wynn, *The African American Experience*, 71.
3. Sybil Lewis, in Mark Jonathan Harris, Franklin Mitchell, and Steven Schechter, eds., *The Homefront: America During World War II* (New York: G.P. Putnam's Sons, 1984), 251; Wynn, *The African American Experience*, 89.
4. Manning Marable, *Race, Reform, and Rebellion: The Second Reconstruction and Beyond in Black America, 1945–2006*, 3rd ed. (Jackson, MS: University Press of Mississippi, 2007), 15.
5. Philip S. Foner, *Organized Labor and the Black Worker, 1619–1973* (New York: International Publishers, 1974), 270; Marable, *Race, Reform, and Rebellion*, 15.
6. Marable, *Race, Reform, and Rebellion*, 15.
7. Eph. 6:5, quoted in Albert J. Raboteau, *Canaan Land: A Religious History of African Americans* (New York: Oxford University Press, 2001), 15.
8. Albert J. Raboteau, *Slave Religion: The 'Invisible Institution' in the Antebellum South*, updated edition (New York: Oxford University Press, 2004), 250.
9. Raboteau, *Canaan Land*, 79.
10. W. E. B. Du Bois, *The Souls of Black Folk* (New York: Penguin Books, 1996), 159.

PROLOGUE

1. President Barack Obama, "Press Conference by the President," *The White House Office of the Press Secretary*, December 20, 2013, https://www.white house.gov/the-press-office/2013/12/20/press-conference-president.

2. President Barack Obama, in discussion with the author, March 2011.

3. June H. Fifield, "Branch Rickey's 'Day of Decision'" (Brooklyn, NY: Plymouth Church, Summer 1966), 2. For a full transcript of Fifield's essay, see Roger Kahn, *Rickey & Robinson: The True, Untold Story of the Integration of Baseball* (New York: Rodale, 2014), 37–42. Few records exist of June Fifield's essay as it was published by Plymouth Church. Thus, all future references to "Branch Rickey's 'Day of Decision'" will refer to the copy reprinted in Roger Kahn's *Rickey & Robinson*.

4. Jackie Robinson, *Breakthrough to the Big League: The Story of Jackie Robinson*, with Alfred Duckett (New York: Harper & Row, Publishers, 1965), 167.

5. Ralph Branca, *A Moment in Time: An American Story of Baseball, Heartbreak, and Grace*, with David Ritz (New York: Scribner, 2011), 70. Reprinted with the permission of Scribner, a division of Simon & Schuster, Inc. Copyright © 2011 Ralph Branca and David Ritz. All rights reserved.

CHAPTER 1: "I'M TAKING A CHANCE HERE"

1. This and all following quotations from Carl Erskine are from a discussion with the author, July 2016.

2. Cal Fussman, *After Jackie: Pride, Prejudice, and Baseball's Forgotten Heroes, An Oral History* (New York: ESPN Books, 2007), ix.

3. Agreement between Jackie Robinson, c/o Lester Lewis Associates and Harper & Brothers over publication of "Untitled Book in the 'Great Day' Series," March 22, 1961. Jackie Robinson Papers (Box 10, Folder 21), Manuscript Division, Library of Congress, Washington, DC; Addenda to the agreement dated March 22, 1961, between Jackie Robinson and Harper & Row Publishers over *The Story of Jackie Robinson (A Breakthrough Book)*, February 4, 1963.

4. Jackie Robinson, *My Greatest Day* (unpublished manuscript, undated), 77. Jackie Robinson Papers (Box 11, Folder 12), Manuscript Division, Library of Congress, Washington, DC.

5. Fussman, *After Jackie*, ix.

6. Martin Luther King Jr., "Address delivered by Martin Luther King Jr., President, Southern Christian Leadership Conference, Atlanta, Georgia, on the occasion of the Hall of Fame Dinner honoring Jackie Robinson," July 20, 1962. Jackie Robinson Papers (Box 2, Folder 7), Manuscript Division, Library of Congress, Washington, DC.

7. "Interview with Rachel Robinson on February 11, 1998," *Scholastic.com*, http://www.scholastic.com/teachers/article/interview-rachel-robinson#top.

8. Robinson, *My Greatest Day*, 84.

9. Ibid., Religion chapter, 3. This line also appears in Robinson, *Breakthrough*, 169.

10. Robinson, *My Greatest Day*, 30.

11. Larry Moffi and Jonathan Kronstadt, *Crossing the Line: Black Major Leaguers, 1947–1959* (Jefferson, NC, and London: McFarland & Company, Inc., Publishers, 1994), 20.

12. Robinson, *My Greatest Day*, 31.

13. "Branch Rickey's Office," *42*, directed by Brian Helgeland (2013; Burbank, CA: Warner Bros. Pictures).

14. Roger Kahn, *Rickey & Robinson: The True, Untold Story of the Integration of Baseball* (New York: Rodale, 2014), 41.

CHAPTER 2: JACKIE IN WINTER

1. Jackie Robinson, "'Cast The First Stone,' Sermon Delivered in New Rochelle, NY on October 15, 1967." Jackie Robinson Papers (Box 7, Folder 21), Manuscript Division, Library of Congress, Washington, DC.

2. Carl Erskine, in discussion with the author, July 2016.

3. This and all following quotations from Larry King are from a discussion with the author, March 2015.

4. Mark Emery, "59 Years After Satchel Paige Pitched at 59, Here Are His Six Tips for Staying Young," *New York Daily News*, September 25, 2015, http://www .nydailynews.com/sports/baseball/satchel-paige-pitched-59-knew-stay-young -article-1.2374681.

5. Grantland Rice, "Jesse Owens, Woodruff Steal Show: Negro Aces Hold 'Spot,'" *Los Angeles Times*, August 4, 1936, A15. *ProQuest Historical Newspapers*.

6. Roger Kahn, *The Boys of Summer* (1972; repr., New York City: Harper Perennial Modern Classics, 2006), xix.

7. Ibid., 393.

8. All excerpts from this speech are from Jackie Robinson, "Untitled Speech," Jackie Robinson Papers (Box 13, Folder 3), Manuscript Division, Library of Congress, Washington, DC. Incidentally, in a book entitled *1947: When All Hell Broke Loose in Baseball*, Red Barber used the Book of Job to describe the problems faced by Branch Rickey in April 1947, when he had to deal with both Robinson's entry into the major league and the suspension of Leo Durocher. See Red Barber, *1947: When All Hell Broke Loose in Baseball* (1982; repr., New York: Da Capo Paperback, 1984), 135.

9. Jackie Robinson, "Guest Speaker at Freedom Dinner of Southern Christian

Leadership Conference—Tuesday Evening, September 25th at Birmingham, Alabama." Jackie Robinson Papers (Box 12, Folder 8), Manuscript Division, Library of Congress, Washington, DC.

10. Ibid.

11. Jackie Robinson, "Address of Mr. Jackie Robinson—Masons—Salem Methodist Church—NYC—7/24/66." Jackie Robinson Papers (Box 13, Folder 3), Manuscript Division, Library of Congress, Washington, DC.

12. Kahn, *Boys of Summer*, xviii–xix.

13. Robinson, "'Cast The First Stone.'"

14. Branch Rickey, "What Makes the Difference?" Lenten Guideposts, *Ottawa Citizen*, February 24, 1955, 21. Reproduced with permission. All rights reserved. For access to the article, see "Branch Rickey on Achieving Success," Guideposts Classics, *Guideposts*, https://www.guideposts.org/guideposts-classics-branch-rickey-on-achieving-success?nopaging=1.

CHAPTER 3: RICKEY HAD A SECRET

1. Donna Shor, in discussion with the author, March 2008.

2. This and all following quotations from Ken Burns are from a discussion with the author, April 2011.

3. Harvey Frommer, *Rickey and Robinson: The Men Who Broke Baseball's Color Barrier* (1982; repr., Lanham, MD: Taylor Trade Publishing, 2015), 12.

4. Branch Rickey III, in discussion with the author, March 2011.

5. Arthur Daley, "Their Magician Was Handcuffed," Sports of the Times, *New York Times*, April 18, 1972, http://www.nytimes.com/1972/04/18/archives/their-magician-was-handcuffed.html.

6. This and all quotations from and descriptions of Branch Rickey's visit with Wendell Fifield are from June H. Fifield, "Branch Rickey's 'Day of Decision,'" in Roger Kahn, *Rickey & Robinson: The True, Untold Story of the Integration of Baseball* (New York: Rodale, 2014), 39.

7. Branch Rickey, "What Makes the Difference?" Lenten Guideposts, *Ottawa Citizen*, February 24, 1955, 21. Reproduced with permission. All rights reserved. For access to the article, see "Branch Rickey on Achieving Success," Guideposts Classics, *Guideposts*, https://www.guideposts.org/guideposts-classics-branch-rickey-on-achieving-success?nopaging=1.

8. Kahn, *Rickey & Robinson*, 39.

9. Roscoe McGowen, "Ringing Up a Run for Dodgers to Help Extend Their Winning Streak," *New York Times*, May 14, 1945, 12. *ProQuest Historical Newspapers*.

10. Harvey Frommer, *New York City Baseball: The Golden Years, 1947–1957* (1980; repr., Lanham, MD: Taylor Trade Publishing, 2013), 57.

11. Carl Erskine, in discussion with the author, July 2016.

12. Red Barber, *1947: When All Hell Broke Loose in Baseball* (1982; repr., New York: Da Capo Paperback, 1984), 61. Used by permission of Doubleday, an imprint of the Knopf Doubleday Publishing Group, a division of Penguin Random House LLC. All rights reserved.

13. Branch Rickey III, in discussion with the author, March 2011.

14. Lee Lowenfish, *Branch Rickey: Baseball's Ferocious Gentleman* (Lincoln: University of Nebraska Press, 2009), 351.

15. Ibid., 358–359.

16. Jimmy Breslin, *Branch Rickey* (New York: Viking, 2011), 6.

17. Don Newcomb, in discussion with Jules Tygiel, *Baseball's Great Experiment: Jackie Robinson and His Legacy* (Oxford and New York: Oxford University Press, 2008), 343.

18. Ibid., 49.

19. Cal Fussman, *After Jackie: Pride, Prejudice, and Baseball's Forgotten Heroes* (New York: ESPN Books, 2007), 3–4.

20. "Dodger Hater" to "Mr. Robinson," September 15, 1953, in *First Class Citizenship: The Civil Rights Letters of Jackie Robinson*, ed. Michael G. Long (New York: Times Books, 2007), 10–11.

21. Jackie Robinson, *I Never Had It Made*, with Alfred Duckett (1972; repr., Hopewell, NJ: Ecco, 1995), 59. Copyright © by Rachel Robinson. Reprinted by permission of HarperCollins Publishers.

22. National Negro Publishers Association, "Churchmen Protest Jacksonville's Stand on Robinson, Wright," *New Journal and Guide*, April 6, 1946: A19. *ProQuest Historical Newspapers;* Tygiel, *Baseball's Great Experiment*, 108.

23. For a description of St. Louis Cardinals' Enos "Country" Slaughter's spiking of Jackie Robinson in 1947, see Arnold Rampersad, *Jackie Robinson: A Biography* (New York: Ballantine Books, 1998), 184.

24. Kahn, *Rickey & Robinson*, 39–40.

25. Sharon Robinson, in discussion with the author, April 2011.

26. Branch Rickey III, in discussion with the author, March 2011.

27. Ibid.

28. Kahn, *Rickey & Robinson*, 42.

CHAPTER 4: JACKIE ON A TRAIN

1. The name was changed to the Chicago Hilton and Towers in 1985, and finally the Hilton Chicago in 1998. Robert V. Allegrini, *Chicago's Grand*

Hotels: The Palmer House Hilton, the Drake, and the Hilton Chicago (Chicago: Arcadia Publishing, 2005), 109.

2. "Hilton Chicago: History," *Historic Hotels of America: National Trust for Historic Preservation*, http://www.historichotels.org/hotels-resorts/hilton -chicago/history.php.

3. Jack Orr, "Jackie Robinson: Symbol of the Revolution," *Sport*, March 1960, 55.

4. "Memorandum of Conversation Between Mr. Rickey and Mr. Sukeforth, Monday, January 16, 1950, Arthur Mann Papers, Library of Congress; Robert C. Cottrell, *Two Pioneers: How Hank Greenberg and Jackie Robinson Transformed Baseball—And America* (Dulles, VA: Potomac Books, 2012), 140.

5. Scott Simon, *Jackie Robinson and the Integration of Baseball* (Hoboken, NJ: John Wiley & Sons, Inc., 2002), 66. Copyright © by Scott Simon. Originally published by John Wiley & Sons. Permission granted by Turner Publishing Company. All rights reserved.

6. Harvey Frommer, *Rickey and Robinson: The Men Who Broke Baseball's Color Barrier* (1982; repr., Lanham, MD: Taylor Trade Publishing, 2015), 4.

7. Carl T. Rowan, *Wait Till Next Year: The Story of Jackie Robinson*, with Jackie Robinson (1960; repr., New York: Ishi Press, 2015), 104.

8. Bill Madden, "Scout's Honor Who Was That in the Middle of Jackie to Brooklyn, Branca to the Mount and Roberto to Pittsburgh? Clyde Sukeforth, of Course!" *New York Daily News*, July 28, 1996, http://www.nydailynews .com/archives/sports/scout-honor-middle-jackie-brooklyn-branca-mound -roberto-pittsburgh-clyde-sukeforth-article-1.733399.

9. Carl Erskine, in discussion with the author, July 2016.

10. The Sukeforth and Robinson dialogue between "You Jack Robinson?" and ". . . the game is over" is from Jackie Robinson, *Breakthrough to the Big League: The Story of Jackie Robinson* (New York: Harper & Row, Publishers, 1965), 61–62.

11. Jackie Robinson, *I Never Had It Made*, with Alfred Duckett (New York: G.P. Putnam's Sons, 1972), 41–42. Copyright © by Rachel Robinson. Reprinted by permission of HarperCollins Publishers.

12. Howard Bryant, *Shout Out: A Story of Race and Baseball in Boston* (New York: Routledge, 2002), 41.

13. Arnold Rampersad, *Jackie Robinson: A Biography* (New York: Ballantine Books, 1998), 123.

14. This back and forth between Robinson and Sukeforth is from Robinson, *Breakthrough*, 62–64.

15. Ibid.

16. Jackie Robinson, *My Greatest Day* (unpublished manuscript, undated), 7. Jackie Robinson Papers (Box 11, Folder 12), Manuscript Division, Library of Congress, Washington, DC.
17. Ibid., 2.
18. Ibid., 1.
19. Roger Kahn, *Rickey & Robinson: The True, Untold Story of the Integration of Baseball* (New York: Rodale, 2014), 101.
20. Robinson, *My Greatest Day*, 2. He also makes this claim in Robinson, *Breakthrough*, 5.
21. Robinson, *My Greatest Day*, Religion chapter, 1–2.
22. Jackie Robinson, "What's Wrong With Negro Baseball?" *Ebony*, June 1, 1948, 16–18; Rampersad, *Jackie Robinson*, 116.
23. Robinson, *My Greatest Day*, 6–7. This line also appears in Robinson, *Breakthrough*, 50.
24. Robinson, *My Greatest Day*, 3. He also makes this claim in Robinson, *Breakthrough*, 10.
25. Ibid., Foreword, 1.
26. Ibid., Religion chapter, 2–3. He also makes this claim in Robinson, *Breakthrough*, xi–xii.
27. Ibid.

CHAPTER 5: "GOD WILL HAVE TO KEEP HIS EYE ON YOU"

1. This and all following quotations from Carl Erskine are from a discussion with the author, July 2016.
2. David Falkner, *Great Time Coming: The Life of Jackie Robinson from Baseball to Birmingham* (1995; repr., New York: Touchstone Books, 1996), 18. Copyright © 1995 by David Falkner. Reprinted with the permission of Simon & Schuster, Inc. All rights reserved.
3. Jackie Robinson, *Breakthrough to the Big League: The Story of Jackie Robinson*, with Alfred Duckett (New York: Harper & Row, Publishers, 1965), 8.
4. Jackie Robinson, *I Never Had It Made*, with Alfred Duckett (1972; repr., Hopewell, NJ: Ecco, 1995), 3. Copyright © by Rachel Robinson. Reprinted by permission of HarperCollins Publishers.
5. Robinson, *Breakthrough*, 7.
6. "Mrs. Robinson's Notes," from Jackie Robinson Papers; Arnold Rampersad, *Jackie Robinson: A Biography* (New York: Ballantine Books, 1998), 15.
7. Jackie Robinson, *My Greatest Day* (unpublished manuscript, undated), 10.

Jackie Robinson Papers (Box 11, Folder 12), Manuscript Division, Library of Congress, Washington, DC.

8. Ibid., Religion chapter, 3.

9. Rampersad, *Jackie Robinson*, 14.

10. Arthur D. Morse, "Jackie Wouldn't Have Gotten to First Base . . ." *Better Homes and Gardens*, May 1950, 279; Anne Schraff, *Jackie Robinson: An American Hero* (Berlin, NJ: Townsend Press, 2008), 8–9.

11. Rampersad, *Jackie Robinson*, 12–13.

12. "Mrs. Robinson's Notes," Jackie Robinson Papers; Rampersad, *Jackie Robinson*, 16.

13. Robinson, *My Greatest Day*, Religion chapter, 1. This line also appears in Robinson, *Breakthrough*, 167–169.

14. Ibid., Religion chapter, 3.

CHAPTER 6: "I RESOLVED NOT TO BE A DOORMAT"

1. Jackie Robinson, *Breakthrough to the Big League: The Story of Jackie Robinson*, with Alfred Duckett (New York: Harper & Row, Publishers, 1965), 12.

2. Jackie Robinson, "Jackie Robinson Tells His Own Story," with Ed Reid, *Washington Post*, August 21, 1949, C1. *ProQuest Historical Newspapers*.

3. Pasadena *Star-News*, April 7, 1987; Arnold Rampersad, *Jackie Robinson: A Biography* (New York: Ballantine Books, 1998), 61.

4. Paraphrased from Rampersad, *Jackie Robinson*, 21.

5. Robinson, *Breakthrough*, 13.

6. Mack Robinson, in discussion with Maury Allen, 1985, quoted in Rampersad, *Jackie Robinson*, 52.

7. Shav Glick, "For Mack Robinson, Memories of Silver Medal Aren't Glittering," *Los Angeles Times*, July 22, 1984, H32. *ProQuest Historical Newspapers*.

8. Anne Schraff, *Jackie Robinson: An American Hero* (Berlin, NJ: Townsend Press, 2008), 21.

9. Sophia Hollander, "Ken Burns Takes a New Look at Jackie Robinson," *Wall Street Journal*, April 8, 2016, http://www.wsj.com/articles/ken-burns-takes-a-new-look-at-jackie-robinson-1460157650.

10. Jessie Maxwell Wills, in discussion with David Falkner, *Great Time Coming: The Life of Jackie Robinson from Baseball to Birmingham* (1995; repr., New York: Touchstone Books, 1996), 25. Copyright © 1995 by David Falkner. Reprinted with the permission of Simon & Schuster, Inc. All rights reserved.

11. Arthur Mann, *The Jackie Robinson Story* (New York: Grosset & Dunlap, 1951), 33; Rampersad, *Jackie Robinson*, 25.

12. Jack Gordon, in discussion with Arnold Rampersad, *Jackie Robinson*, 52.

13. Ibid., 53.

14. Ibid.

15. Jackie Robinson, *I Never Had It Made*, with Alfred Duckett (1972; repr., Hopewell, NJ: Ecco, 1995), 8. Copyright © by Rachel Robinson. Reprinted by permission of HarperCollins Publishers.

16. Jackie Robinson, "Robinson Never Forgets Mother's Advice," with Ed Reid, *Washington Post*, August 23, 1949, 12. *ProQuest Historical Newspapers.*

17. Robinson, *I Never Had It Made*, 9.

18. Ibid., 8.

19. Ibid., 7.

20. "Mrs. Robinson's Notes," from Jackie Robinson Papers; Rampersad, *Jackie Robinson*, 25.

21. Jackie Robinson, *My Greatest Day* (unpublished manuscript, undated), 30. Jackie Robinson Papers (Box 11, Folder 12), Manuscript Division, Library of Congress, Washington, DC. In *Breakthrough to the Big League*, Jackie writes, somewhat less dramatically: "Even before I went to high school and college I resolved not to take insults without retaliating." Robinson, *Breakthrough*, 13.

22. Shav Glick, "The Walls Came Tumbling Down," *Los Angeles Times*, April 12, 1977, D1. *ProQuest Historical Newspapers.*

23. Robinson, *I Never Had It Made*, 5.

24. Falkner, *Great Time Coming*, 20.

25. Jackie Robinson, *Washington Post*, August 23, 1949; Rampersad, *Jackie Robinson*, 33.

26. Jackie Robinson, *My Greatest Day* (unpublished manuscript, undated), Religion chapter, 3, Jackie Robinson Papers (Box 11, Folder 12), Manuscript Division, Library of Congress, Washington, DC.

27. Ibid., 59.

CHAPTER 7: BRANCH FINDS GOD

1. This and all following quotations from Branch Rickey III are from a discussion with the author, March 2011.

2. Arthur Daley, "Their Magician Was Handcuffed," Sports of the Times, *New York Times*, April 18, 1972, http://www.nytimes.com/1972/04/18/archives /their-magician-was-handcuffed.html.

3. Carl Erskine, in discussion with the author, July 2016.

4. Nancy Rickey Keltner, in e-mail discussion with Lee Lowenfish, *Branch Rickey:*

    Baseball's Ferocious Gentleman (Lincoln: University of Nebraska Press, 2007), 15–16.

5. Arthur Mann, *Branch Rickey: American in Action* (Boston: Houghton Mifflin, 1957), 11.

6. Jackie Robinson, *Breakthrough to the Big League: The Story of Jackie Robinson*, with Alfred Duckett (New York: Harper & Row, Publishers, 1965), 53.

7. Mary Rickey Eckler, in discussion with Lowenfish, *Baseball's Ferocious Gentleman*, 16.

8. "John Wesley, 1703–1791: Thoughts upon Slavery," *Documenting the American South*, http://docsouth.unc.edu/church/wesley/wesley.html; Roger Kahn, *Rickey & Robinson: The Untold Story of the Integration of Baseball* (New York: Rodale, 2014), 28; *General Conference of 1784*, Rev. William L. Harris, ed., *General Conference of the Methodist Episcopal Church, Held in Buffalo, N.Y., 1860* (New York: Carlton & Porter, 1860), 420.

9. Branch Rickey, (Allegheny) *Campus*, May 22, 1906; Lowenfish, *Baseball's Ferocious Gentleman*, 36.

10. Branch Rickey to Emily Rickey and Frank Rickey, March 4, 1906. Branch Rickey Papers (Box 2, Folder 1), Manuscript Division, Library of Congress, Washington, DC.

11. "Man of Empire," Sports, *Newsweek*, August 8, 1949, 66.

12. Lowenfish, *Baseball's Ferocious Gentleman*, 39.

13. "Well, This Is Queer: Our Boys Trounce New York Pitchers and Win a Game," *Washington Post*, June 28, 1907, 8, quoted in Lowenfish, *Baseball's Ferocious Gentleman*, 40.

14. Gertrud Hopping to Robert Haig, describing postcards sent to her from Jane, March 15, April 6, and April 14, 1909. Branch Rickey Papers, Manuscript Division, Library of Congress, Washington, DC; Lowenfish, *Baseball's Ferocious Gentleman*, 46.

15. Branch Rickey to Emily Rickey and Frank Rickey, January 1, 1910. Branch Rickey Papers (Box 2, Folder 1), Manuscript Division, Library of Congress, Washington DC.

16. Lowenfish, *Baseball's Ferocious Gentleman*, 52.

17. Ibid., 105.

18. John Heidenry, *The GasHouse Gang: How Dizzy Dean, Leo Durocher, Branch Rickey, Pepper Martin, and their Colorful, Come-from-Behind-Ball Club Won the World Series—and America's Heart—During the Great Depression* (New York: Perseus, 2007), 25.

19. Frank Rickey to "My Darling Loved Ones," January 30, 1937. Branch Rickey Papers (Box 2, Folder 1), Manuscript Division, Library of Congress, Washington, DC.
20. John Wesley, "The Uses of Money," in *John Wesley*, ed. Albert C. Outler (New York: Oxford University Press, 1964), 238–250.
21. Branch Rickey to Frank Rickey, November 25, 1936. Branch Rickey Papers.
22. Ibid., January 3, 1938.
23. Ibid., 1937.
24. Scott Simon, *Jackie Robinson and the Integration of Baseball* (Hoboken, NJ: John Wiley & Sons, Inc., 2002), 71. Copyright © by Scott Simon. Originally published by John Wiley & Sons. Permission granted by Turner Publishing Company. All rights reserved.
25. George Vecsey, in discussion with the author, December 2014.
26. Branch Rickey III, in discussion with the author, March 2011.
27. Jackie Robinson, *My Greatest Day* (unpublished manuscript, undated), Religion chapter, 3, Jackie Robinson Papers (Box 11, Folder 12), Manuscript Division, Library of Congress, Washington, DC. Part of these lines, from "Some people have" until "brotherhood of man," also appear in Robinson, *Breakthrough*, 167.

CHAPTER 8: JACKIE MEETS MR. RICKEY

1. "Weather History Results for Brooklyn, NY (11201) August 28th, 1945," *Farmers' Almanac*, http://farmersalmanac.com/weather-history/search-results/.
2. For the price of Branch Rickey's cigars, see "Man of Empire," Sports, *Newsweek*, August 8, 1949, 63.
3. Robinson offers a description of the pictures that bedecked Rickey's office wall in Jackie Robinson, "Trouble Ahead Needn't Bother You," in *Faith Made Them Champions,* edited by Norman Vincent Peale (Carmel, NY: Guideposts Associates, 1954), 238–241; Michael G. Long, ed., *Beyond Home Plate: Jackie Robinson on Life After Baseball* (Syracuse: Syracuse University Press, 2013), 2. For another description of the portraits hanging in Rickey's office, see Scott Simon, *Jackie Robinson and the Integration of Baseball* (Hoboken, NJ: John Wiley & Sons, Inc., 2002), 71–72.
4. Long, *Beyond Home*, 2.
5. "Man of Empire," 62. That quote is a reference to a line from Shakespeare's *Macbeth* and how, in a play about a man under heavy stress, sleep can repair the daily struggles.

6. For various and varying accounts of the meeting between Branch Rickey and Jackie Robinson at 215 Montague Street, see Falkner, *Great Time Coming,* 107–115; Frommer, *Rickey and Robinson,* 2–16; Kahn, *Rickey & Robinson,* 103–108; Rampersad, *Jackie Robinson,* 125–128; Jeff Nilsson, "Grace Under Pressure: Jackie Robinson," *Saturday Evening Post,* January 29, 2011, http://www.saturdayeveningpost.com/2011/01/29/history/post-perspective/grace-pressure-jackie-robinson.html; Robinson, *Breakthrough to the Big League,* 66–78; Robinson, *I Never Had It Made,* 30–34; Simon, *Integration of Baseball,* 76–83.

7. Simon, *Integration of Baseball,* 76.

8. Ibid.

9. The Robinson and Rickey dialogue between "do you have a girl?" and "marry her as quick as you can" is from Harvey Frommer, *Rickey and Robinson: The Men Who Broke Baseball's Color Barrier* (1982; repr., Lanham, MD: Taylor Trade Publishing, 2015), 5.

10. The Robinson and Rickey dialogue between "but sit down" and "chance with the Brooklyn Dodgers" is from Nilsson, "Grace Under Pressure."

11. The Robinson and Rickey dialogue between "do you think . . . ?" and "willing to sign it" is from Roger Kahn, *Rickey & Robinson: The Untold Story of the Integration of Baseball* (New York: Rodale, 2014), 104.

12. The Robinson and Rickey dialogue between "Mr. Rickey, it sounds like a dream" and "tact and common sense" is from Robinson, "Trouble Ahead Needn't Bother You," 2–3.

13. The Robinson and Rickey dialogue between "I want to win" and "Yes" is from Simon, *Integration of Baseball,* 80.

14. The description of Sukeforth witnessing the scene, as well as the subsequent discussion over whether Robinson can "take it" is paraphrased and quoted from Nilsson, "Grace Under Pressure."

15. Branch Rickey's hypothetical accusations appear in Paul Roth, *The Game: How Baseball Overcame Segregation* (2013), 47, https://issuu.com/paulyroth/docs/the_game.

16. "Five Years in White Man's Baseball: An Exclusive *Focus* Interview," *Focus,* July 1952, 5.

17. This and all following quotations from Erskine are from a discussion with the author, July 2016.

18. Giovanni Papini, *The Life of Christ,* trans. Dorothy Canfield Fisher (NY: Harcourt Brace, 1923), 104–105; Rampersad, *Jackie Robinson,* 127.

19. Branch Rickey, *The American Diamond: A Documentary of the Game of Baseball* (New York: Simon & Schuster, 1965), 46.
20. "Montreal Signs Negro Shortstop," *New York Times*, October 24, 1945, 17; Rampersad, *Jackie Robinson*, 129.
21. "Rickey Claims that 15 Clubs Voted to Bar Negroes from the Majors," *New York Times*, February 18, 1948, 37.
22. The Robinson and Rickey dialogue between "I'm a hotheaded player!" and "I've got two cheeks" is from Nilsson, "Grace Under Pressure."
23. For descriptions of the various incidents at Pasadena Junior College, see Rampersad, *Jackie Robinson*, 48–50.
24. Jackie Robinson, *My Greatest Day* (unpublished manuscript, undated), 29. Jackie Robinson Papers (Box 11, Folder 12), Manuscript Division, Library of Congress, Washington, DC.
25. Roth, *The Game*, 47.
26. Robinson, *My Greatest Day*, 30.
27. Alexander Pope, "Essay on Man" in *The Works of Alexander Pope Esq. Volume III Containing His Moral Essays* (London: C. Bathurst, 1787), 64; Lowenfish, *Baseball's Ferocious Gentleman*, 429.
28. Jackie Robinson, interview with Reverend Dana F. Kennedy, *Viewpoint*, December 14, 1957. Jackie Robinson Papers (Box 1, Folder 23), Manuscript Division, Library of Congress, Washington, DC.
29. Kahn, *Rickey & Robinson*, 102.
30. Jackie Robinson, *My Greatest Day*, Religion chapter, 4. A similar version of this line appears in Robinson, *Breakthrough*, 169.

CHAPTER 9: NO DOUBTING THOMAS

1. This and all following quotations from Branch Rickey III are from a discussion with the author, March 2011.
2. "Looking Back at the Oliver Hotel, Throwback Thursday," *South Bend Tribune*, February 4, 2016, http://www.southbendtribune.com/news/local/history/throwback-thursday-looking-back-at-the-oliver-hotel/article_3297ff10-c9ed-11e5-b661-83c3231ccbbd.html.
3. For a summary of Barber's slang, see Bob Edwards, "The Ole Redhead," The Blog, *Huffington Post*, February 13, 2008, http://www.huffingtonpost.com/bob-edwards/the-ole-redhead_b_86514.html.
4. Branch Rickey III, in discussion with the author, March 2011.
5. Red Barber, *1947: When All Hell Broke Loose in Baseball* (1982; repr., New

York: Da Capo Paperback, 1984), 49. Used by permission of Doubleday, an imprint of the Knopf Doubleday Publishing Group, a division of Penguin Random House LLC. All rights reserved.

6. Ibid., 51–52.

7. Roger Kahn, *Rickey & Robinson: The True, Untold Story of the Integration of Baseball* (New York: Rodale, 2014), 36–37.

8. Ibid., 49–50.

9. Ibid., 48.

10. Lee Lowenfish, *Branch Rickey: Baseball's Ferocious Gentleman* (Lincoln: University of Nebraska Press, 2007), 23.

11. Barber, *When All Hell Broke Loose*, 50.

12. Jules Tygiel, *Baseball's Great Experiment: Jackie Robinson and His Legacy* (Oxford and New York: Oxford University Press, 2008), 52.

13. Lowenfish, *Baseball's Ferocious Gentleman*, 24.

14. Tygiel, *Baseball's Great Experiment*, 52.

15. Lowenfish, *Baseball's Ferocious Gentleman*, 24.

16. Chris Lamb, "Did Branch Rickey Sign Jackie Robinson to Right a 40-Year Wrong?" *Black Ball* 6, no. 1 (Spring 2013): 5–18.

17. Bill Mardo, "Robinson-Robeson," in *Jackie Robinson: Race, Sports, and the American Dream*, edited by Joseph Dorinson and Joram Warmund (New York: Routledge, 2015), 102–103; Lamb, "Did Branch Rickey," 8.

18. Mardo, "Robinson-Robeson," 103; Lamb, "Did Branch Rickey," 8.

19. Lamb, "Did Branch Rickey," 9.

20. A.S. "Doc" Young, "The Black Athlete in the Golden Age of Sports," *Ebony*, November 1968, 156; Lamb, "Did Branch Rickey," 12.

21. Lamb, "Did Branch Rickey," 16.

22. Lowenfish, *Baseball's Ferocious Gentleman*, 600, fn. 29.

23. Dr. C. L. Thomas "Tommy" to Friend Rickey, October 26, 1921. Branch Rickey Papers (Box 29, Folder 5), Manuscript Division, Library of Congress, Washington, DC.

24. Ibid., Branch Rickey to Dr. C. L. Thomas, November 1, 1921.

25. Young, "The Black Athlete," 156; Lamb, "Did Branch Rickey," 11.

26. Murray Polner, *Branch Rickey: A Biography*, rev. ed. (Jefferson, NC: McFarland & Company, Inc., 2007), 36.

27. Jim Reisler, *Black Writers/ Black Baseball: An Anthology of Articles from Black Sportswriters Who Covered the Negro Leagues*, rev. ed. (Jefferson, NC: McFarland & Company, Inc., 2007), 81.

28. Lamb, "Did Branch Rickey," 16.

29. Carl Erskine, in discussion with the author, July 2016.

30. Red Barber, *When All Hell Broke Loose*, 50–51.

31. Ibid., 63.

32. Ibid., 135–136.

33. Ibid., 63.

34. Ibid., 64.

CHAPTER 10: "ALL HEAVEN WILL REJOICE"

1. Carl Erskine, in discussion with the author, July 2016.

2. Branch Rickey III, in discussion with the author, March 2011.

3. Associated Press, "Griffith Attacks Rickey: Sees Attempt by Dodger Chief to 'Dictate' in Negro Baseball," *New York Times*, May 16, 1945, 23. *ProQuest Historical Newspapers*; Roger Kahn, "The Ten Years of Jackie Robinson," *Sport*, October 1955, 79.

4. Jackie Robinson, *I Never Had It Made*, with Alfred Duckett (1972; repr., Hopewell, NJ: Ecco, 1995), 35. Copyright © by Rachel Robinson. Reprinted by permission of HarperCollins Publishers.

5. Ibid.

6. Jackie Robinson, *Jackie Robinson: My Own Story*, with Wendell Smith (1948; repr., Pickle Partners Publishing, 2016), 19; David Falkner, *Great Time Coming: The Life of Jackie Robinson from Baseball to Birmingham* (1995; repr., New York: Touchstone Books, 1996), 116.

7. "Montreal Signs Negro Shortstop," *New York Times,* October 24, 1945, 17; Falkner, *Great Time Coming*, 116.

8. "Montreal Signs Negro Shortstop"; Arnold Rampersad, *Jackie Robinson: A Biography* (New York: Ballantine Books, 1998), 129.

9. Ibid.

10. Robinson refers to Reese as "probably [his] best friend on the club" in a 1955 piece in *Look*. Jackie Robinson, "Now I Know Why They Boo Me!," *Look*, January 25, 1955, 28.

11. Scott Simon, *Jackie Robinson and the Integration of Baseball* (Hoboken, NJ: John Wiley & Sons, Inc., 2002), 25. Copyright © by Scott Simon. Originally published by John Wiley & Sons. Permission granted by Turner Publishing Company. All rights reserved.

12. Ibid., 30.

13. Ibid., 30–31.

14. Ibid., 31.

15. Fay Young, "End of Baseball's Jim Crow Seen with Signing of Jackie Robinson," *Chicago Defender*, November 3, 1945, 9. *ProQuest Historical Newspapers*; Lee Lowenfish, *Branch Rickey: Baseball's Ferocious Gentleman* (Lincoln: University of Nebraska Press, 2007), 392.

16. Associated Press, "Robinson's Chances Slim, Says Feller," *Washington Post*, November 1, 1945, 12; Tygiel, *Great Experiment*, 76.

17. Larry Lester, "J. L. Wilkinson: 'Only the Stars Come out at Night,'" in *Satchel Paige and Company: Essays on the Kansas City Monarchs, Their Greatest Star and the Negro Leagues*, edited by Leslie A. Heaphy (Jefferson, NC: McFarland & Company, Inc., 2007), 132.

18. "Smokey" to Branch Rickey, October 24, 1945. Branch Rickey Papers (Box 24, Folder 12), Library of Congress, Manuscript Division, Washington, DC.

19. Ibid., Alexa D. N. Nancy Duval to Branch Rickey, October 24, 1945.

20. Ibid., Branch Rickey to Frank C. Clemens, November 15, 1945.

21. For Branch Rickey's description of the August 1946 meeting in Chicago, see the Associated Press, "Rickey Claims That 15 Clubs Voted to Bar Negroes From the Majors," *New York Times*, February 17, 1946, 37.

22. Ibid.

23. Ibid.

24. Ibid.

25. Associated Press, "Text of MacPhail Statement," *New York Times*, February 20, 1948, 16; Roger Kahn, *Rickey & Robinson: The True, Untold Story of the Integration of Baseball* (New York: Rodale, 2014), 112.

26. Chris Lamb, *Blackout: The Untold Story of Jackie Robinson's First Spring Training* (Lincoln: University of Nebraska Press, 2004), 23–41.

27. Bill Gibson, "Hear Me Talkin' To Ya," *Baltimore Afro-American*, February 18, 1933, 17. *ProQuest Historical Newspapers*; Lamb, *Blackout*, 25.

28. "Heydler Says Creed or Color Has Not Been Bar," *Pittsburgh Courier*, February 25, 1933, 5. *ProQuest Historical Newspapers*; Lamb, *Blackout*, 27.

29. Earl J. Morris, "No Rule Barring Colored Players Exists in Major Leagues, Says Leslie M. O'Connor," *Pittsburgh Courier*, March 11, 1933, 5. *ProQuest Historical Newspapers*; Lamb, *Blackout*, 27.

30. Carl Erskine, in discussion with the author, July 2016.

31. Roger Kahn, *Rickey & Robinson: The True, Untold Story of the Integration of Baseball* (New York: Rodale, 2014), 108.

32. Jackie Robinson, *Breakthrough to the Big League*, with Alfred Duckett (New York: Harper & Row, Publishers, 1965), 25.

33. Ibid., 28.

34. Rachel Robinson, "I Live with a Hero," *McCall's*, March 1951, 39.

35. Rachel Robinson, *Jackie Robinson: An Intimate Portrait*, with Lee Wilkins (New York: Harry M. Abrams, 1996), 46.

36. Robinson, "I Live with a Hero," 39.

37. Ibid., 40.

38. Ibid., 39.

39. Ibid., 40.

40. Ibid.

41. Roger Kahn, "The Ten Years of Jackie Robinson," *Sport*, October 1955, 78.

42. Jackie Robinson, *My Greatest Day*, 32.

43. Ibid., 33. This line also appears in Jackie Robinson, *Breakthrough to the Big League*, 77.

44. Kahn, *Rickey & Robinson*, 105.

CHAPTER 11: THE CONVERSION OF CLAY HOPPER

1. Carl Erskine, in discussion with the author, July 2016.

2. Sam Lacy, "Looking 'Em Over," *Baltimore Afro-American*, March 2, 1946, 18. *ProQuest Historical Newspapers*.

3. Wendell Smith, "Cordial Welcome Awaits Jackie Robinson in Florida," *Pittsburgh Courier*, March 2, 1946, 2. *ProQuest Historical Newspapers*.

4. Associated Press, "Jackie Robinson Fails to Attend Montreal Drill," March 2, 1946, 18. *ProQuest Historical Newspapers*.

5. Smith, "Cordial Welcome."

6. Peter Golenbock, *Bums: An Oral History of the Brooklyn Dodgers* (Mineola, NY: Dover Publications, Inc., 2010), 128.

7. Roger Kahn, *Rickey & Robinson: The True, Untold Story of the Integration of Baseball* (New York: Rodale, 2014), 201–202.

8. Ibid., 202.

9. Arnold Rampersad, *Jackie Robinson: A Biography* (New York: Ballantine Books, 1998), 147.

10. Jackie recounts the story of the boy who encourages him after his 1946 attempt to steal home in Jackie Robinson, "We're Winning the One That Counts," *Look*, September 19, 1950, 56.

11. Kahn, *Rickey & Robinson*, 64.

12. Ibid., 202.

13. For Robinson's account of his poor hitting spring training and Paul Derringer's

attempt to snap him out of it, see Jackie Robinson, "Now I Know Why They Boo Me!," *Look*, January 25, 1955, 24.

14. Kahn, *Rickey & Robinson*, 202.

15. Ibid.

16. Ibid.

17. Ibid., 202–203.

18. "Untitled Speech," Jackie Robinson Papers (Box 13, Folder 3), Manuscript Division, Library of Congress, Washington, DC.

19. Dave Anderson, "50 Years Ago: Robinson's Jersey Debut," Sports of the Times, *New York Times*, April 18, 1996, http://www.nytimes.com/1996/04/18/sports /sports-of-the-times-50-years-ago-robinson-s-jersey-debut.html.

20. Jackie Robinson, "Trouble Ahead Needn't Bother You," in *Faith Made Them Champions*, edited by Norman Vincent Peale (Carmel, NY: Guideposts Associates, 1954), 238–241; Michael G. Long, ed. *Beyond Home Plate: Jackie Robinson on Life After Baseball* (Syracuse, NY: Syracuse University Press, 2013), 3.

21. Clay Hopper's pre-game talk and Jackie Robinson's reaction to it appear in Kahn, *Rickey & Robinson*, 204–205.

22. Robinson, "Trouble Ahead Needn't Bother You"; Long, *Beyond Home Plate*, 3.

23. Dave Stubbs, "Greeting History at Home Plate," *Montreal Gazette*, April 18, 2006, A1.

24. Richard Goldstein, "George Shuba, 89, Dies; Handshake Heralded Racial Tolerance in Baseball," *New York Times*, September 30, 2014, http://www .nytimes.com/2014/10/01/sports/baseball/george-shuba-whose-handshake -heralded-racial-tolerance-in-baseball-dies-at-89.html.

25. Kahn, *Rickey & Robinson*, 206.

26. Red Barber, *1947: When All Hell Broke Loose in Baseball* (1982; repr., New York: Da Capo Paperback, 1984), 81. Used by permission of Doubleday, an imprint of the Knopf Doubleday Publishing Group, a division of Penguin Random House LLC. All rights reserved.

27. In a 1955 article in *Sport*, sportswriter Roger Kahn recalls Dixie Howell telling Rube Walker how rough pitchers were on Robinson while he played for the Royals. Roger Kahn, "The Ten Years of Jackie Robinson," *Sport*, October 1955, 79.

28. Kahn, "The Ten Years of Jackie Robinson," 80.

29. Robinson, "Trouble Ahead Needn't Bother You;" Long, *Beyond Home Plate*, 3–4.

30. Kahn, "The Ten Years of Jackie Robinson."

31. Jackie Robinson, *My Greatest Day* (unpublished manuscript, undated), 32.

Jackie Robinson Papers (Box 11, Folder 12), Manuscript Division, Library of Congress, Washington, DC.

32. For Jackie's various confrontations at Fort Riley and Fort Hood, see Scott Simon, *Jackie Robinson and the Integration of Baseball* (Hoboken, NJ: John Wiley & Sons, Inc., 2002), 14–16.

33. Ibid., 17.

34. The dialogue from this account of Robinson's run-in with the Texas bus driver appears in Simon, *Integration of Baseball*, 18–23.

35. Simon, *Integration of Baseball*, 24.

36. Kahn, *Rickey & Robinson*, 223. For another account of Montreal fans chasing Robinson around the field in 1946 following the Little World Series, see Jackie Robinson, "Now I Know Why They Boo Me!," *Look*, January 25, 1955, 24.

CHAPTER 12: NO SLEEP TILL BROOKLYN

1. Betsy Streisand, "L.A., Here They Came," *U.S. News & World Report*, August 13, 2007, 57.

2. For information on Charles Ebbets' financial troubles, Stephen and Edward McKeever's interest in the construction of Ebbets Field, and their partnership with Charles Ebbets, see Glenn Stout, *The Dodgers: 120 Years of Dodgers Baseball* (New York: Houghton Mifflin Company, 2004): 53–57.

3. Larry King, in discussion with the author, March 2015.

4. Enos Slaughter, as remembered by Larry King, in discussion with the author, March 2015. For a published account of this story, see Enos Slaughter, in discussion with Larry King, *Why I Love Baseball* (Beverly Hills: New Millennium Entertainment, 2004), 46–47.

5. Jonathan Eig, *Opening Day: The Story of Jackie Robinson's First Season* (New York: Simon & Schuster Paperbacks, 2007), 36.

6. Jackie Robinson, *My Greatest Day* (unpublished manuscript, undated), 24. Jackie Robinson Papers (Box 11, Folder 12), Manuscript Division, Library of Congress, Washington, DC.

7. Roger Kahn, *The Boys of Summer* (1972; repr., New York City, Harper Perennial Modern Classics, 2006), 43.

8. Roger Kahn, *Rickey & Robinson: The True, Untold Story of the Integration of Baseball* (New York: Rodale, 2014), 237.

9. Leo Durocher, *Nice Guys Finish Last*, with Ed Linn (1975; repr., Chicago: University of Chicago Press, 2009), 204. Reprinted by permission The Estate of Leo Durocher™ by CMG Worldwide.

10. Few authors spend much time discussing who, in particular, wrote the petition; most mention it in passing. Authors Jonathan Eig, Peter Golenbock, Roger Kahn, and Jules Tygiel attribute the petition's origin to Dixie Walker. See Jonathan Eig, *Opening Day*, 41–42; Peter Golenbock, "Men of Conscience," in *Jackie Robinson: Race, Sports, and the American Dream*, edited by Joseph Dorinson and Joram Warmund (London: Routledge, 1998), 17; Kahn, *The Era*, 34; Jules Tygiel, *Baseball's Great Experiment: Jackie Robinson and His Legacy* (Oxford and New York: Oxford University Press, 2008), 170. Others spread the blame more widely. In *Nice Guys Finish Last*, Leo Durocher attributes it to Dixie Walker and Eddie Stanky. See Durocher, *Nice Guys Finish Last*, 203. Both Ralph Branca and Arnold Rampersad attribute it to the Southern players on the team: Walker, as well as Hugh Casey, Kirby Higbe, and Bobby Bragan. See Branca, *A Moment in Time*, 71; Arnold Rampersad, *Jackie Robinson: A Biography* (New York: Ballantine Books, 1998), 175.

11. This account of the Dodgers' petition to bar Jackie Robinson, and Leo Durocher's role in stopping it, is based on and quotes material from Durocher, *Nice Guys Finish Last*, 204–205.

12. Ralph Branca, *A Moment in Time: An American Story of Baseball, Heartbreak, and Grace*, with David Ritz (New York: Scribner, 2011), 45. Reprinted with the permission of Scribner, a division of Simon & Schuster, Inc. Copyright © 2011 Ralph Branca and David Ritz. All rights reserved.

13. For a description of Durocher's flashy lifestyle, see Branca, *Moment in Time*, 47.

14. Ibid., 46.

15. Ibid.

16. Ibid., 71.

17. For a full transcript of the letter, see Maury Allen and Susan Walker, *Dixie Walker of the Dodgers: The People's Choice* (Tuscaloosa: The University of Alabama Press, 2010), 4.

18. Kahn, *Boys of Summer*, 323.

19. Ibid., 324.

20. Ibid., 325.

21. Eig, *Opening Day*, 104.

22. Robinson, *My Greatest Day*, 25. These lines also appear in Jackie Robinson, *Breakthrough to the Big League: The Story of Jackie Robinson*, with Alfred Duckett (New York: Harper & Row, Publishers, 1965), 106.

23. Roger Kahn, *The Era, 1947–1957: When the Yankees, the Giants, and the Dodgers Ruled the World* (Lincoln: University of Nebraska Press, 2002), 35.

24. Robinson, *My Greatest Day*, Religion chapter, 3. He also makes this claim in Robinson, *Breakthrough*, 169.

CHAPTER 13: "GOOSE PIMPLES" AT EBBETS FIELD

1. This and all following quotes from Jerry Reinsdorf are from a discussion with the author, July 2016.
2. Carl Erskine, in discussion with the author, July 2016.
3. For a description of the advertisements that bedecked Ebbets Field, see Andrew Paul Mele, *"Tearin' Up The Pea Patch": The Brooklyn Dodgers, 1953* (Jefferson, NC: McFarland & Company, Inc., Publishers, 2015), 182.
4. Vin Scully, video linked from Twitter post, September 24, 2014, 8:53 p.m., https://twitter.com/vinscullytweet/status/514986059877203970.
5. Ralph Branca, *A Moment in Time: An American Story of Baseball, Heartbreak, and Grace*, with David Ritz (New York: Scribner, 2011), 24–25. Reprinted with the permission of Scribner, a division of Simon & Schuster, Inc. Copyright © 2011 Ralph Branca and David Ritz. All rights reserved.
6. Arthur Daley, "Return to Brooklyn," Sports of the Times, *New York Times*, April 9, 1947, 32. *ProQuest Historical Newspapers*.
7. Red Barber, *1947: When All Hell Broke Loose in Baseball* (1982; repr., New York: Da Capo Paperback, 1984), 126. Used by permission of Doubleday, an imprint of the Knopf Doubleday Publishing Group, a division of Penguin Random House LLC. All rights reserved.
8. Barber, *When All Hell Broke Loose*, 126–136.
9. Ibid., 135.
10. Jackie Robinson, *I Never Had It Made*, with Alfred Duckett (1972; repr., Hopewell, NJ: Ecco, 1995), xiii. Copyright © by Rachel Robinson. Reprinted by permission of HarperCollins Publishers.
11. Donald Graf, e-mail message to author, October 23, 2016.
12. Graf, in follow-up discussion with the author, November 2016.
13. Jackie Robinson, in discussion with Ward Morehouse, "Debut 'Just Another Game' to Jackie," *Sporting News*, April 23, 1947; Jonathan Eig, *Opening Day: The Story of Jackie Robinson's First Season* (New York: Simon & Schuster Paperbacks, 2007), 60–61.
14. Jerry Reinsdorf, in discussion with the author, July 2016.
15. Jackie Robinson, "Trouble Ahead Needn't Bother You," in *Faith Made Them Champions*, edited by Norman Vincent Peale (Carmel, NY: Guideposts

Associates, 1954), 238–241; Michael G. Long, ed. *Beyond Home Plate: Jackie Robinson on Life After Baseball* (Syracuse, Syracuse University Press, 2013), 4.

16. Branca, *Moment in Time*, 74.

17. Roger Kahn, *Rickey & Robinson: The True, Untold Story of the Integration of Baseball* (New York: Rodale, 2014), 37.

18. Ibid., 64–65.

CHAPTER 14: PRAYERS FOR JACKIE

1. Ken Burns, interview by Evan Smith, *Overheard with Evan Smith*, PBS, May 14, 2016, https://archive.org/details/KCSM_20160514_233000_Overheard_With_Evan_Smith.

2. Jackie Robinson, "Five Years in White Man's Baseball: An Exclusive *Focus* Interview," *Focus*, July 1952, 7.

3. Jackie Robinson, "A Kentucky Colonel Kept Me in Baseball," *Look*, February 8, 1955, 82–90.

4. Ralph Branca, *A Moment in Time: An American Story of Baseball, Heartbreak, and Grace*, with David Ritz (New York: Scribner, 2011), 75. Reprinted with the permission of Scribner, a division of Simon & Schuster, Inc. Copyright © 2011 Ralph Branca and David Ritz. All rights reserved.

5. "Quick Facts: Philadelphia County, Pennsylvania," *United States Census Bureau*, http://www.census.gov/quickfacts/table/INC910214/42101.

6. Harold Parrott, *The Lords of Baseball: A Wry Look at a Side of the Game the Fan Seldom Sees—The Front Office* (New York: Praeger, 1976), 193; Arnold Rampersad, *Jackie Robinson: A Biography* (New York: Ballantine Books, 1998), 175.

7. Ibid.

8. Robinson, "Five Years in White Man's Baseball," 7.

9. Robinson, "A Kentucky Colonel Kept Me in Baseball."

10. Ibid.

11. Ibid.

12. Robinson, "Five Years in White Man's Baseball," 7. For another description of Stanky standing up for Robinson in Philadelphia, see Jackie Robinson, "We're Winning the One That Counts," *Look*, September 19, 1950, 60.

13. Jackie Robinson, *My Greatest Day* (unpublished manuscript, undated), 54, Jackie Robinson Papers (Box 11, Folder 12), Manuscript Division, Library of Congress, Washington, DC.

14. Carl Erskine, in discussion with the author, July 2016.

15. Mrs. Bernice Franklin to Jackie Robinson, August 20, 1947. Jackie Robinson

Papers (Box 1, Folder 290), Manuscript Division, Library of Congress, Washington, DC.

16. Ibid., Harold MacDowell to Jackie Robinson, May 16, 1947.

17. Ibid., Reverend John F. Curran to Jackie Robinson, October 7, 1947.

18. Ibid., Eugene Carey to Jackie Robinson, May 9, 1947.

19. Branca, *Moment in Time*, 77–78.

20. Robinson, "A Kentucky Colonel Kept Me in Baseball."

21. For a description of Robinson's encounter with Joe Garagiola, as well as his back and forth with the umpire, see Tim Cohane, "Jackie Robinson's First Year With the Dodgers," *Look*, January 6, 1948, 50.

22. Branca, *Moment in Time*, 82.

23. Robinson, "A Kentucky Colonel Kept Me in Baseball."

24. Jackie Robinson, "I Was Part of the Team," *Reader's Digest*, April 1953, back cover.

25. Branca, *Moment in Time*, 82.

26. Robinson, *My Greatest Day*, 34.

27. Jackie Robinson, "Now I Know Why They Boo Me!," *Look*, January 25, 1955, 24.

28. Robinson, "A Kentucky Colonel Kept Me in Baseball."

29. Roger Kahn, "The Ten Years of Jackie Robinson," *Sport*, October, 1955, 78.

30. Robinson, *My Greatest Day*, 39–40. This anecdote, except the bit about "Uncle Tom for Uncle Tomming's sake," also appears in Robinson, *Breakthrough*, 121–122.

31. Jackie Robinson, "Trouble Ahead Needn't Bother You," in *Faith Made Them Champions*, edited by Norman Vincent Peale (Carmel, NY: Guideposts Associates, 1954), 238–241; Michael G. Long, ed. *Beyond Home Plate: Jackie Robinson on Life After Baseball* (Syracuse, Syracuse University Press, 2013), 4.

32. Robinson, *My Greatest Day*, 44–45. Robinson also makes this claim in *Breakthrough*, 138–139.

33. Ibid., 31.

34. These figures appear in Cohane, "Jackie Robinson's First Year with the Dodgers," 51.

CHAPTER 15: UNEASY ALLIANCE WITH CAMPY

1. Joe Reichler to Jackie Robinson, February 17, 1958. Jackie Robinson Papers (Box 2, Folder 21), Manuscript Division, Library of Congress, Washington, DC.

2. Roger Kahn, *The Boys of Summer* (1972; repr., New York City, Harper Perennial Modern Classics, 2006), 105.

3. This and all following quotations from Paul Reichler are from a discussion with the author, December 2015.

4. Associated Press, "Jackie Robinson Confident He Will Make Dodger Grade," *Christian Science Monitor*, April 11, 1947, 14. *Proquest Historical Newspapers*. See also a copy of the piece held in the Jackie Robinson Papers (Box 2, Folder 21), Manuscript Division, Library of Congress, Washington, DC.

5. Branch Rickey to Dick Young, February 5, 1952. Branch Rickey Papers (Box 24, Folder 14), Manuscript Division, Library of Congress, Washington, DC.

6. Carl Erskine, in discussion with the author, July 2016.

7. William C. Kashatus, *Jackie and Campy: The Untold Story of Their Rocky Relationship and the Breaking of Baseball's Color Line* (Lincoln: University of Nebraska Press, 2014), 4.

8. Sam Lacy, in discussion with Arnold Rampersad, *Jackie Robinson*, 291.

9. Ralph Branca, *A Moment in Time: An American Story of Baseball, Heartbreak, and Grace*, with David Ritz (New York: Scribner, 2011), 90. Reprinted with the permission of Scribner, a division of Simon & Schuster, Inc. Copyright © 2011 Ralph Branca and David Ritz. All rights reserved.

10. Carl Erskine, in discussion with the author, July 2016.

11. Joe Reichler to Jackie Robinson, February 17, 1958. Jackie Robinson Papers.

12. Ibid.

13. Tim Cohane, "Jackie Robinson's First Year With the Dodgers," *Look*, January 6, 1948, 50.

14. Branca, *Moment in Time*, 91.

15. Jackie Robinson, "A Kentucky Colonel Kept Me in Baseball," *Look*, February 8, 1955, 82–90.

16. Jackie Robinson, "Jackie Says," *Pittsburgh Courier*, July 24, 1948, 10. *ProQuest Historical Newspapers*; Arnold Rampersad, *Jackie Robinson: A Biography* (New York: Ballantine Books, 1998), 202.

17. Robinson, "A Kentucky Colonel Kept Me in Baseball."

18. Jack Orr, "Jackie Robinson: Symbol of the Revolution," *Sport*, March 1960, 54.

19. "Negroes Are Americans: Jackie Robinson Proves It in Words and on the Ball Field," *LIFE*, August 1, 1949, 22–23.

20. Associated Press, "Robeson Assaults Stettinius," April 20, 1949; Rampersad, *Jackie Robinson*, 211.

21. Jackie Robinson, *I Never Had It Made*, with Alfred Duckett (1972; repr., Hopewell, NJ: Ecco, 1995), 83. Copyright © by Rachel Robinson. Reprinted by permission of HarperCollins Publishers.

22. "Sworn Testimony of Jack Roosevelt Robinson," *Hearings Before the Committee on Un-American Activities, House of Representatives Eighty-First*

Congress First Session (Washington, DC: Government Printing Office, 1949), 479–483, quoted in "Negroes Are Americans," 22.

23. "Negroes Are Americans," 22.

24. "He Fights and Steals," *Quick,* August 1, 1949, 57.

25. "Negroes Are Americans," *LIFE*, August 1, 1949, 22.

26. Joe DiMaggio, "It's Great to be Back," *LIFE*, August 1, 1949, 66.

CHAPTER 16: LOSING RICKEY

1. This and all following quotations from Carl Erskine are from a discussion with the author, July 2016.

2. Jackie Robinson, *My Greatest Day* (unpublished manuscript, undated), 72, Jackie Robinson Papers (Box 11, Folder 12), Manuscript Division, Library of Congress, Washington, DC.

3. Ralph Branca, *A Moment in Time: An American Story of Baseball, Heartbreak, and Grace*, with David Ritz (New York: Scribner, 2011), 110. Reprinted with the permission of Scribner, a division of Simon & Schuster, Inc. Copyright © 2011 Ralph Branca and David Ritz. All rights reserved.

4. For the full story of Robinson's teammates joking around with him from behind home plate, see Jackie Robinson, "We're Winning the One That Counts," *Look*, September 19, 1950, 56. For Roger Kahn's description of Furillo, see Roger Kahn, *The Boys of Summer* (1972; repr., New York City, Harper Perennial Modern Classics, 2006), xviii.

5. Robinson, "We're Winning the One That Counts," 56.

6. Ibid., 64.

7. Jackie Robinson, "Five Years in White Man's Baseball: An Exclusive *Focus* Interview," *Focus*, July 1952, 7.

8. Robinson, "We're Winning the One That Counts," 58.

9. Ibid., 76.

10. *The Jackie Robinson Story*, directed by Alfred E. Green (Jewel Pictures, 1950).

11. For a description of Robinson's work on the film, as well as the quotes from his teammates riding him after his return to baseball, see "Jackie Robinson's Double Play," *LIFE*, May 8, 1950, 129–135.

12. Jackie Robinson to Branch Rickey, undated. Branch Rickey Papers (Box 24, Folder 13), Manuscript Division, Library of Congress, Washington, DC.

13. Ibid., Branch Rickey to Jackie Robinson, December 31, 1950.

14. Jeremiah 12:5, unknown translation, as quoted in Dr. F. Gerald Ensley, "When Life Gets Tougher as It Goes Along" (sermon, North Broadway Methodist

Church, Columbus, OH, September 17, 1950). Branch Rickey Papers (Box 24, Folder 13), Manuscript Division, Library of Congress, Washington, DC.

15. Ibid.

CHAPTER 17: "THE GIANTS WIN THE PENNANT!"

1. Jerry Reinsdorf, in discussion with the author, July 2016.
2. Bill Gutman, *Giants of Baseball* (New York: Tempo Books, 1975).
3. Carl Erskine, in discussion with the author, July 2016.
4. Roger Kahn, *The Boys of Summer* (1972; repr., New York City, Harper Perennial Modern Classics, 2006), 190.
5. Chuck Dressen, in discussion with Kahn, Ibid., 143–144.
6. Joshua Prager, "The Giants Steal the Pennant!" *Chicago Tribune*, February 2, 2001.
7. Carl Erskine, in discussion with the author, July 2016.
8. Jerry Reinsdorf, in discussion with the author, July 2016.
9. Ralph Branca, *A Moment in Time: An American Story of Baseball, Heartbreak, and Grace*, with David Ritz (New York: Scribner, 2011), 118. Reprinted with the permission of Scribner, a division of Simon & Schuster, Inc. Copyright © 2011 Ralph Branca and David Ritz. All rights reserved.
10. Ibid., 122.
11. Ibid., 127.
12. Ibid., 138.
13. Ibid., 140.
14. Jackie Robinson, "A Kentucky Colonel Kept Me in Baseball," *Look*, February 8, 1955, 82–90.
15. Branca, *Moment in Time*, 141.
16. Ibid., 146–147.
17. Jerry Reinsdorf, in discussion with the author, July 2016.
18. Branca, *Moment in Time*, 150.
19. Ibid., 151.
20. Joshua Prager, *The Echoing Green: The Untold Story of Bobby Thomson, Ralph Branca and the Shot Heard Round the World* (2006, repr., New York: Vintage Books, 2008), 217.
21. Carl Erskine, in discussion with the author, November 2016.
22. Branca, *Moment in Time*, 152.
23. WMCA, recording of game, October 3, 1951; Prager, *Echoing Green*, 220.
24. Richard Sandomir, "The Shot Heard 'Round the World; A Call is Born, and Saved by a Mom," *New York Times*, October 1, 2001, http://www.nytimes.com

/2001/10/01/sports/the-shot-heard-round-the-world-a-call-is-born-and-saved
-by-a-mom.html.

25. Branca, *Moment in Time*, 152.

26. Jerry Reinsdorf, in discussion with the author, July 2016.

27. Vin Scully, in discussion with the author, December 2016. For a published account of Scully's time spent with Barber, Branca, and Ann Mulvey, see Tom Verducci, "Vin Scully," *Sports Illustrated*, May 16, 2016, 58. For a published account of the "Shot Heard 'Round the World" as seen by Scully, see Branca, *Moment in Time*, 153.

28. Branca, *Moment in Time*, 153.

29. Scully, in discussion with the author, December 2016.

30. Ibid.

31. Branca, *Moment in Time*, 154.

32. Carl Erskine, in discussion with the author, July 2016.

33. Scully, in discussion with the author, December 2016.

CHAPTER 18: "HOW DO YOU LIKE *THAT* GARBAGE?!"

1. This and all following quotes from Carl Erskine are from a discussion with the author, July 2016.

2. Carl Erskine, *What I Learned from Jackie Robinson: A Teammate's Reflections On and Off the Field*, with Burton Rocks (New York: McGraw-Hill, 2005), 87.

3. Jackie Robinson, "Now I Know Why They Boo Me!," *Look*, January 25, 1955, 26.

4. For the story of Jackie and Rachel Robinson's attempts to buy property in Westchester and North Stamford, see ibid.

5. Ibid., 25–26.

6. For Robinson's account of this incident at Wrigley Field in 1954, see Robinson, "Now I Know Why They Boo Me!," 23. He gives another account of the incident in Jackie Robinson, *I Never Had It Made*, with Alfred Duckett (1972; repr., Hopewell, NJ: Ecco, 1995), 117–118.

7. Jackie Robinson, "A Kentucky Colonel Kept Me in Baseball," *Look*, February 8, 1955, 82–90.

8. For Robinson's account of the two 1954 incidents in Milwaukee, see Robinson, "Now I Know Why They Boo Me!," 24.

9. Ibid.

10. Ibid.

11. Ibid.

12. Ibid.

13. Ed Fitzgerald, "Can Jackie Robinson Make the Hall of Fame?," *Saga*, August 1953, 52.

14. Paul Reichler, in discussion with the author, December 2015.

15. Roger Kahn, "The Ten Years of Jackie Robinson," *Sport*, October 1955, 76.

16. Francis Miller, John Dominis, and Ralph Morse, "The Overpowering Dodgers," *LIFE*, May 23, 1955, 142.

17. "The Disabled Dodgers: They Suffer But Do Not Sink," *LIFE*, August 1, 1955, 69.

18. Jackie Robinson, "How We Won," *Dell Baseball Annual*, 1956.

19. Ibid.

20. Ibid.

21. Jackie Robinson, "There's Only One Way to Beat the Yankees," *LIFE*, October 4, 1963, 112.

22. Robert Creamer and Roy Terrell, "Preview: The World Series. This Year the Dodgers?" *Sports Illustrated*, September 26, 1955, 19.

23. Ibid.

24. Joey Nowak, "Jackie Safe at Home? Not According to Yogi," *MLB.com*, September 24, 2015, http://m.mlb.com/news/article/151385362/yogi-berra -jackie-robinson-and-stealing-home/.

25. Carl Erskine, in discussion with the author, July 2016.

CHAPTER 19: ROBINSON TRADED TO THE . . . GIANTS?

1. This and all following quotations from Jerry Reinsdorf are from a discussion with the author, July 2016.

2. Roger Kahn, *Rickey & Robinson: The True, Untold Story of the Integration of Baseball* (New York: Rodale, 2014), 272.

3. For a full transcript of the letter, see Kahn, *Rickey & Robinson*, 273.

4. Jerry Reinsdorf, in discussion with the author, July 2016.

5. Carl Erskine, in discussion with the author, July 2016.

6. Jackie Robinson, "Why I'm Quitting Baseball," *Look*, January 22, 1957, 91.

7. Roger Kahn, "Man of the 25 Years: Jackie Robinson," *Sport*, December 1971, 66.

8. Jack Kelley, "Tulsa Students Impress Jackie: Will Rogers Tops Them All," *Tulsa World*, February 13, 1954, 11. Jackie Robinson Papers (Box 7, Folder 21), Manuscript Division, Library of Congress, Washington, DC.

9. Ibid.

10. Robinson, "Why I'm Quitting Baseball," 92.

11. Dan Burley, "Did Jackie Robinson Betray Baseball?," *Jet*, January 24, 1957, 55–56.

12. Kahn, *Rickey & Robinson*, 274.

13. Burley, "Did Jackie Robinson Betray Baseball?," 54.

14. Ibid., 56–57.

15. "Does Jackie Robinson Talk Too Much?," *Jet*, January 31, 1957, 52.

16. Associated Press, "Sorry Now He Mentioned It: Night Clubbing Cost Braves Title Last Year, Says Jackie Robinson," *Washington Post*, January 12, 1957, C2. *ProQuest Historical Newspapers*.

17. Charles Phillips to Jackie Robinson, December 13, 1956. Jackie Robinson Papers (Box 2, Folder 16), Manuscript Division, Library of Congress, Washington, DC.

18. Ibid., Thomas Kirksey to Jackie Robinson, December 21, 1956.

19. Ibid., Bill Mac Gibbon to Jackie Robinson, December 18, 1956.

20. Ibid., unidentified couple to Jackie Robinson, December 20, 1956.

21. Ibid.

22. Ibid., Benn Sah to Jackie Robinson, December 26, 1956.

23. Ibid., "Jackie Fan" to Jackie Robinson, December 25, 1956.

24. Ibid., Hyman Silverman to Jackie Robinson, December 14, 1956.

25. Ibid., Dr. Sol Melnick to Jackie Robinson, December 19, 1956.

26. Ibid., Bil Mac Gibbon to Jackie Robinson, December 18, 1956.

27. Robinson, "Why I'm Quitting Baseball," 92.

28. Roy Terrell, "Brooklyn's Money Men Come Through Again," *Sports Illustrated*, August 13, 1956, 8.

29. Ibid., 55.

30. Hank Aaron, "Guideposts Classics: Hank Aaron on Sacrificing for Others," *Guideposts,* September 1973, accessed September 29, 2016, https://www .guideposts.org/positive-living/guideposts-classics-hank-aaron-on-sacrificing -for-others?nopaging=1.

CHAPTER 20: THEIR BELIEF IN GOD'S SPIRIT

1. Rachel Robinson, in discussion with the author, April 2011.

2. Jackie Robinson, *My Greatest Day* (unpublished manuscript, undated), 18, Manuscript Division, Library of Congress, Washington, DC. Robinson also makes this claim in Jackie Robinson, *Breakthrough to the Big League: The Story of Jackie Robinson,* with Alfred Duckett (New York: Harper & Row, Publishers, 1965), 89.

3. Rachel Robinson, *Jackie Robinson: An Intimate Portrait*, with Lee Wilkins (New York: Harry M. Abrams, 1996), 48.

4. Jackie Robinson, "Now I Know Why They Boo Me!," *Look*, January 25, 1955, 24.

5. Robinson, *My Greatest Day*, 15.

6. Ralph Branca, *A Moment in Time: An American Story of Baseball, Heartbreak, and Grace*, with David Ritz (New York: Scribner, 2011), 48. Reprinted with the permission of Scribner, a division of Simon & Schuster, Inc. Copyright © 2011 Ralph Branca and David Ritz. All rights reserved.

7. Vin Scully, in discussion with the author, December 2016.

8. Robinson, *My Greatest Day*, 10.

9. Jackie Robinson, *I Never Had It Made*, with Alfred Duckett (1972; repr., Hopewell, NJ: Ecco, 1995), 99. Copyright © by Rachel Robinson. Reprinted by permission of HarperCollins Publishers.

10. "Jackie Robinson: The Man and the Legacy He Leaves," *Jet*, November 16, 1972, 56.

11. Jackie Robinson, "Address by Mr. Jackie Robinson, Fourth General Synod of the United Church of Christ" (speech, Denver, CO, July 10, 1963). Jackie Robinson Papers (Box 13, Folder 3), Manuscript Division, Library of Congress, Washington, DC.

12. Ibid.

13. Jackie Robinson, "'Cast the First Stone,' sermon delivered in New Rochelle, NY on October 15, 1967." Jackie Robinson Papers, (Box 7, Folder 21), Manuscript Division, Library of Congress, Washington, DC.

14. Jackie Robinson, "The Church and the World" (81st Annual Assembly of the Texas Association of Christian Churches, Austin, TX, May 3, 1968). Jackie Robinson Papers (Box 8, Folder 3), Manuscript Division, Library of Congress, Washington, DC.

15. Ibid.

16. Michael Beschloss, "Jackie Robinson and Nixon: Life and Death of a Political Friendship," The Upshot, *New York Times*, June 6, 2014, http://www.nytimes.com/2014/06/07/upshot/jackie-robinson-and-nixon-life-and-death-of-a-political-friendship.html?_r=0.

17. Beschloss, "Jackie Robinson and Nixon."

18. Robinson, "The Church and the World."

19. Jackie Robinson to Dwight Eisenhower, May 13, 1958, *First Class Citizenship: The Civil Rights Letters of Jackie Robinson*, edited by Michael G. Long (New York: Times Books, 2007), 56–57.

20. Jackie Robinson to Richard Nixon, March 21, 1972; Long, *First Class Citizenship*, 313.

21. Carl Erskine, in discussion with the author, July 2016.

22. The story of Robinson's trip to Birmingham in May 1963 is recounted in Bill Stephenson, "I Flew into Birmingham with Jackie Robinson," *Star Weekly Magazine*, June 8, 1963, 1–9.

23. Jackie Robinson to Branch Rickey, April 12, 1965. Branch Rickey Papers (Box 24, Folder 15), Manuscript Division, Library of Congress, Washington, DC.

24. Lee Lowenfish, *Branch Rickey: Baseball's Ferocious Gentleman* (Lincoln: University of Nebraska Press, 2007), 5.

25. Roger Kahn, "The Ten Years of Jackie Robinson," *Sport*, October 1955, 77–78.

26. United Press International, "Frick Calls Rickey Man of Dedication," *Chicago Tribune*, December 10, 1965, 2. *ProQuest Historical Newspapers*.

27. Branch Rickey, *The American Diamond: A Documentary of the Game of Baseball* (New York: Simon & Schuster, 1965), 40.

28. Branch Rickey III, in discussion with the author, March 2011.

CHAPTER 21: "MY SON DESERVED BETTER"

1. Larry King, in discussion with the author, March 2015.

2. Brian Carroll, *The Black Press and Black Baseball: A Devil's Bargain* (New York: Routledge, 2015), 2.

3. Jackie Robinson, *I Never Had It Made*, with Alfred Duckett (1972; repr., Hopewell, NJ: Ecco, 1995), 261. Copyright © by Rachel Robinson. Reprinted by permission of HarperCollins Publishers.

4. Dan Burley, "Dodger Brass, Writers Cry 'Foul,' But Jackie Scores Clean 'Steal,'" *Jet*, January 24, 1957, 57.

5. C. R. Brookbank to Jackie Robinson, October 25, 1956. Jackie Robinson Papers (Box 7, Folder 21), Manuscript Division, Library of Congress, Washington, DC.

6. Jack Orr, "Jackie Robinson: Symbol of the Revolution," *Sport*, March 1960, 53–54.

7. "Jackie Continues Pioneering—This Time in Hall of Fame," *Jet*, February 8, 1962, 57.

8. Jackie Robinson, in "Remembering Jackie," *National Baseball Hall of Fame*, http://baseballhall.org/discover/remembering-jackie.

9. Paul Reichler, in discussion with the author, December 2015.

10. Robinson, "Remembering Jackie."

11. Cordell M. Thompson, "Jackie Robinson Joins War Against Dope in Ghettos," *Jet*, September 10, 1970, 24–28.

12. Robinson, *I Never Had It Made*, 89.

13. Thompson, "Jackie Robinson Joins War Against Dope."

14. Jackie Robinson, *I Never Had It Made*, 155.

15. Ibid., 156.
16. Ibid.
17. Ibid., 218.
18. Ibid., 248.
19. Ibid., 255.
20. "Board of Directors," *The Jackie Robinson Foundation*, http://www.jackie robinson.org/about/board-of-directors/.
21. Ed Goren and Jerry Reinsdorf, in discussion with the author, July 2016.
22. Paul Reichler, in discussion with the author, December 2015.
23. Ralph Branca, *A Moment in Time: An American Story of Baseball, Heartbreak, and Grace*, with David Ritz (New York: Scribner, 2011), 196–197. Reprinted with the permission of Scribner, a division of Simon & Schuster, Inc. Copyright © 2011 Ralph Branca and David Ritz. All rights reserved.
24. Ibid., 198.
25. Ibid., 197.
26. Carl Erskine, in discussion with the author, July 2016.

CHAPTER 22: "CARL, I PRAY FOR YOU EVERY DAY"

1. Carl Erskine, *The Parallel: Witnessing Two of the Greatest Social Changes in My Lifetime* (2012).
2. Ralph Branca, *A Moment in Time: An American Story of Baseball, Heartbreak, and Grace*, with David Ritz (New York: Scribner, 2011), 206. Reprinted with the permission of Scribner, a division of Simon & Schuster, Inc. Copyright © 2011 Ralph Branca and David Ritz. All rights reserved.
3. Ted Gray was close to Earl Rapp, who briefly played for the Giants in 1951. See Branca, *Moment in Time*, 170.
4. Ibid.
5. Jerry Reinsdorf, in discussion with the author, July 2016.
6. Branca, *Moment in Time*, 155.
7. Ibid., 175.
8. Ibid., 203–207.
9. Bobby Valentine, in discussion with Christopher "Mad Dog" Russo, *Mad Dog Unleashed*, Sirius XM, November 23, 2016.
10. Bobby Valentine, in discussion with the author, December 2016.
11. Joshua Prager, "For Branca, an Asterisk of a Different Kind," *New York Times*, August 11, 2011, http://www.nytimes.com/2011/08/15/sports/baseball/for-branca -an-asterisk-of-a-different-kind.html?_r=0.

12. Joshua Prager, *The Echoing Green: The Untold Story of Bobby Thomson, Ralph Branca and the Shot Heard Round the World* (2006, repr., New York: Vintage Books, 2008), 85.
13. Carl Erskine, in discussion with the author, July 2016.
14. Branca, *Moment in Time*, 154.
15. Bobby Valentine, in discussion with the author, December 2016.
16. Branca, *Moment in Time*, 154.
17. Carl Erskine, in discussion with the author, July 2016.
18. Jerry Reinsdorf, in discussion with the author, July 2016.
19. Carl Erskine, in discussion with the author, July 2016.

CHAPTER 23: THE LAST HURRAH

1. Roger Kahn, "Man of the 25 Years: Jackie Robinson," *Sport*, December 1971, 86.
2. Jackie Robinson, in "Remembering Jackie," *National Baseball Hall of Fame*, http://baseballhall.org/discover/remembering-jackie.
3. Rachel Robinson, *Jackie Robinson: An Intimate Portrait*, with Lee Daniels (New York: Harry Abrams Publishing, 1996), 216.
4. Jackie Robinson, words spoken on October 15, 1972, quoted in Lori Latrice Martin, ed. *Out of Bounds: Racism and the Black Athlete* (Santa Barbara: Praeger, 2014), 139.
5. Robinson, *Intimate Portrait*, 216.
6. Roger Kahn, "The Boys Turn 26," *Los Angeles Times*, February 22, 1998, http://articles.latimes.com/1998/feb/22/sports/sp-22009/3.
7. Sharon Robinson, *Stealing Home: An Intimate Family Portrait by the Daughter of Jackie Robinson* (New York: HarperCollins, 1996).
8. Bill Russell, "Sports: Leveling the Playing Field" (lecture, McGarr Symposium on Sports and Society, LBJ Presidential Library, Austin, TX, April 2014), https://www.c-span.org/video/?318483–2/sports-race.
9. This and all following quotations from Rachel Robinson are from a discussion with the author, April 2011.
10. Roger Kahn, *Rickey & Robinson: The Untold Story of the Integration of Baseball*, by Roger Kahn (New York: Rodale, 2014), 42.
11. Jackie Robinson, *My Greatest Day*, Religion chapter, 4. Part of these lines, from "the promise was" until "major leagues," also appears in Jackie Robinson, *Breakthrough to the Big League: The Story of Jackie Robinson,* with Alfred Duckett (New York: Harper & Row, Publishers, 1965), 169.
12. Robinson revealed these superstitions to an audience in Tulsa, Oklahoma

in February 1954 while serving as national chairman of Brotherhood Week. See Jack Kelley, "Tulsa Students Impress Jackie: Will Rogers Tops Them All," *Tulsa World*, February 13, 1954, 11. Jackie Robinson Papers (Box 7, Folder 21), Manuscript Division, Library of Congress, Washington, DC.

13. Duke Snider, *The Duke of Flatbush,* with Bill Gilbert (New York: Citadel Press, 2002), 63.

ABOUT THE AUTHOR

ED HENRY serves as Fox News Channel's chief national correspondent. He joined the network in June 2011. Throughout his tenure at FNC, Henry has covered all major news stories involving President Trump and former president Obama.

Henry has won numerous journalism honors, including the Everett McKinley Dirksen Award for Distinguished Reporting of Congress and the White House Correspondents' Association's Merriman Smith Award for excellence in presidential coverage under deadline pressure in 2008.

Henry also served in the prestigious post of president of the White House Correspondents' Association from 2012 to 2013. Prior to joining FNC, Henry was at CNN from 2004 to 2011, where he served as the network's senior White House correspondent and a congressional correspondent.

Henry began his career working for Pulitzer Prize–winning journalist Jack Anderson and later joined the newspaper *Roll Call* as a reporter, where he rose to senior editor.

Henry graduated from Siena College with a BA in English.